Lecture Notes in Computer Science   13165

More information about this subseries at https://link.springer.com/bookseries/7408

James Cheney · Simona Perri (Eds.)

Practical Aspects of Declarative Languages

24th International Symposium, PADL 2022
Philadelphia, PA, USA, January 17–18, 2022
Proceedings

Editors
James Cheney (iD)
University of Edinburgh
Edinburgh, UK

Simona Perri (iD)
University of Calabria
Rende, Italy

ISSN 0302-9743   ISSN 1611-3349 (electronic)
Lecture Notes in Computer Science
ISBN 978-3-030-94478-0   ISBN 978-3-030-94479-7 (eBook)
https://doi.org/10.1007/978-3-030-94479-7

LNCS Sublibrary: SL2 – Programming and Software Engineering

This Springer imprint is published by the registered company Springer Nature Switzerland AG
The registered company address is: Gewerbestrasse 11, 6330 Cham, Switzerland

Preface

This volume contains the papers presented at the 24th International Symposium on Practical Aspects of Declarative Languages (PADL 2022). The symposium was co-located with the 49th ACM SIGPLAN Symposium on Principles of Programming Languages (POPL 2022), and took place during January 17–18, 2022. The conference was planned to be held in Philadelphia, Pennsylvania, and as of this writing it is planned to go ahead as a traditional in-person event following the nearly two years of disruption caused by the COVID–19 pandemic.

PADL is a well-established forum for researchers and practitioners to present original work emphasizing novel applications and implementation techniques for all forms of declarative programming, including programming with sets, functions, logics, and constraints. The contributions to PADL 2022 were particularly focused on new ideas and approaches for principled implementation, fuzzing and declarative debugging, domain specific languages, and real-world applications ranging from blockchain to web programming.

Originally established as a workshop (PADL 1999 in San Antonio, Texas), the PADL series developed into a regular annual symposium; previous editions took place in San Antonio, Texas (1999), Boston, Massachusetts (2000), Las Vegas, Nevada (2001), Portland, Oregon (2002), New Orleans, Louisiana (2003), Dallas, Texas (2004), Long Beach, California (2005), Charleston, South Carolina (2006), Nice, France (2007), San Francisco, California (2008), Savannah, Georgia (2009), Madrid, Spain (2010), Austin, Texas (2012), Rome, Italy (2013), San Diego, California (2014), Portland, Oregon (2015), St. Petersburg, Florida (2016), Paris, France (2017), Los Angeles, California (2018), Lisbon, Portugal (2019), New Orleans, Louisiana (2020), and Copenhagen, Denmark (2021, virtual event due to COVID-19 pandemic).

This year, the Program Committee accepted nine full papers, four application papers, and one short paper (extended abstract), selected from 22 submissions. Each submission was reviewed by at least three Program Committee members and went through a five-day online discussion period by the Program Committee before a final decision was made. The selection was based only on the merit of each submission and regardless of scheduling or space constraints.

We would like to express thanks to the Association for Logic Programming (ALP) and the Association for Computing Machinery (ACM) for their continuous support of the symposium, and Springer for their longstanding, successful cooperation with the PADL series. We are very grateful to all members of the PADL 2022 Program Committee and external reviewers for their invaluable work. Many thanks to Marco Gavanelli, the ALP Conference Coordinator. We are happy to note that the conference was successfully managed with the help of EasyChair.

We note that this was an unusual year due to the continued disruption and uncertainty of the COVID–19 pandemic, although with the development of vaccines and widespread vaccination programs the outlook is considerably more hopeful than a year ago. Many (if not most) members of our research community have been adversely affected, in a variety of ways, and while the situation has improved, the pandemic has undoubtedly had an impact on the amount of scientific activity that people have been able to engage in. We are therefore even more thankful to our reviewers for their time and care, and to all contributors to this year's PADL.

January 2022   Simona Perri
                                                                   James Cheney

Organization

Program Chairs

James Cheney   University of Edinburgh, UK
Simona Perri   University of Calabria, Italy

Program Committee

Andres Löh   WellTyped, Germany
Chiaki Sakama   Wakayama University, Japan
Daniela Inclezan   Miami University, USA
Ekaterina Komendantskaya   Heriot-Watt University, UK
Esra Erdem   Sabanci University, Turkey
Francesco Calimeri   University of Calabria, Italy
Jan Christiansen   Flensburg University of Applied Sciences, Germany
Konstantin Schekotihin   University of Klagenfurt, Austria
Lukasz Ziarek   University at Buffalo, USA
Lionel Parreaux   Hong Kong University of Science and Technology, China

Marco Maratea   University of Genoa, Italy
Marina De Vos   University of Bath, UK
Martin Erwig   Oregon State University, USA
Martin Gebser   University of Klagenfurt, Austria
Michael Greenberg   Stevens Institute of Technology, USA
Paul Tarau   University of North Texas, USA
Pavan Kumar Chittimalli   TCS Research, India
Pedro Cabalar   University of Corunna, Spain
Roly Perera   The Alan Turing Institute, UK
Tomas Petricek   University of Kent, UK
Torsten Grust   University of Tübingen, Germany
Tran Cao Son   New Mexico State University, USA
Yukiyoshi Kameyama   University of Tsukuba, Japan

Additional Reviewers

Mohammed El-Kholany   Jack Pattison
Danila Fedorin   Bhargav Shivkumar
Elena Mastria   Pierre Tassel
Maria Concetta Morelli   Jessica Zangari

Abstracts of Invited Talks

People, Ideas, and the Path Ahead

Marcello Balduccini

Saint Joseph's University, Elemental Cognition
marcello.balduccini@gmail.com

Abstract. While recent advances in machine learning have yielded impressive results, researchers, practitioners, and even companies are beginning to recognize that true artificial intelligence requires much more sophisticated reasoning capabilities. Knowledge representation and declarative programming are arguably in a premier position to aid in the achievement of such capabilities. In this paper, I reflect on people and ideas that have had a great influence on my view of knowledge representation and of declarative programming. Through these lenses, I will discuss what I consider to be some of the most important milestones in the evolution of the field over the past years. I will conclude my reflection with my take on what this may tell us about the path that lies ahead and about areas where research efforts may yield considerable benefits.

Declarative Programming and Education

Shriram Krishnamurthi

Brown University, Providence, RI, USA

Abstract. Education has always been one of the major uses of advanced programming languages. However, the impact of declarative techniques is now threatened by multiple forces: the rise of Python, large codebases in conventional languages, the growth of synthesis, and more.

This talk will take stock of where we stand, and suggest ways in which programming problems may have finally caught up with where declarative techniques shine. It will also discuss some open problems in programming education that have for too long been overlooked by many segments of the declarative community. Making progress on these challenges can lead to much more widespread use of declarative languages, while failure to do so could lead to fresh bouts of exclusion.

Contents

Declarative Solutions

Invited Talk

People, Ideas, and the Path Ahead

Marcello Balduccini[1,2]([✉])

[1] Saint Joseph's University, Philadelphia, PA, USA
[2] Elemental Cognition, Wilton, CT, USA
marcello.balduccini@gmail.com

Abstract. While recent advances in machine learning have yielded impressive results, researchers, practitioners, and even companies are beginning to recognize that true artificial intelligence requires much more sophisticated reasoning capabilities. Knowledge representation and declarative programming are arguably in a premier position to aid in the achievement of such capabilities. In this paper, I reflect on people and ideas that have had a great influence on my view of knowledge representation and of declarative programming. Through these lenses, I will discuss what I consider to be some of the most important milestones in the evolution of the field over the past years. I will conclude my reflection with my take on what this may tell us about the path that lies ahead and about areas where research efforts may yield considerable benefits.

Keywords: Knowledge representation · Answer set programming · Non-monotonic reasoning · Declarative programming · Practical applications

1 Introduction

I was honored to be asked to give an invited talk to PADL 2022. This article summarizes the key points of my talk.

I decided to structure my talk as reflection on people and ideas that have had a great influence on my view of knowledge representation and of declarative programming. Interestingly, these ideas have corresponded to important milestones in the evolution of the field over the past years. While many researchers have contributed to these milestones, in this article I will refer specifically to the people who have communicated those idea to me first-hand, as a way to honor their impact on my views: Michael Gelfond's idea that the Knowledge Representation (KR) methodology and Answer Set Programming (ASP) [15,23] itself were viable for practical applications; Henry Kautz's suggestion that declarative languages of different nature could be hybridized into languages suitable for use in industrial applications; and David Ferrucci's idea that agents can be thought partners, capable of intelligently engaging humans when faced with problems beyond their individual capabilities. I conclude my reflection with my take on the path that lies ahead and about areas where research efforts may yield considerable benefits.

© Springer Nature Switzerland AG 2022
J. Cheney and S. Perri (Eds.): PADL 2022, LNCS 13165, pp. 3–12, 2022.
https://doi.org/10.1007/978-3-030-94479-7_1

2   KR Methodology and Practical Applications

At the time it was conceived, Michael Gelfond's idea was a bold one: that ASP, coupled with a rigorous KR methodology, would be viable for practical applications, both in terms of convenience of use and in terms of scalability.

I was exposed to this idea when I joined Michael's lab at Texas Tech University as a fresh Ph.D. student, and got involved in Michael's and Monica Nogueira's research on the USA Advisor reasoning system [4]. At the time we started working on the USA Advisor, demonstrations of ASP were mostly limited to the level of academic exercises and initial performance evaluations (e.g., [11]). There were some concerns that ASP programs would not scale enough to be usable in practical applications, particularly when the programs were written following a rigorous KR methodology and, even more so in the case of an action-language based approach [16].

The rigorous KR methodology I am referring to is what Michael was very careful in instilling all of his students. When one is formalizing a dynamic domain, one should first of all answer the questions: What are the objects of the domain? What are the relations? What are the actions? Following this categorization, one would then proceed to representing the effects of actions in terms of dynamic causal laws, state constraints and executability conditions, either directly encoded in an action language or translated to ASP. Very importantly, fluents and actions should have a precise informal meaning stated in English. The problem should, then, be formulated first using precise English statements that (a) follow the expression patterns of laws of action languages, and (b) leverage the English phrases associated with fluents and actions. The English statements should then be translated into ASP in a direct way, so that every ASP statement, when it was read back into English, would match the original English statement.

This approach is designed to yield elegant and fully declarative specifications, which was in fact the case in the USA Advisor. Two of my favorites:[1]

```
% Tank node N1 is pressurized by tank X if it is connected
% by an open valve to a node which is pressurized by tank X.

h(pressurized_by(N1,X),T) :- time(T),
                             tank_of(N1,R),
                             link(N2,N1,V),
                             h(in_state(V,open),T),
                             tank_of(X,R),
                             h(pressurized_by(N2,X),T).

% If the input value of a NOT gate is S1 at time t and its delay
% is d then its output value is opposite value S2 at time t+d.

h(value(W2,S2),T1) :-
```

---

[1] For historical faithfulness, I copy them here in their entirety, including the original comments from the formalization of the USA Advisor.

```
        of_type(G,not_gate),
        delay(G,D),
        time(T),
        time(T1),
        T1 = T+D,
        input(W1,G),
        output(W2,G),
        opposite(S1,S2),
        h(value(W1,S1),T),
        not is_stuck(W2,G).
```

At the time when we created the USA Advisor, the first rule was a striking example of ASP's ability to elegantly capture complex kinds of knowledge. Not only the rule was part of a recursive definition, which would have been a challenge in many other languages at the time, it embedded such a recursive definition within a state constraint, thus capturing the evolution of the state of the domain over time in a way that mirrored faithfully the intuition. The second rule was, too, related to recursive definitions, but my fascination with it lies in the fact that it was in fact not a rule that we had written for the USA Advisor.

Some time before we focused on the USA Advisor, we had worked on using ASP and the KR methodology for representing digital circuits and reasoning about them [3]. This rule is part of what we called the "General Theory of Digital Circuits in A-Prolog."

Thus, what is striking to me is that, even at that time, Michael had such a clear conception of modularity in ASP, that it allowed us to reuse in the USA Advisor a rather sophisticated module that we had previously created independently of it, and we were able to do so without any substantial modifications.

But what was the scalability of the formalization? Did it scale to the needs of this first industrial application of ASP? Indeed, it was, and to some extent it surprised even us by how well it performed. We had been given a time threshold of 20 minutes for every problem instance and we found that the system was, on average, orders of magnitude faster than that and never got even close to that threshold even in the most challenging cases.

The fact that we were concerned about scalability is clearly visible in certain statements. For instance, we preferred to ground manually the rules encoding the law of inertia and in doing so we restricted the groundings only to the fluents that we knew "mattered", e.g.

```
% Tanks maintain correct pressure unless some leak
% occurs along their path for some time.

h(pressurized_by(X,X),T1) :- next(T,T1),
                             tank_of(X,R),
                             h(pressurized_by(X,X),T),
                             not nh(pressurized_by(X,X),T1).
```

This would be unnecessary nowadays. In fact, given what we learned later about the performance of the system, in hindsight we could have probably trusted the grounding of the rules of inertia to the lparse grounder. However, this shows the level of concern and lack of a generally clear picture of what might affect performance and what might not.

Something that is important to remark is that this success was not only due to Michael's great KR capabilities and intuition. Instrumental to the success of this project was also the excellent work by Illka Niemela, Tommi Syrjanen, and others that had given us grounder lparse and solver smodels [25].

3   Hybrid Declarative Languages for Practical Applications

Henry Kautz was my supervisor when I joined the Eastman Kodak Research Labs. I had been asked to investigate ways to automate decision-making processes of commercial print shops: given a set of print jobs (e.g., books or magazines), which presses, cutters, binders, and other devices should be used, which device configurations would minimize waste and costs, and what was the best schedule for the work? The agent should also be able to respond to sudden unexpected events, such as devices becoming unavailable or "rush jobs" coming it while others are already in production. The response should consist of incremental changes that minimize disruptions and additional costs.

It was known in the industry that, when humans experts were carrying out those decision-making processes, an important factor of their success was the heuristic knowledge that they had accumulated over the years – so much so that (I was told) experienced people were paid substantial salaries and were regarded as key elements of the manufacturing process. Because of this, an additional constraint I was given was that the system should make it possible to easily incorporate heuristic knowledge as it might be provided by human experts.

On the one side, I expected the expert knowledge to be in the form of commonsensical statements, possibly defaults and their exceptions, and so it was clear to me that a non-monotonic language like ASP would be most appropriate. On the other hand, intuition and preliminary experiments showed me that ASP-based formalizations of this underlying "planning-while-scheduling" problem would not scale well for practical use. It seemed clear that a representation based on Constraint Satisfaction Problems (CSP) [19] would be most appropriate for that.

Of course, the underlying problem was that whichever approach I adopted, would need to be viable for a practical, industry-sized application. I was explaining all of this to Henry in a meeting, when he pointed me to the approach taken in Satisfaction Modulo Theories (SMT) [26] as a possible solution.

SMT had demonstrated that it was possible to overcome the expressive shortcomings and performance shortcomings of individual declarative languages by hybridizing them. The bet was that ASP and Constraint Programming could be hybridized in a way that allowed us to solve this "planning-while-scheduling" problem augmented with expert knowledge, and to do so in a way that was scalable.[2]

The idea of hybridizing ASP and CP was not entirely new. A couple of years earlier, Baselice, Bonatti and Gelfond had published a paper proposing a possible approach [9], and I was aware that Veena Mellarkod, Michael Gelfond and Yuanlin Zhang had been working for some time on a related implementation [24]. However, what was surprising – almost shocking – to me was the proposal of using such a hybrid for a practical application, when the work I was aware of had been limited to academic exercises.

Sure enough, preliminary tests on Mellarkod's system showed that it would not scale to the type of application we were building. Additionally, Veena's system leveraged specific solving algorithms. That was a problem for me, since there was substantial uncertainty in my mind on exactly which solvers to use. Lparse and smodels? The new gringo grounder [12] and clasp solver [13]? And which constraint solver? Ilog, to which I had been introduced in a previous Kodak project? The constraint solver embedded in some Constraint Logic Programming (CLP) system? And should the constraint solver need to support finite domains only or larger domain variables?

This prompted me to develop EZCSP [1,5,6], which I literally intended as an easy (hence "EZ") way of encoding CSP by means of a host language featuring strong KR foundations and support for non-monotonic constructs. The view of ASP as a host language for a constraint satisfaction language allowed me to adopt a loosely coupled view of the two languages and of the underlying solvers, making it possible to experiment with multiple combinations of ASP solvers and constraint solvers, as well as different types of variable domains.

Henry's intuition proved to be a good one. Developing EZCSP as a lightweight layer that leveraged existing solvers without modifications allowed me to conduct experiments with various solver combinations and quickly identify one that scaled to the level needed for our application. Remarkably, the first use of EZCSP coincided with its first industrial-sized, deployed application [1], which to the best of my knowledge was also the first deployed application of what we later came to call Constraint ASP [5]. The final product, which was running EZCSP at its core, even came with a user interface designed by UX expert Stacie Hibino.

I think all of this is an amazing demonstration of the power of constraint-based languages, a term that I use to denote both ASP and CP languages, as well as of Henry's intuition about the potential of a hybrid solution of ASP and CP.

---

[2] As an aside, our work on the USA Advisor had also been influenced by one of Henry's ideas, specifically Kautz and Selman's work on solving planning problems by reducing them to satisfiability problems [20].

4   Intelligent Agents as Thought Partners

David Ferrucci, the creator of IBM Watson, currently heads Elemental Cognition[3] (EC), a research-driven company aiming at developing and using a full spectrum of AI techniques to deliver revolutionary products that solve challenging, real-world problems.

When I first started collaborating with EC, two aspects fascinated me: on one side, David and EC fully understood the importance of KR, non-monotonic reasoning and declarative programming in achieving sophisticated agent capabilities. On the other side, David was adamant in his vision that agents should be "thought partners." As such, they should collaborate with humans rather than just acting autonomously. One particularly striking instance of this is that it may well happen that agent may sometimes be unable to solve a certain problem, either due to lack of knowledge or to performance limitations. In those cases, the agent should be capable of recognizing the issue and of engaging the humans in intelligent ways, in order to overcome the obstacle together.

This latter idea was quite striking to me, as it was in partial divergence with idea of agents as fully autonomous, to which I had subscribed since my early steps in AI. Then again, while at a first glance it may seem that giving up full autonomy might be an indication of a reduced level of intelligence, David's idea of agents as thought partners requires in fact even greater intelligence.

David's vision has struck a chord with a several parties, and has already led to successful projects. One of my favorite is a project that contributed to making the Superbowl possible in 2021 in spite of having been held in the midst of the covid-19 pandemic.[4] EC's PolicyPath app and underlying systems were involved in enforcing the access policy for corporate-level employees – approximately 40,000 people.

There were a number of important lessons that we learned from this project in relation to the use of KR, some of which are discussed in more details in [2]. In a nutshell, we faced even more challenges than I had faced before, or than I had expected.

On the one side, intelligent interaction with a user requires a level of introspection by the agent that is extremely challenging. Together with that comes the agent's need to explain its reasoning and its conclusions in terms that the user can understand – likely in an interactive dialogue – which is another very challenging task.

However, there are also challenges at the level of more typical KR and reasoning tasks, which were surprising to me. While reasoning about actions and change has made enormous progress since John McCarthy's seminal papers [17], some types of statements that are straightforward for humans are still difficult to formalize precisely and efficiently. I will summarize here some of these observations.

---

[3] https://ec.ai.

[4] https://www.billboard.com/pro/super-bowl-halftime-show-covid-safety-coronavirus/.

Consider for instance the statement "after international travel, one is not allowed access to the office for 14 days." Formalizing such statements requires some notion of "wall-clock" time and mechanisms allowing fluents to change value without intervening observations.

Action languages such as $\mathcal{H}$ [10], while possibly suitable, have a complex semantics and can reduce performance considerably due to the complexity of the underlying implementation. Additionally, in all access policies we studied, time and change were simpler than in typical uses of $\mathcal{H}$ and did not justify its use. Additive fluents [21] offer a potential solution, but once again appeared to be more sophisticated than needed, and it is unclear how to conveniently cause value changes in fluents, even if one were to formalize them via triggers. For instance, the statement "one is not allowed access to the office for 14 days" requires the ability to count down the given amount of time and to cause a fluent, say, has_access to be false for that duration and to become true at the end unless other causes intervene. While additive fluents could be used to represent the amount of time left, changing that value over time in a convenient way seems less straightforward. An additional challenge was that one would also want somehow to ensure that has_access is allowed to revert to true at the end of that period.

We were able to solve this challenge by introducing the notion of "timed" fluents – essentially, numerical fluents whose value naturally decays (or, in principle, increases) over time. However, this raised a performance problem: representing explicitly every state and state transition related to the evolution of a timed fluent becomes problematic when one is considering a long period of time, e.g. in the order of months or years. That is because, in principle, every change in the value of a timed fluent causes a state transition. It should be noted that this is strongly related to the problem faced in formalizing hybrid domains discussed in [10] and preceding articles.

With inspiration from that line of research, we realized that only part of those state transitions are critical to the evolution of the domain. In the example above, states remain "sufficiently" similar to each other until the timed fluent reaches 0, unless of course other causes intervene. We were thus able to refine the representation in such a way that only the "relevant" states were explicitly considered, and rules of the formalization itself were responsible for determining which states were relevant. For instance, in our example, there is only one "relevant" state 14 days from now.

While this approach yielded a satisfactory solution for medium-sized problem instances, our experiments showed that in the presence of larger time horizons or when more complex policies were considered, near real-time interaction with the user was still beyond reach.

One particularly interesting case was that of a subject for whose state the agent has already calculated the evolution over time, possibly for several months. Note that this evolution does not necessarily need to be only future-facing. It may contain past observations for a prolonged amount of time and the agent needs to be able to consider how the subject's state evolved in response to those observations – as the user may want to ask questions about them – and how those observations may affect future states.

Suppose now that a new observation is received, such as a covid test result. The information might be about the current moment in time, but could also be previously unavailable information about a past moment. Recomputing the entire evolution from scratch was found to take several minutes, making near real-time interaction impossible.

The obvious solution was to adopt the approach of an incremental computation, especially leveraging clingo's incremental solving capabilities [18]. Indeed, clingo's incremental solving has been demonstrated to yield substantial performance improvements. For instance, in planning problems, one can look for a plan up to a certain maximum length and, if no such plan is found, one can have the solver incrementally consider additional time steps, and do so by reusing and extending the search space built for the prior computation rather than recreating it from scratch every time.

Unfortunately, this approach did not quite seem to work for our use case, where the observations may trigger a recomputation of past states or may cause the discovery of new "relevant" states between states that had already been computed. Situations of these types violate the conditions of the Module Theorem [27] and are thus not directly solvable with clingo's incremental solving capabilities.

We were eventually able to solve the problem by developing algorithms that essentially "roll back" the search space to the latest point in the search process from which incremental computations could be applied. While this allowed us to solve the problem at hand – and, in fact, improve performance by multiple orders of magnitude – the solution was quite specific to the particular formulation and problem domain, and to the best of our knowledge, no general solution is currently available.

EC's efforts have highlighted a number of additional, and very interesting, challenges, which are outside of the scope of this article, such as those related to the prevalence of incomplete knowledge in practical applications, more so than research exercises typically consider, and to the need to draw at least partial inferences in spite of such incomplete knowledge – all while maintaining the ability to interact with the user in near real-time.

5   Conclusion

In this paper, I have reflected on people and ideas that have had a great influence on my view of knowledge representation and of declarative programming, and that have coincided with what I consider to be important milestones in the evolution of our field, some of which I have been honored to be involved with at least in part: the idea that a rigorous KR methodology and ASP itself could be viable for practical applications, the idea that declarative languages of different nature could be hybridized into languages suitable for use in industrial applications, and the idea that agents could be thought partners, capable of intelligently engaging humans when faced with problems beyond their individual capabilities.

While enormous progress has been made over the past decades, much work still remains in order to design agents that are truly intelligent and can act as such thought partners. Work has already been under way for several years on explanatory reasoning and on building more efficient ASP solvers that rely on non-ground solving techniques. However, research will also be needed in other directions. In particular, the research on incremental solving so far seem to have only scratched the surface and will need to be extended beyond the confines of the Module Theorem. Additionally, research is needed on representation, and specifically on techniques for declaratively, but efficiently, stating the conditions under which an agent should stop reasoning and seek assistance – and what to ask for. At least in part, prior work on sensing actions is a starting point (e.g., [7,8,22], as is the research on epistemic specification (e.g., [14]).

References

1. Balduccini, M.: Industrial-size scheduling with ASP+CP. In: Delgrande, J.P., Faber, W. (eds.) LPNMR 2011. LNCS (LNAI), vol. 6645, pp. 284–296. Springer, Heidelberg (2011). https://doi.org/10.1007/978-3-642-20895-9_33
2. Balduccini, M., Barborak, M., Ferrucci, D.: Action languages and COVID-19: lessons learned. In: 2nd Workshop on Causal Reasoning and Explanation in Logic Programming (CAUSAL2020) (2020)
3. Balduccini, M., Gelfond, M., Nogueira, M.: A-Prolog as a tool for declarative programming. In: Proceedings of the 12th International Conference on Software Engineering and Knowledge Engineering (SEKE2000), pp. 63–72 (2000)
4. Balduccini, M., Gelfond, M., Nogueira, M.: Answer set based design of knowledge systems. Ann. Math. Artif. Intell. **47**(1–2), 183–219 (2006)
5. Balduccini, M., Lierler, Y.: Constraint answer set solver EZCSP and why integration schemas matter. J. Theory Pract. Logic Program. (TPLP) **17**(4), 462–515 (2017)
6. Balduccini, M., Lierler, Y., Schüller, P.: Prolog and ASP inference under one roof. In: Cabalar, P., Son, T.C. (eds.) LPNMR 2013. LNCS (LNAI), vol. 8148, pp. 148–160. Springer, Heidelberg (2013). https://doi.org/10.1007/978-3-642-40564-8_15
7. Baral, C., McIlraith, S.A., Son, T.C.: Formulating diagnostic problem solving using an action language with narratives and sensing. In: Proceedings of the 2000 KR Conference, pp. 311–322 (2000)
8. Baral, C., Son, T.C.: Formalizing sensing actions - a transition function based approach. Artif. Intell. J. **125**(1–2), 19–91 (2001)
9. Baselice, S., Bonatti, P.A., Gelfond, M.: Towards an integration of answer set and constraint solving. In: Gabbrielli, M., Gupta, G. (eds.) ICLP 2005. LNCS, vol. 3668, pp. 52–66. Springer, Heidelberg (2005). https://doi.org/10.1007/11562931_7
10. Chintabathina, S., Watson, R.: Logic Programming, Knowledge Representation, and Nonmonotonic Reasoning: Essays Dedicated to Michael Gelfond on the Occasion of His 65th Birthday, chap. A New Incarnation of Action Language H, pp. 560–575. LNAI (LNCS), Springer Verlag, Berlin (2011). https://doi.org/10.1007/978-3-642-30743-0_38
11. Erdem, E.: Application of Logic Programming to Planning: Computational Experiments (1999). http://www.cs.utexas.edu/users/esra/papers.html

12. Gebser, M., Kaminski, R., Ostrowski, M., Schaub, T., Thiele, S.: On the input language of ASP grounder *Gringo*. In: Erdem, E., Lin, F., Schaub, T. (eds.) LPNMR 2009. LNCS (LNAI), vol. 5753, pp. 502–508. Springer, Heidelberg (2009). https://doi.org/10.1007/978-3-642-04238-6_49

13. Gebser, M., Kaufmann, B., Neumann, A., Schaub, T.: Conflict-driven answer set solving. In: Veloso, M.M. (ed.) Proceedings of the Twentieth International Joint Conference on Artificial Intelligence (IJCAI 2007), pp. 386–392 (2007)

14. Gelfond, M.: New semantics for epistemic specifications. In: Delgrande, J.P., Faber, W. (eds.) LPNMR 2011. LNCS (LNAI), vol. 6645, pp. 260–265. Springer, Heidelberg (2011). https://doi.org/10.1007/978-3-642-20895-9_29

15. Gelfond, M., Lifschitz, V.: Classical negation in logic programs and disjunctive databases. New Gener. Comput. **9**, 365–385 (1991). https://doi.org/10.1007/BF03037169

16. Gelfond, M., Lifschitz, V.: Representing action and change by logic programs. J. Logic Program. **17**(2–4), 301–321 (1993)

17. Hayes, P.J., McCarthy, J.: Some philosophical problems from the standpoint of artificial intelligence. In: Meltzer, B., Michie, D. (eds.) Machine Intelligence, vol. 4, pp. 463–502. Edinburgh University Press (1969)

18. Kaminski, R., Schaub, T., Wanko, P.: A tutorial on hybrid answer set solving with *clingo*. In: Ianni, G., et al. (eds.) Reasoning Web 2017. LNCS, vol. 10370, pp. 167–203. Springer, Cham (2017). https://doi.org/10.1007/978-3-319-61033-7_6

19. Katriel, I., van Hoeve, W.J.: Handbook of Constraint Programming, Chap. 6. Global Constraints, pp. 169–208. Foundations of Artificial Intelligence. Elsevier (2006)

20. Kautz, H., Selman, B.: Planning and satisfiability. In: Proceedings of the 10th European Conference on Artificial Intelligence (ECAI92), pp. 359–363 (1992)

21. Lee, J., Lifschitz, V.: Additive fluents. In: Provetti, A., Son, T.C. (eds.) Answer Set Programming: Towards Efficient and Scalable Knowledge Representation and Reasoning. AAAI 2001 Spring Symposium Series, March 2001

22. Levesque, H.J.: What is planning in the presence of sensing? In: Proceedings of the 13th National Conference on Artificial Intelligence, pp. 1139–1146 (1996)

23. Marek, V.W., Truszczynski, M.: The Logic Programming Paradigm: a 25-Year Perspective, chap. Stable Models and an Alternative Logic Programming Paradigm, pp. 375–398. Springer Verlag, Berlin (1999). https://doi.org/10.1007/978-3-642-60085-2_17

24. Mellarkod, V.S., Gelfond, M., Zhang, Y.: Integrating answer set programming and constraint logic programming. Ann. Math. Artif. Intell. **53**, 251–287 (2008). https://doi.org/10.1007/s10472-009-9116-y

25. Niemelä, I., Simons, P.: Logic-Based Artificial Intelligence, chap. Extending the Smodels System with Cardinality and Weight Constraints, pp. 491–521. Kluwer Academic Publishers (2000)

26. Nieuwenhuis, R., Oliveras, A., Tinelli, C.: Solving SAT and SAT module theories: from an abstract Davis-Putnam-Longemann-Loveland procedure to DPLL(T). J. Artif. Intell. Res. **53**(6), 937–977 (2006)

27. Oikarinen, E., Janhunen, T.: Modular equivalence for normal logic programs. In: Proceedings of the Seventeenth European Conference on Artificial Intelligence (ECAI 2006), pp. 412–416 (2006)

Answer Set Programming

Modelling the Outlier Detection Problem in ASP(Q)

Pierpaolo Bellusci, Giuseppe Mazzotta[✉], and Francesco Ricca

University of Calabria, Rende, Italy
giuseppe.mazzotta@unical.it, ricca@mat.unical.it

Abstract. Knowledge discovery techniques had important impact in several relevant application domains. Among the most important knowledge discovery tasks is *outlier detection*. Outlier detection is the task of identifying anomalous individuals in a given population. This task is very demanding from the computational complexity point of view, being located in the second level of the polynomial hierarchy. Angiulli et al. in 2007 proposed to employ Answer Set Programming (ASP) to compute outliers. Their solution is based on the saturation technique and, as a consequence, it is very hard to evaluate by ASP systems. In this paper we resort to Answer Set Programming with Quantifiers (ASP(Q)) to provide a more declarative, compact and efficient modeling of the outlier detection problem. An experiment on syntetic benchmarks proves that our ASP(Q)-based solution can handle databases that are three order of magnitude larger than the ASP-based one proposed by Angiulli et al.

Keywords: Answer Set Programming · Outlier detection · Knowledge representation

1 Introduction

The development of effective knowledge discovery techniques has become a very active research area in recent year due to the important impact it has had in several relevant application areas [8]. One interesting task is to identify anomalous individuals from a given population, for example, for bank fraud detection, network robustness analysis or intrusion detection. For the detection of these values, called *outliers*, several techniques have been already developed [2,7,9], typically through Data Mining methods, such as clustering, where large amounts of data are examined looking for values that could create inconsistencies.

These techniques are based on statistical factors that could lead to models with poor generalization capabilities. So, there are approaches in the literature that tried to exploit declarativity and expressiveness of logic programming in order to describe, in a more general way, the normal behaviour of individuals [3].

Partially supported by MISE under project MAP4ID "Multipurpose Analytics Platform 4 Industrial Data", N. F/190138/01-03/X44.

J. Cheney and S. Perri (Eds.): PADL 2022, LNCS 13165, pp. 15–23, 2022.
https://doi.org/10.1007/978-3-030-94479-7_2

In this article, we start from the work on outlier detection by Angiulli and colleagues [3], that was based on Answer Set Programming (ASP) [4,6], and we aim at providing a revised logic-based method for computing outliers that allows us to deal with instances that the previous approach is not able to treat, and in general it is more efficient in terms of execution time.

The Outlier detection task is very demanding from the computational complexity point of view, being located in the second level of the polynomial hierarchy [3]. For this reason the approach proposed by Angiulli and colleagues was based on an encoding technique called saturation [5]. As a consequence, it is a very involved solution that is also hard to evaluate by ASP systems [1].

In this paper we resort to Answer Set Programming with Quantifiers (ASP(Q)) [1] to provide a more declarative, compact and efficient modeling of the outlier detection problem focusing on the *brave* semantics [3]. An experiment on synthetic benchmarks proves that our ASP(Q)-based solution can handle databases that are three order of magnitude larger than the ASP-based one proposed by Angiulli et al.

2   Preliminaries

In this section we recall some basic notions about Answer Set Programming (ASP) and ASP with Quantifiers (ASP(Q)).

ASP. A *variable* is a string starting with uppercase letter, a *constant* instead is any integer number or any string starting with lowercase letter. A *term* is either a constant or a variable. An atom a is of the form $p(t_1, ..., t_n)$ where p is a predicate of ariety n and $t_1, ..., t_n$ are terms. If $t_1, ..., t_n$ are constants then a is a *ground* atom. A rule r is of the form:

$$a_1 \vee ... \vee a_n \leftarrow b_1, ..., b_m, not\ c_1, ...,\ not\ c_l \tag{1}$$

where *not* represents the *negation as failure*, $H_r = \{a_1, ..., a_n\}$ is a set of atoms, referred as *head*, $B_r^+ = \{b_1, ..., b_m\}$ and $B_r^- = \{c_1, ..., c_l\}$ are set of atoms, referred as *positive* and *negative body*, respectively. Given a rule r, if $H_r = \emptyset$ then r is a *constraint*; if $B_r^+ \cup B_r^- = \emptyset$ then r is a *fact*; if $|H_r| \leq 1$ then r is a *normal rule*. A *program* P is a finite set of rules. If P contains only normal rules then P is a *normal program*. The *dependency graph* of a program P is a labeled directed graph in which nodes are predicates in P and there will be a positive (resp. negative) edge from p to p' if p appears in the positive (resp. negative) body of a rule where p' appears in the head. A program P is *stratified* if the dependency graph of P does not contain cycles with negative edges. Given a program P, the *Herbrand Universe* is the set of constants appearing in P, denoted by U_P; the *Herbrand Base* is the set of all ground atoms that can be built by using predicate in P and constants in U_P, denoted by B_P; the ground instantiation of P, $ground(P)$, is the union of all possible ground instantiations of rules in P. A ground instantiation of a rule $r \in P$ is defined by a variable substitution σ that maps variables in r to constant in U_P. An *interpretation* I

for the program P is a set of ground atoms such that $I \subseteq B_P$. I is a *model* for P if for each rule $r \in ground(P)$, if $B_r^+ \subseteq I \wedge B_r^- \cap I = \emptyset$ then $H_r \cap I \neq \emptyset$. A model M is a *minimal model* if for each $M' \subset M$, M' is not a model for P. Given an interpretation I for a program P we define *Gelfond-Lifschitz reduct*, P^I, as the set of rules of the form $H_r \leftarrow B_r^+$, such that $r \in ground(P)$, $B_r^- \cap I = \emptyset$ and $H_r \neq \emptyset$. I is an *answer set* (*stable model*) of P, if I is a model for P and it is a minimal model of P^I. We denote by $AS(P)$ the set of all answer sets (or stable models) of P. A program P is *coherent* if it admits at least one answer set, otherwise it is *incoherent*.

Let W be a set of atoms. Then, P *bravely entails* W (resp. $\neg W$), denoted by $P \models_b W$ (resp. $P \models_b \neg W$), if there exists $M \in AS(P)$ such that each atom in W is evaluated true (resp. false) in M. Conversely, P *cautiously entails* W (resp. $\neg W$), denoted by $P \models_c W$ (resp. $P \models_b \neg W$), if for each model $M \in AS(P)$, each atom in W is true (resp. false) in M. For a stratified program P, $P \models_c W$ iff $P \models_b W$.

Example 1. Let P be the following ASP program:

$$r_1 : a \vee b.$$
$$r_2 : c.$$

We have that, $AS(P) = \{\{a, c\}, \{b, c\}\}$. If $W = \{c\}$ then P cautiously entails W, $P \models_c W$, since c is true in each $M \in AS(P)$; if $W = \{a\}$ then P bravely entails W, $P \models_b W$, since there is an answer set where a is true, that is $M = \{a, c\}$, but a is not true in all answer sets.

ASP(Q). An *ASP with Quantifiers* program Π is of the form:

$$\square_1 P_1 \ \square_2 P_2 \ \cdots \ \square_n P_n : C \tag{2}$$

where, for each $i = 1, \ldots, n$, $\square_i \in \{\exists^{st}, \forall^{st}\}$, P_i is an ASP program, and C is a stratified normal ASP program. $\exists^{st}$ and $\forall^{st}$ are named *existential* and *universal answer set quantifiers*, respectively. An ASP(Q)program Π of the form (2) is *existential* if $\square_1 = \exists^{st}$, otherwise if $\square_1 = \forall^{st}$ then Π in *universal*. Given a program P and an interpretation I over B_P, and an ASP(Q)program Π the form (2), we denote by $fix_P(I)$ the set of facts and constraints $\{a \mid a \in I\} \cup \{\leftarrow a \mid a \in B_P \setminus I\}$, and by $\Pi_{P,I}$ the ASP(Q)program of the form (2), where P_1 is replaced by $P_1 \cup fix_P(I)$, that is, $\Pi_{P,I} = \square_1(P_1 \cup fix_P(I)) \cdots \square_n P_n : C$. Coherence of ASP(Q) programs is defined inductively:

- $\exists^{st} P : C$ is coherent, if $\exists \ M \in AS(P)$ such that $C \cup fix_P(M)$ is coherent;
- $\forall^{st} P : C$ is coherent, if $\forall \ M \in AS(P)$, $C \cup fix_P(M)$ is coherent;
- $\exists^{st} P \ \Pi$ is coherent, if $\exists \ M \in AS(P)$ such that $\Pi_{P,M}$ is coherent;
- $\forall^{st} P \ \Pi$ is coherent, if $\forall \ M \in AS(P)$, $\Pi_{P,M}$ is coherent.

Example 2. Consider the ASP(Q) program $\Pi = \exists^{st} P_1 \forall^{st} P_2 : C$, where

$$P_1 = \{x(1) \vee x(2)\}$$

$$P_2 = \{y(1) \vee y(2) \leftarrow x(1); \; y(2) \leftarrow x(2)\}$$
$$C = \{\leftarrow y(1), \; not \; y(2)\}$$

The program P_1 has two answer sets $\{x(1)\}$ and $\{x(2)\}$. Hence, to establish the coherence of Π, we have to check if at least one of $\{x(1)\}$ and $\{x(2)\}$ is a quantified answer set of Π. Considering $\{x(1)\}$, we have $fix_{P_1}(\{x(1)\}) = \{x(1); \leftarrow x(2)\}$. Under the notation used above, $P_2' = P_2 \cup fix_{P_1}(\{x(1)\})$. Thus, $AS(P_2') = \{\{x(1), y(1)\}, \{x(1), y(2)\}\}$. For $M = \{x(1), y(1)\}$ we have $fix_{P_2'}(M) = \{x(1); y(1); \leftarrow x(2); \leftarrow y(2)\}$, and it is clear that the program $C \cup fix_{P_2'}(M)$ is not coherent. Therefore, $\{x(1)\}$ is not a quantified answer set of Π. On the other hand, a similar analysis for the other answer set of P_1, $\{x(2)\}$, shows that it is a quantified answer set of Π.

3   Outlier Detection

Outlier detection is the task of identifying anomalous individuals in a given population. We now recall the formalization of the problem proposed in [3].

Let P^{rls} be a logic program encoding general knowledge about the world, called *rule component*, and let P^{obs} be a set of facts encoding some *observations* of the current state of the world, called *observation component*. Then, the structure $\mathcal{P} = \langle P^{rls}, P^{obs} \rangle$ is a *rule-observation pair* that establish a relation between the general knowledge encoded in P^{rls} and the observations of the world encoded in P^{obs}. Given a rule-observation pair $\mathcal{P}$, the goal is to identify a set $\mathcal{O}$, if there is one, of observations, facts in P^{obs}, that are 'anomalous' (i.e., outliers) according to the general theory P^{rls} and the other facts in $P^{obs} \backslash \mathcal{O}$. The basic idea of identifying $\mathcal{O}$ is to find a *witness set* $\mathcal{W} \subseteq P^{obs}$, that is, a set of facts that a theory can explain, if and only if all the facts in $\mathcal{O}$ were not observed. This intuition is formalized in the following definition.

Definition 1. *[3] Let $\mathcal{P} = \langle P^{rls}, P^{obs} \rangle$ be a rule-observation pair and let $\mathcal{O} \subseteq P^{obs}$ be a set facts. Then, $\mathcal{O}$ is an outlier in $\mathcal{P}$ if there is a nonempty set $\mathcal{W} \subseteq P^{obs}$ with $\mathcal{W} \cap \mathcal{O} = \emptyset$, called outlier witness for $\mathcal{O}$ in $\mathcal{P}$, such that:*

1. $P(\mathcal{P})_{\mathcal{W}} \models \neg \mathcal{W}$
2. $P(\mathcal{P})_{\mathcal{W},\mathcal{O}} \not\models \neg \mathcal{W}$

where $P(\mathcal{P}) = P^{rls} \cup P^{obs}$, $P(\mathcal{P})_{\mathcal{W}} = P(\mathcal{P}) \backslash \mathcal{W}$, $P(\mathcal{P})_{\mathcal{W},\mathcal{O}} = P(\mathcal{P})_{\mathcal{W}} \backslash \mathcal{O}$, and $\models$ denotes entailment under either cautious semantics ($\models_c$) or brave semantics ($\models_b$).

An important feature accounted in Definition 1 is the possibility of dealing with the two different semantics that are commonly used in the logic programming framework, which are *brave* and *cautious semantics*. Comparing the two semantics, we can notice that *under cautious* reasoning the Definition 1 is strict in requiring that for each stable model, the witness set $\mathcal{W}$ is not entailed by the theory obtained by removing $\mathcal{W}$ itself (cond. 1), but then it just requires the

1: $down(X) \leftarrow computer(X), not\, predecessorUp(X).$
2: $predecessorUp(X) \leftarrow wired(Y, X), up(Y).$
3: $up(X) \leftarrow computer(X), not\, down(X).$
4: $computer(s).\, computer(a).\, ...\, computer(t).$
5: $wired(s, a).\, ...\, wired(g, t).$
6: $up(s).$

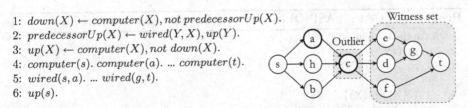

(a) Agent's background knowledge   (b) Instance of agent's observation

Fig. 1. Computer network example from [3]

existence of a model explaining some facts in $\mathcal{W}$ after the removal of the outlier $\mathcal{O}$ (cond. 2). Conversely, under *brave semantics* the definition is loose in the first point, because it requires that $\mathcal{W}$ is true in at least one stable model, but, for the condition 2, it requires that each model of $P(\mathcal{P})_{\mathcal{W},\mathcal{O}}$ entails some facts in $\mathcal{W}$. As example for the Definition 1, let us consider the problem in Fig. 1.

Example 3. (from [3]) Consider an agent A that is in charge of monitoring the connectivity status of the computer network N shown in Fig. 1b. The agent's background knowledge is modelled by a logic program P_N^{rls} in Fig. 1a, which is used by A to check whether the computer s is connected to t.

In order to monitor the network, A observes the actual status of each computer X in the network using a set of observed facts, say P_N^{obs}, defined on the *down* and *up* predicates. Assume now that P_N^{obs} comprises the facts $\{down(a),\ up(b),\ down(c),\ up(d),\ up(e),\ up(f),\ up(g),\ up(h),\ up(t)\}$; in the figure, the computers observed as down are marked in bold.

Let us consider $\mathcal{P}_N = \langle P_N^{rls}, P_N^{obs} \rangle$ as the rule-observation pair. We can notice two anomalous things in P_N^{obs}, which are *down(a)* and *down(c)*. These observations may be clearly viewed as unexpected according to the background knowledge, although only one lead to an inconsistency. Indeed, let $\mathcal{W}$ be the witness set $\{up(d),\ up(e),\ up(f),\ up(g),\ up(t)\}$ and $\mathcal{O}$ be the outlier set $\{down(c)\}$, then it is easy to see that $P(\mathcal{P}_N)_{\mathcal{W}} \models_b \neg \mathcal{W}$ and $P(\mathcal{P}_N)_{\mathcal{W},\mathcal{O}} \not\models_b \neg \mathcal{W}$ are satisfied. Therefore, $\{down(c)\}$ is an outlier in $P(\mathcal{P}_N)$, and $\mathcal{W}$ is an outlier witness for $\mathcal{O}$ in $\mathcal{P}_N$ (under the brave semantics). Actually, since the program has exactly one stable model, it is the case that *down(c)* is an outlier and $\mathcal{W}$ its witness also under cautious semantics.

4 ASP(Q) Encoding

Starting from the formal definition of outlier detection problem [3] and Quantified ASP [1], we provide a more declarative, compact and efficient modeling of the outlier detection problem exploiting the ASP with Quantifiers. Let us consider the case of a pair $\mathcal{P} = \langle P^{rls}, P^{obs} \rangle$ such that P^{rls} is a generic logic program, and therefore may have more than one model. Specifically we focus on brave semantics, where it is necessary to check if there exists a stable model

Program 1. General ASP(Q) encoding schema for brave sematics

```
1: %@exists (defines P₁)
2:      ρc1(P^rls)
3:      ρobs(P^obs)
4:
5:      {o(X):obs(X)}.
6:      {w(X):obs(X),not o(X)}.
7:
8:      c1(X) :- not w(X), obs(X).
9:      bad_c1 :- w(X), c1(X).
10:
11: %@forall (defines P₂)
12:      ρc2(P^rls)
13:
14:      c2(X) :- not o(X), not w(X), obs(X).
15:      sat_c2 :- w(X), c2(X).
16:
17: %@constraint (defines C)
18:      :- bad_c1.
19:      :- not sat_c2.
```

for condition 1 (of Definition 1) such that for all stable models of condition 2 (of Definition 1) is valid. Hence, we model a ASP(Q)program Π of the form $\exists^{st} P_1 \forall^{st} P_2 : C$ such that P_1 is used for checking condition 1 in Definition 1, while P_2 is used for checking condition 2 in the same definition, and C is used to impose some constraints. The encoding Π is shown in Program 1. We present the encoding in the syntax of the *qasp* solver by Amendola et.al, where *%@keyword* where $keyword \in \{forall, exists, constraint\}$ indicate the scope of the logic programs in plain text files. In order to better understand, the idea behind our approach let us define ρ_x as a rewriting function that given a ASP program P, it replaces each atom $p \in P$ with $x(p)$ where the atom p became a function-symbol and x is an arbitrary predicate. For example let $P = \{a(D) \leftarrow b(D), \; not \; c(D).\}$, $\rho_x(P) = \{x(a(D)) \leftarrow x(b(D)), \; not \; x(c(D)).\}\}$.

This allows us to exploit the grounding phase of the ASP system to simulate the programs $P(\mathcal{P})_\mathcal{W}$ and $P(\mathcal{P})_{\mathcal{W},\mathcal{O}}$, and also gives us the opportunity to make the encoding more general. In particular, under the existential quantifier we compute $\rho_{c1}(P^{rls})$ for checking condition 1 and $\rho_{obs}(P^{obs})$ to generalize observed facts. Finally, under the forall quantifier we use $\rho_{c2}(P^{rls})$ for checking condition 2. Analyzing in more detail the encoding, in the program P_1 there are two choice rules for guessing the outlier and the witness sets. The first choice rule guesses a set of outliers from the set of observations, such that for each observation in the set the rule can decide whether to instantiate $o(X)$ or not. Since from Definition 1, the set of outliers $\mathcal{O}$ and the set of witness $\mathcal{W}$ have to be disjoint, the second choice rule performs the guess of a set of witness from the observations, such that for each observation, which is not an outlier, the rule can decide whether to instantiate $w(X)$ or not. At the end of P_1, there are the

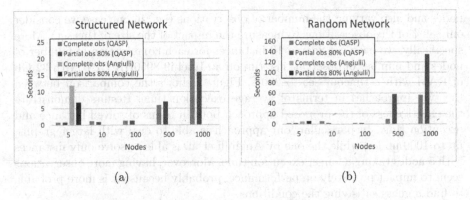

Fig. 2. Graphs comparing the tests performed on the Network dataset

main rules for checking condition 1. The first rule aims to simulate the $P(\mathcal{P})_{\mathcal{W}}$, adding to $c1$ all the observations that are not witness. The second rule is used to evaluate if condition 1 is not satisfied using the atom bad_c1, which is true if in $c1$ there is at least an observation that is also true in the witness set violating the condition $P(\mathcal{P})_{\mathcal{W}} \models \neg\mathcal{W}$. Program P_2, instead, contains only the rules necessary for checking condition 2. The first rule aims to simulate the $P(\mathcal{P})_{\mathcal{W,O}}$, adding to $c2$ all the observations that are neither outlier nor witness. The second rule is used to evaluate if the condition 2 is satisfied using the atom sat_c2, which is true if in $c2$ there is an observation that is also true in the witness set, and therefore satisfying the condition $P(\mathcal{P})_{\mathcal{W,O}} \not\models \neg\mathcal{W}$. Hence, we can deduce that the interest is only in stable models in which bad_c1 is false and sat_c2 is true, and this is modeled by the program under the *constraint* keyword. Summarizing, the program P_1 encodes the observations P^{obs}, generates the possible outlier and witness set and evaluates condition 1. Afterward, the program P_2 evaluated condition 2 and, finally, the program C imposes that the previous encoded conditions have to be satisfied. In this way, for a candidate answer set of P_1 we impose that observations, outlier and witness facts must be true in every model of P_2.

5   Experiments

[1]In this section we analyze the results obtained with the new approach for outlier detection running *qasp* solver by Amendola et al. by comparing it with the one proposed in [3]. The two implementations have been evaluated on a dataset based on Example 3 in which two types of graph are used. In particular we have structured graphs, in which the architecture is close to a real network simulating connection between different subnets, and random graphs, in which each node is connected to at most with 10% of the network. The entire evaluation has been conducted considering graph of different dimension in terms of the number of

---

[1] https://github.com/MazzottaG/QASP-OutlierDetection.

nodes and also varying the number of observations (i.e., in one case we consider only 80% of the observations to measure the impact of the size of this set). More specifically, we have considered 10 instances for each combination of number of nodes and number of observations, run on an Intel i9-8950HK CPU with 32 Gb of RAM with a timeout set to 200 s. Figure 2 shows the comparison between the two approaches in terms of average execution time. Results demonstrate the effectiveness of the proposed approach both in terms of solved instance and execution time. In particular, our approach is able to deal with larger graphs, up to 1000 nodes, while the one by Angiulli et al. is able to solve only instances with 5 nodes taking a longer execution time. Moreover, having more observations seem to impact positively on performance, probably because it is more probable to find a guess satisfying the conditions.

6 Conclusion

Inspired by the way the work done by Angiulli et al. [3], we have introduced a new declarative approach for computing outliers that is based on ASP(Q). Comparing our encoding with the one employed by Angiulli et al. it becomes clear that we use less symbols (number of atoms and rules in the program). Indeed, the ASP encoding of Angiulli et al. has to resort to the saturation techniques [5], thus resulting in a less readable and computationally-expensive encoding. Instead, our solution, that is based on ASP(Q), offers an alternative and more efficient approach. An experiment proves empirically that our ASP(Q)-based solution can handle databases that are three order of magnitude larger than previous approach. As future work we plan to extend our approach to cautious semantics.

References

1. Amendola, G., Ricca, F., Truszczynski, M.: Beyond NP: quantifying over answer sets. Theory Pract. Logic Program. **19**(5–6), 705–721 (2019)
2. Angiulli, F., Fassetti, F., Serrao, C.: ODCA: an outlier detection approach to deal with correlated attributes. In: Golfarelli, M., Wrembel, R., Kotsis, G., Tjoa, A.M., Khalil, I. (eds.) DaWaK 2021. LNCS, vol. 12925, pp. 180–191. Springer, Cham (2021). https://doi.org/10.1007/978-3-030-86534-4_17
3. Angiulli, F., Greco, G., Palopoli, L.: Outlier detection by logic programming. ACM Trans. Comput. Logic **9**(1), 7 (2007)
4. Brewka, G., Eiter, T., Truszczynski, M.: Answer set programming at a glance. Commun. ACM **54**(12), 92–103 (2011)
5. Eiter, T., Gottlob, G.: On the computational cost of disjunctive logic programming: Propositional case. Ann. Math. Artif. Intell. **15**(3–4), 289–323 (1995). https://doi.org/10.1007/BF01536399
6. Gelfond, M., Lifschitz, V.: Classical negation in logic programs and disjunctive databases. New Gener. Comput. **9**(3/4), 365–386 (1991). https://doi.org/10.1007/BF03037169

7. Gupta, M., Gao, J., Aggarwal, C.C., Han, J.: Outlier detection for temporal data: a survey. IEEE Trans. Knowl. Data Eng. **26**(9), 2250–2267 (2014)
8. Maimon, O., Rokach, L. (eds.): Data Mining and Knowledge Discovery Handbook, 2nd edn. Springer, Boston (2010). https://doi.org/10.1007/978-0-387-09823-4
9. Ord, K.: Outliers in statistical data. Int. J. Forecast. **12**(1), 175–176 (1996)

Multi-agent Pick and Delivery with Capacities: Action Planning Vs Path Finding

Nima Tajelipirbazari[1] , Cagri Uluc Yildirimoglu[2] , Orkunt Sabuncu[1] ,
Ali Can Arici[3], Idil Helin Ozen[3], Volkan Patoglu[2] , and Esra Erdem[2(✉)]

[1] Department of Computer Engineering, TED University, Ankara, Turkey
[2] Faculty of Engineering and Natural Sciences, Sabanci University, Istanbul, Turkey
esra.erdem@sabanciuniv.edu
[3] Ekol Logistics, Istanbul, Turkey

Abstract. Motivated by autonomous warehouse applications in the real world, we study a variant of Multi-Agent Path Finding (MAPF) problem where robots also need to pick and deliver some items on their way to their destination. We call this variant the Multi-Agent Pick and Delivery with Capacities (MAPDC) problem. In addition to the challenges of MAPF (i.e., finding collision-free plans for each robot from an initial location to a destination while minimizing the maximum makespan), MAPDC asks also for the allocation of the pick and deliver tasks among robots while taking into account their capacities (i.e., the maximum number of items one robot can carry at a time). We study this problem with two different approaches, action planning vs path finding, using Answer Set Programming with two different computation modes, single-shot vs multi-shot.

Keywords: Multi-agent path finding · Pick and delivery with capacities · Action planning · Answer set programming

1 Introduction

Most warehouses share the same general pattern of material flow [1]: they receive bulk shipments, put them away for quick retrieval, pick them in response to customer requests, and then pack and ship them out to customers. The third component of this flow, i.e., order-picking, typically accounts for about 55% of warehouse operating costs. With increasing demand on e-commerce due to the pandemic, the importance and effect of order-picking also increase [9]. Furthermore, among the three main phases of order-picking (i.e., traveling to the location of the product, searching for the product at that location, and grabbing/collecting the product), traveling comprises the greatest part of the expense of order-picking.

With these motivations, we study a variant of Multi Agent Pathfinding (**MAPF**) problem, where the agents need to pick and deliver some items on their way to their destination. We call this problem **MAPDC**. In addition to the challenges of MAPF (i.e., finding collision-free plans for each agent from its initial location to a goal destination

This work has been partially supported by Tubitak Grant 118E431.

while minimizing the maximum makespan), **MAPDC** asks also for the allocation of the pick and deliver tasks among agents while taking into account their capacities (i.e., the maximum number of items one agent can carry at a time).

We study this problem with two different approaches, action planning vs path finding, based on Answer Set Programming (ASP) [2,7,11,15,17].

In the planning approach, we represent the agents' actions (i.e., moving to a location, picking a product, delivering a product), and the change in the warehouse (i.e., over the locations and the bags of agents) by an action domain description in ASP. This description takes into account the collision constraints and the capacity constraints. After that, we model **MAPDC** as a planning problem, with its initial state description (i.e., initial locations of agents and the order-picking tasks) and goal description (i.e., destinations of agents while enforcing all the tasks are completed).

In the path finding approach, we model **MAPDC** as a graph problem. We view the warehouse environment as a graph, allocate tasks to each agent, and compute a path and its traversal recursively for each agent, respecting the collision and capacity constraints and ensuring the completion of all tasks, while minimizing the maximum makespan.

We compare these two approaches empirically with randomly generated instances over various sizes and types of warehouses (e.g., where shelves are shorter/longer, closer/farther to/from each other). We use the ASP solver CLINGO [5] in our experiments, considering single-shot vs multi-shot computations.

2   Related Work

MAPF is a well-studied problem with various optimizations, using different approaches, such as ASP [4], ILP [21], SAT [19], and search-based [18] methods.

Considering pick and delivery tasks assigned to agents, some variants of **MAPF** have been studied. For instance, **TAPF** [13] generalizes **MAPF** by assigning targets to teams of agents, while **G-TAPF** [16] further allows greater number of tasks per agent. **MAPDC** differs from **G-TAPF** in that it does not consider teams of agents or assumes an order of tasks. **MAPDC** considers capacity constraints of the agents and asks for the order of tasks as well.

Liu et al. [12] study **MAPD** problems (i.e., **MAPDC** where the capacity of each agent is 1) by first assigning tasks to agents, and then using a search-based path finding algorithm to compute collision-free paths. The search stage tries to minimize the makespan after committing to the task assignment found in the first stage. Although dividing the overall problem into two stages scales better, it does not guarantee optimal solutions for the overall problem. **MAPDC** considers capacity constraints and guarantees optimal solutions without dividing the problem into two parts.

For the offline setting, Honig et al. [10] propose a Conflict Based Search (CBS) approach to solve **MAPD**. It is complete and optimal for the sum of path lengths, a metric different from the one we consider in our approaches. CBS is known to scale poorly as the number of conflicts among agents increases [16]. Along these lines, authors have also presented a bounded sub-optimal approach (ECBS) to improve scalability.

In online versions of **MAPD** [14], agents have to fulfil a stream of delivery tasks. The tasks are allocated to free agents such that every agent can execute at most one task. Then, a path from the initial location to the pick-up location, and then to the delivery location, and finally to the destination, is computed. The agents cannot rest in their destinations after they finish executing tasks. Grenouilleau et al. [8] also address online **MAPD** problems where new tasks appear whenever they arrive. They first assign tasks to agents using an heuristics approach and use a modified A* search algorithm so that one search call is sufficient, instead of two calls, for finding the two paths of the agent: one from its current location to the pickup location and the other one from the pickup location to the delivery one.

Different from these studies, we focus on an offline method that allocates tasks to compute plans, and that computes plans to pick and deliver the allocated tasks. Therefore, in our approach, task allocation and planning are not decoupled: they are handled at the same time. Furthermore, an agent can handle more than one task at a time, and it is not assumed to disappear when it reaches its destination.

Chen et al. [3] solve **MAPD** problem in both offline and online settings. Similar to **MAPDC** problem, they also consider capacities where agents can carry multiple items at a time. Unlike the previous **MAPD** solution techniques, their search-based algorithm handles task assignment and path finding simultaneously. Even though considering actual path costs while assigning tasks to agents improves the quality of solutions found, in its current form, their algorithm does not guarantee optimality, unlike our proposed solutions for the **MAPDC** problem. Regarding optimality of solutions, they propose a variant of the algorithm where local search techniques are used to further improve the best solution at hand.

Another related study is by Vodrazka et al. [20] since they introduce a planning approach to solve and study **MAPF**. They consider a special case of a planning problem with only two actions, move and wait, subject to the constraint that there is no collision between the agents. They present a method that first computes a sequential plan where at most one agent moves to a free location at a time, and cuts the sequential plan into sub-plans, and parallelize them so that several agents can move at a time without any vertex collision. These authors also present another method that splits the move action into start-move and finish-move actions, and ensures that, for each action, the agents need to have a token as a precondition and pass the token to another agent as an effect. Our planning method for **MAPDC** considers picks and delivers as well. Thanks to the expressive formalism of ASP, concurrent plans can be generated without further need to split sequential plans or actions.

Overall, different from the related work, both of our action planning and path finding based approaches address the offline version of **MAPDC** while considering the capacities of agents, solve the task assignment and path finding problems simultaneously to ensure the optimality of solutions in terms of the overall completion time (the maximum makespan) of tasks.

3   MAPDC-P: Solving MAPDC with a Planning Approach

We model the **MAPDC** as a planning problem by representing actions of agents and changes in the warehouse by an action domain description which also considers all collision and capacity constraints. Agents use these plans to navigate from their starting locations to destinations while picking up and delivering items. Our goal is to pick-up and deliver every item in tasks, while optimizing the overall completion time of tasks.

3.1 MAPDC as a Planning Problem

We consider the environment of agents as a graph $G = (V, E)$ where the set V of locations form a 4-neighbour grid and the edges E are based on the adjacent locations in this grid. Some of the locations may be occupied with shelves and they are treated as static obstacles for the agents.

The functional fluent *position* represents the locations of agents. Specifically, for an agent $i \in A$ the fluent value $pos(i) = l@x$ represents the location of i at time step $x \leq u \in \mathbb{Z}^+$ is $l \in V$. Consequently, $pos(i) = init(i)@0$ and $pos(i) = goal(i)@u$ hold, where *init* and *goal* functions specify the initial and goal locations of agents, respectively.

Agents move along the edges of the graph. Considering the grid structure of the environment, we model $move(i, dir)$ action of agent i, where dir is among four cardinal directions. Specifically, an action occurrence $move(i, dir)@x$ represents a movement of agent i in direction dir at time step x. Whenever $pos(i) = l_1@x - 1$ holds, a $move(i, dir)@x$ action occurrence changes the position of the agent i such that $pos(i) = l_2@x$ holds where $(l_1, l_2) \in E$ and position l_2 is adjacent to l_1 in the direction dir[1].

In a **MAPDC** problem, we consider vertex and edge collisions. A vertex collision occurs whenever $pos(i) = l@x$ and $pos(j) = l@x$ hold for two different agents i and j at time point x. Similarly, an edge collision occurs whenever $pos(i) = l_1@x$, $pos(j) = l_2@x$, $pos(i) = l_2@y$, and $pos(j) = l_1@y$ hold s.t. $i \neq j$, $y = x + 1$ and $(l_1, l_2) \in E$.

Each task $t \in T$ of the form (id, p, d) has a unique identifier id, a pick up location $p \in V$, and a delivery location $d \in V$. A task must be assigned to a unique agent and the agent fulfils it by picking up a product from the task's pick up location and carrying the product until delivered to the task's delivery location. To this end, an agent may perform *pickup* and *deliver* actions with the condition that the agent must be at the pick up and delivery locations, respectively. Specifically, for a task (id, p, d) action occurrences $pickup(i, id)@x$ and $deliver(i, id)@x$ are possible if $pos(i) = p@x - 1$ and $pos(i) = d@x - 1$ hold, respectively. Additionally, for the latter action to be possible the agent must be carrying the product respective to the task. The boolean fluent *carrying* is used for representing the products an agent carries. The occurrence $pickup(i, id)@x$ causes $carrying(i, id)@x$ to hold and the fluent keeps holding until $deliver(i, id)@y$ occurs such that $y > x$. Note that a task with identifier id is fulfilled whenever a $deliver(i, id)$ action occurs by an agent i at time step x. Moreover, the product related to a task cannot be picked up more than one time by an agent. To this end, for an action $pickup(i, id)$ occurrence, neither the task with id id is fulfilled before nor the agent i is carrying the product related to the task.

A plan, which is composed of occurrences of actions *move*, *pickup* and *deliver*, is a solution of a **MAPDC** problem, if and only if there are no vertex or edge collisions considering the *position* fluent values projected by the actions in the plan, all agents are at their goal locations at the last time step of the plan, all tasks are fulfilled, and each agent carries at most c number of products at any time step, where capacity c is given as an input of the problem. The last condition constrains that for any agent i and any

---

[1] The effects of an action appear at the same time step as the occurrence of the action, instead of the next time step, to comply with the multi-shot ASP formulation of **MAPDC-P** explained in the next section.

time step x, $\left|\{id \mid carrying(i,id)@x\ holds\}\right| \leq c$. Based on these notations, **MAPDC** problem can be defined as a planning problem (i.e., **MAPDC-P**) as illustrated in Fig. 1.

3.2   Solving MAPDC-P Using Multi-shot ASP

We rely on multi-shot ASP [5] for solving the **MAPDC-P** problem. Multi-shot solving is used to encode dynamic domains, such as planning problems, where the logic program changes during the solving process. Given a planning problem, one can encode a multi-shot ASP program by partitioning the whole program into three parts; the static part where knowledge that does not change with time is represented, the cumulative part corresponding to knowledge that accumulates at increasing time steps, and the volatile part where we represent knowledge that is added for a specific time step and retracted when the time step is increased during the multi-shot solving process. As a planning problem, **MAPDC-P** is naturally suitable for encoding via multi-shot ASP.

MAPDC-P

Input:
- A graph $G = (V, E)$ where the set V of locations form a 4-neighbour grid and the edges E are based on adjacent locations in this grid.
- A set $O \subseteq V$ (to denote the parts of the environment occupied by shelves).
- A set A of agents.
- A function $init : A \mapsto V$ (to describe the initial locations of agents).
- A function $goal : A \mapsto V$ (to describe the goal locations of agents).
- A set T of tasks (id, p, d) (with unique identifier id, and pick up and delivery locations $p, d \in V$).
- A positive integer t (to specify the maximum makespan).
- A positive integer c (to specify the capacity of each agent).

Output: For some positive integer $u \leq t$, a plan W of length u, i.e., a sequence $\langle A_1, ..., A_u \rangle$ where each A_x, $1 \leq x \leq u$ is a set of action occurrences among the following ones:
- $move(i, dir)@x$ (to describe that agent i moves in direction dir at time step x),
- $pickup(i, id)@x$ (to describe that agent i picks up a product for task id at time step x),
- $deliver(i, id)@x$ (to describe that agent i delivers a product for task id at time step x),

such that the following hold:
- No parallel move actions are allowed for an agent at any time step, i.e., for any A_x, there are no $move(i, dir_1)@x \in A_x$ and $move(i, dir_2)@x \in A_x$ s.t. $dir_1 \neq dir_2$.
- All tasks are complete, i.e., $\forall\ task(id, p, d) \in T$ there exists a time step $x \leq u$ and an agent $i \in A$ s.t. $deliver(i, id)@x \in A_x$.
- Agents do not carry more than their capacity, i.e., $\left|\{id \mid carrying(i, id)@x\ holds\}\right| \leq c$.
- All agents are at their goal locations at the last time step, i.e., $\forall i \in A, pos(i) = goal(i)@u$ holds.
- There are no vertex or edge collisions, i.e., whenever $pos(i) = l_i@x$ and $pos(j) = l_j@x$ hold for $i \neq j$, $l_i \neq l_j$ also holds and whenever $pos(i) = l_i@x$ and $pos(j) = l_j@x$ hold for $i \neq j$, $(l_i, l_j) \in E$, $pos(i) = l_j@x+1$ and $pos(j) = l_i@x+1$ cannot hold together.

Fig. 1. MAPDC-P: MAPDC as a planning problem.

During multi-shot solving, CLINGO increases the time step until it finds an answer set, which corresponds to a plan for the problem. This way of solving has the advantage that the computed plan will be optimal in terms of the time steps. Hence, a plan for a **MAPDC-P** problem found by multi-shot solving will be optimal regarding its makespan.

In our encoding unlike the common practice in ASP community where actions are executed at time step x and its effects are seen at time step $x + 1$, we encode effects of an action at the same time step as the occurrence of the action to eliminate the extra grounding and solving step that otherwise multi-shot solver would need in order to work with the atoms of the next time step.

Similar to a multi-shot ASP encoding of a general planning problem, our **MAPDC-P** encoding has three parts. The static part is mainly composed of the grid environment and facts from the **MAPDC-P** instance. For this part, we rely on the encoding of M domain in asprilo for the instance format and some domain predicate signatures. Asprilo is a framework for experimenting with logistic domains in ASP [6]. Briefly, we use predicates isRobot/1, task/3, shelfPos/3, and finalPos/2 for representing agents, tasks, locations of shelves (these will be used as pick up and delivery locations of tasks), and goal locations of agents, respectively. Additionally, we have instances of pos/1 and nextto/3 predicates to represent set V of grid locations and subset of edges E, where each edge has no location occupied by an obstacle.

The static part also includes the following rule. This choice rule succinctly assigns each task to a unique agent. Later, the assign/2 predicate will be used as preconditions for representations of actions *pickup* and *deliver*. Note that the #program directive groups a set of rules as a program part. Here the static part is named as base.

```
#program base.
1{assign(I,ID): isRobot(I)}1 :- task(ID,P,D).
```

In the cumulative part, we represent dynamic knowledge of **MAPDC-P** accumulating with each increasing time point. Specifically, in this part we represent actions and fluents of the domain. Below, an instance move(i,dir,x) of the move/3 predicate represents the action occurrence $move(i, dir)@x$ and the predicate direction/1 represents cardinal movement directions. Note that parameter x in all the remaining rules is a program part parameter. It represents time steps in our domain and is controlled by CLINGO during incremental grounding of the program part named as step by the #program directive. Basically, it is instantiated with value 1 and incremented by 1 in each grounding stage of multi-shot solving. Hence, the choice rule below encodes that each agent can move in any of the directions at a time step. The upper bound in the choice rule head neatly represents the constraint that no parallel movement actions are allowed for an agent. The second rule represents the effect of movement action. An instance pos(i,l,x) of the pos/3 predicate represents the fluent valuation $pos(i) = l@x$ holds. The third rule constrains that no agent moves in a direction where there is no edge from the current position of the agent.

```
#program step(x).
{move(I,DIR,x): direction(DIR)} 1 :- isRobot(I), time(x).
pos(I,L,x) :- move(I,DIR,x), pos(I,L',x-1), nextto(L',DIR,L).
:- move(I,DIR,x), pos(I,L ,x-1), not nextto(L ,DIR,_).
```

Next two rules represent the *position* fluent is inertial and functional, respectively. For any agent, when there is no reason to change its location (whenever it does not move), its location from the previous time step stays the same for this time step. Related to this, an agent must be at exactly one location at each time step.

```
{pos(I,L,x)} :- pos(I,L,x-1), isRobot(I), time(x).
:- {pos(I,L,x)}!=1, isRobot(I), time(x).
```

The following group of rules guarantees that there are no edge or vertex collisions in the plan found as an answer set. The moveto(1',1,x) instance in an answer set represents that an agent has moved from 1' to 1 at time step *x*.

```
moveto(L',L,x) :- nextto(L',DIR,L), pos(I,L',x-1), move(I,DIR,x).
:- moveto(L',L,x), moveto(L,L',x), L < L'.
:- {pos(I,L,x): isRobot(I)}>1, pos(L), time(x).
```

The rules presented upto now in the cumulative part are based on the encoding of asprilo's M domain [6], which basically encodes the **MAPF** problem.

In a **MAPDC-P** problem, agents can perform additional pick up and deliver actions. The following rule represents that an agent *i* can choose to pick up a product for the task *id* at time step *x* if the task *id* has been assigned to *i* (assign/2 predicate in the body), agent *i* is not already carrying the product for *id* (negative carrying/3 predicate), and the task *id* has not been fulfilled yet (negative delivered/3 predicate).

```
{pickup(I,ID,x)} :- pos(I,P,x-1), task(ID,P,D),
    assign(I,ID), not delivered(ID,x), not carrying(I,ID,x-1).
```

Similarly, the following choice rule represents *deliver* actions where deliver(i,id,x) basically corresponds to the action occurrence *deliver(i,id)@x* in a plan. Note that, for a *deliver* action, we need the agent must be carrying the respective product (represented by the carrying/3 predicate in rule body).

```
{deliver(I,ID,x)} :- carrying(I,ID,x-1), pos(I,D,x-1),
    task(ID,P,D), assign(I,ID).
```

Considering the previous rules defining *pickup* and *deliver* actions, an atom of the form carrying(i,id,x) represents that the fluent *carrying(i,id)* holds at time step *x*. The first rule in the following group states that *carrying* fluent is a direct effect of *pickup* action. Similarly, delivered(id,x) represents that task *id* has been fulfilled via *delivered* fluent. This fluent is an effect of *deliver* action (represented by third rule). While the second rule represents that *carrying* fluent does not change its value until the agent delivers the respective package, the last rule represents that the *delivered* fluent persists after becoming true.

```
carrying(I,ID,x)  :- pickup(I,ID,x).
carrying(I,ID,x)  :- carrying(I,ID,x-1), not deliver(I,ID,x).
delivered(ID,x)   :- deliver(I,ID,x).
delivered(ID,x)   :- delivered(ID,x -1).
```

Thanks to the powerful construct of aggregates in ASP, the following constraint rule prevents any agent carry more products than the capacity *c* at any time step.

```
:- isRobot(I),time(x),#count{ID : carrying(I,ID,x)} > c.
```

The following rules comprises the volatile part where we represent knowledge that does not accumulate and is related to a specific time step. In a typical multi-shot encoding of a planning problem, this part is used for representing goal conditions of the problem. While the first rule guarantees that all tasks are fulfilled, the second one assures all agents are at their destination locations at the last time step u. Note that the query/1 predicate is an external one that is controlled by CLINGO. Given an instance of it (e.g., query(y)), CLINGO sets its truth value as true when searching for a plan at horizon y. In case no plan is found for horizon y, the truth value of query(y) becomes false and the current horizon is incremented.

```
#program check(x).
:- ordered(ID), not delivered(ID,x), query(x).
:- finalPos(I,L), not pos(I,L,x), query(x).
```

4   MAPDC-G: Solving MAPDC with a Path Finding Approach

We model the **MAPDC** problem as a graph problem. The idea is to view the warehouse environment as a graph, allocate tasks to each agent, and compute a path and its traversal for each agent, respecting the collision constraints and ensuring the completion of all tasks, while minimizing the maximum makespan.

4.1   MAPDC as a Graph Problem

We view the environment as a graph $G = (V, E)$. A path P_i that an agent $i \in A$ traverses in this graph is characterized by a sequence $\langle w_{i,1}, w_{i,2}, \ldots, w_{i,n_i} \rangle$ of vertices such that $\{w_{i,j}, w_{i,j+1}\} \in E$ for all $j < n$. A traversal $traversal_i$ of a path P_i by an agent i within some time u_i ($u_i \in \mathbb{Z}^+$) is a function that maps each time step $x \leq u_i$, to a vertex in P_i describing the location of agent i at time x.

For two agents $i, j \in A$, they collide with each other at time step x if they are at the same location (i.e., $traversal_i(x) = traversal_j(x)$) or when they are swapping their locations (i.e., $traversal_i(x) = traversal_j(x-1)$ and $traversal_i(x-1) = traversal_j(x)$).

Each given task (id, p, d) is associated by a product id that needs to be picked up at some location $p \in V$ and delivered at some other location $d \in V$. We suppose that each pickup and delivery takes one unit of time. Each agent has a limited capacity to carry at most c number of tasks. We describe the *bag of an agent* $i \in A$ by a function $carry_i$ that maps every time step $x \leq u_i$ to a set of tasks (i.e., products) that the agent is carrying at that time step.

As the tasks are completed during the traversal $traversal_i$ of P_i, we need to pay attention to that the tasks are picked up before they are delivered, and the number of items carried by agent i is not more than its capacity c. We say that an agent i *completes a task* $(id, p, d) \in T_i$ within time u_i if there exist a pickup time x and a delivery time y ($0 \leq x < y \leq u_i$) such that $traversal_i(x) = p$, $traversal_i(y) = d$ and $(id, p, d) \in carry_i(z)$ for every time step z between x and y only.

An agent i finishes its traversal in $u_i < t$ time steps. After time step u_i, the agent stays at its goal location. We define $traversal_i$ for time steps greater than u_i as a constant function: $traversal_i(x) = goal(i), u_i \leq x \leq t$.

MAPDC-G

Input:
- A graph $G = (V,E)$ (to describe the environment).
- A set $O \subseteq V$ (to denote the obstacles in the environment).
- A set A of agents.
- A function $init : A \mapsto V$ (to describe the initial locations of agents).
- A function $goal : A \mapsto V$ (to describe the goal locations of agents).
- A set T of tasks (id, p, d) (with unique identifier id, and pick-up and delivery locations $p, d \in V$).
- A positive integer t (to specify the maximum makespan).
- A positive integer c (to specify the capacity of each agent).

Output: For every agent $i \in A$, for some positive integer $u_i \leq t$,
- a set T_i of tasks allocated to the agent i where $\bigcup_{j \in A} T_j = T$ and
  - for every $j \in A$, $i \neq j$ implies $T_i \cap T_j = \emptyset$;
- a path $P_i = \langle w_{i,1}, \ldots, w_{i,n_i} \rangle$ of length n_i ($n_i \leq u_i$) that the agent i can traverse
  - to reach its goal location $w_{i,n_i} = goal(i)$ from its initial location $w_{i,1} = init(i)$,
  - to complete the allocated tasks T_i (i.e., for every $(id, p, d) \in T_i$, there exists $w_{i,j}, w_{i,k} \in P_i$ where $j \leq k$, $w_{i,j} = p$ and $w_{i,k} = d$,
  - without colliding with any obstacles (i.e., $w_{i,j} \in V \setminus O$); and
- a collision-free traversal $traversal_i$ of the path P_i within time u_i and how the bag of the agent i changes during this traversal (i.e., $carry_i$) such that
  - every task in T_i is completed by the agent i with respect to its traversal, and
  - for every $x \leq u_i$, the agent i can carry as many tasks as its capacity: $|carry_i(x)| < c$.

Fig. 2. MAPDC-G: MAPDC as a graph problem.

Based on these notations, **MAPDC** problem can be defined as a graph problem (i.e., **MAPDC-G**) as illustrated in Fig. 2. Given the environment G whose some parts are occupied by obstacles O, the initial and goal locations for each agent, a set T of all tasks to be handled by the agents, the goal is to allocate the tasks in T to all agents, and, for each agent i, to find a path P_i and a collision-free traversal $traversal_i$ of P_i ensuring that agent i completes the allocated set T_i of tasks by a time step $u_i \leq t$.

4.2 Solving MAPDC-G Using Multi-shot ASP

We present a multi-shot formulation of **MAPDC-G** in ASP, based on the definition in Fig. 2. The input graph G of the problem is described by predicates `node/1` and `edge/2`; the obstacles, agents, and tasks are described by the predicates `obs/1`, `agent/1`, `task/3`, respectively; and the initial and goal locations of agents are described by predicates `init/2` and `goal/2`.

The traversal of a path, and the bag of an agent are described by predicates `traverse/3` and `carry/3`. Here, `traverse(I,T,N)` expresses that the agent `I` is at the location `N` at time step `T`, whereas `carry(I,T,ID)` expresses that the agent `I` carries the product specified by the task `ID` at time step `T`.

The ASP formulation for **MAPDC-G** consists of three parts: `base, step, check`. Note that Listing 7 in [5] should be included at the beginning of the formulation.

The base program is grounded only once. It consists of the rules expressing that the traversals start at the initial locations of agents, and each task is assigned to one agent:

```
traverse(I,0,S):- agent(I), init(I,S).
1{assign(I,ID): agent(I)}1 :- task(ID,P,D).
```

The step program is grounded incrementally for t=1,2,3,.... For each agent, a path and its traversal are generated recursively ensuring that the agent cannot be at two different locations.

```
1{traverse(I,t,X); traverse(I,t,Y):edge(X,Y)}1 :- traverse(I,t-1,X).
:- traverse(I,t,X), traverse(I,t,Y), agent(I), node(X), node(Y), Y<X.
```

Then the following constraints are used to ensure that agents do not collide with each other at a node or an edge, or with obstacles.

```
:- traverse(I,t,X), traverse(J,t,X), node(X), agent(I), agent(J), I<J.
:- traverse(I,t-1,X), traverse(I,t,Y), traverse(J,t-1,Y),
   traverse(J,t,X), agent(I), agent(J), edge(X,Y), I<J.
:- traverse(I,t,X), obs(X).
```

For the scheduling of the tasks, we use the predicates taskStart/3 and taskFinish/3. An agent can start a task if the agent is at the picking location of the product of that task. An agent can finish a task if the agent is at the delivery location of the product of that task, provided that the task is already started at a previous time-step.

```
{taskStart(I,ID,t)}1 :- agent(I), task(ID,P,D), assign(I,ID),
   traverse(I,t,P).
{taskFinish(I,ID,t)}1 :- agent(I), task(ID,P,D), assign(I,ID),
   traverse(I,t,D), taskStart(I,ID,T), time(T), T<t.
```

Agents start carrying the products at the scheduled start times and continue carrying them until the scheduled finish times. Agents cannot carry more than their capacities.

```
carry(I,t,ID) :- taskStart(I,ID,t).
carry(I,t,ID) :- carry(I,t-1,ID), not taskFinish(I,ID,t).
:- agent(I), {carry(I,t,ID):task(ID,P,D)} > c.
```

The check program is grounded for each value of t until a solution is computed. In particular, we need to ensure that every task is completed, and that agents should end up at their destinations.

```
:- {taskFinish(I,ID,T):time(T)}!=1, agent(I), assign(I,ID), query(t).
:- agent(I), goal(I,X), not traverse(I,t,X), query(t).
```

Table 1. Warehouse configurations used in our experiments.

Configuration	1	2	3	4	5	6	7
Grid size	10×10	10×10	10×10	10×10	10×20	10×40	20×20
Shelf width	1	1	2	2	2	2	2
Vertical distance	1	1	1	2	2	2	2
Horizontal distance	1	2	1	2	2	2	2

5   Experimental Evaluations

We have experimentally evaluated **MAPDC-P** and **MAPDC-G** to better understand their scalability in terms of the computation time. To this end, we have generated 7 different warehouse environments, varying the grid size, shelf width and horizontal/vertical distances between shelves as described in Table 1.

For each such warehouse configuration, we have created 9 instances that vary the number of agents, the number of tasks and the capacity of the agents. For every combination of configuration, agent number, task number and capacity, we have randomly generated 5 instances and reported the average computation times and makespans.

In each instance, the initial and goal locations of agents lie at the bottom row of the layout and were chosen randomly. Picking and delivery locations of tasks are selected from a pool of nodes that are vertically adjacent to the shelf nodes. In order to have predictable hardness for tasks, picking and delivery locations of the tasks pass through exactly one shelf in the vertical direction. Combinations that only differ in capacity have the same instances except for the capacity values.

For the experiments, we have used CLINGO (4.5.4) with *default* and *handy* configurations, on a Linux server with dual 2.4 GHz Intel E5-2665 CPUs and 64 GB memory.

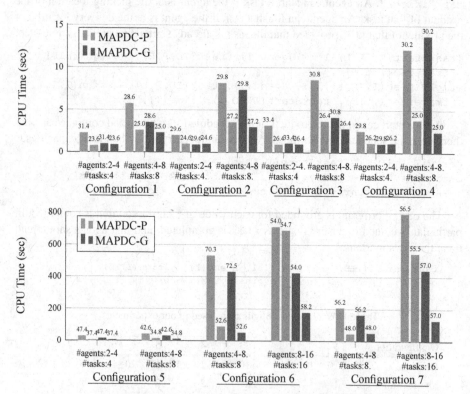

Fig. 3. Scalability as the number of agents increases when capacity = 1 (Table 2).

Table 2. Results with CLINGO's `default` configuration

Configuration	Agents	Tasks	Capacity	MAPDC-G		MAPDC-P	
				CPU time	Makespan (#solved)	CPU time	Makespan (#solved)
Configuration 1	2	2	1	0.46	24.4 (5)	0.53	24.4 (5)
	2	4	1	0.96	31.4 (5)	2.57	31.4 (5)
	2	4	2	0.69	29.8 (5)	2.19	29.8 (5)
	4	4	1	0.86	23.6 (5)	0.79	23.6 (5)
	4	8	1	3.52	28.6 (5)	4.33	28.6 (5)
	4	8	2	1.45	27.0 (5)	2.69	27.0 (5)
	8	8	1	2.29	25.0 (5)	2.55	25.0 (5)
	8	16	1	128.86	28.2 (5)	71.54	28.2 (5)
	8	16	2	6.72	26.2 (5)	12.27	26.2 (5)
Configuration 2	2	2	1	0.39	21.2 (5)	0.37	21.2 (5)
	2	4	1	0.88	29.6 (5)	2.28	29.6 (5)
	2	4	2	0.81	29.2 (5)	2.34	29.2 (5)
	4	4	1	0.98	24.6 (5)	0.96	24.6 (5)
	4	8	1	7.36	29.8 (5)	6.75	29.8 (5)
	4	8	2	1.66	27.4 (5)	3.10	27.4 (5)
	8	8	1	2.95	27.2 (5)	3.87	27.2 (5)
	8	16	1	95.61	27.6 (5)	59.76	27.6 (5)
	8	16	2	6.53	26.6 (5)	11.92	26.6 (5)
Configuration 3	2	2	1	0.40	22.8 (5)	0.44	22.8 (5)
	2	4	1	1.04	33.4 (5)	4.01	33.4 (5)
	2	4	2	0.76	31.4 (5)	2.68	31.4 (5)
	4	4	1	0.95	26.4 (5)	1.05	26.4 (5)
	4	8	1	4.13	30.8 (5)	7.15	30.8 (5)
	4	8	2	2.66	29.8 (5)	6.28	29.8 (5)
	8	8	1	2.78	26.4 (5)	3.65	26.4 (5)
	8	16	1	286.58	29.4 (5)	165.75	29.4 (5)
	8	16	2	6.95	27.8 (5)	21.45	27.8 (5)
Configuration 4	2	2	1	0.45	23.4 (5)	0.48	23.4 (5)
	2	4	1	1.01	29.8 (5)	2.48	29.8 (5)
	2	4	2	0.74	27.4 (5)	1.69	27.4 (5)
	4	4	1	1.07	26.2 (5)	0.96	26.2 (5)
	4	8	1	13.74	30.2 (5)	8.87	30.2 (5)
	4	8	2	2.31	26.4 (5)	3.49	26.4 (5)
	8	8	1	2.39	25.0 (5)	3.05	25.0 (5)
	8	16	1	201.95	28.8 (5)	107.11	28.8 (5)
	8	16	2	7.02	26.4 (5)	19.34	26.4 (5)
Configuration 5	2	2	1	1.92	35.4 (5)	2.69	35.4 (5)
	2	4	1	13.23	47.4 (5)	44.88	47.4 (5)
	2	4	2	3.84	41.6 (5)	23.37	41.6 (5)
	4	4	1	4.66	37.4 (5)	6.19	37.4 (5)
	4	8	1	30.69	42.6 (5)	38.96	42.6 (5)
	4	8	2	11.81	41.0 (5)	29.34	41.0 (5)
	8	8	1	9.73	34.8 (5)	17.99	34.8 (5)
	8	16	1	410.00	39.5 (4)	429.42	39.5 (4)
	8	16	2	38.94	36.6 (5)	139.65	36.6 (5)

(*continued*)

Table 2. (*continued*)

Configuration	Agents	Tasks	Capacity	MAPDC-G		MAPDC-P	
				CPU time	Makespan (#solved)	CPU time	Makespan (#solved)
Configuration 6	4	4	1	27.82	56.6 (5)	70.44	56.6 (5)
	4	8	1	429.16	**72.5 (4)**	440.65	**70.3 (3)**
	4	8	2	110.65	65.0 (5)	253.01	65.0 (5)
	8	8	1	50.86	52.6 (5)	212.67	52.6 (5)
	8	16	1	422.37	**54.0 (1)**	timeout	timeout
	8	16	2	187.27	**57.6 (5)**	138.18	**48.0 (1)**
	16	16	1	176.37	**58.2 (5)**	timeout	timeout
	16	32	1	timeout	timeout	timeout	timeout
	16	32	2	440.93	**55.2 (4)**	timeout	timeout
Configuration 7	4	4	1	16.99	43.0 (5)	16.21	43.0(5)
	4	8	1	162.02	56.2 (5)	233.99	56.2 (5)
	4	8	2	42.35	52.4 (5)	127.96	52.4 (5)
	8	8	1	48.76	48.0 (5)	64.74	48.0 (5)
	8	16	1	440.30	**57.0 (3)**	816.92	**56.5 (2)**
	8	16	2	72.97	**51.4 (5)**	511.79	**49.8 (4)**
	16	16	1	128.51	**49.4 (5)**	544.47	**47.0 (4)**
	16	32	1	timeout	timeout	timeout	timeout
	16	32	2	264.36	**52.2 (4)**	timeout	timeout

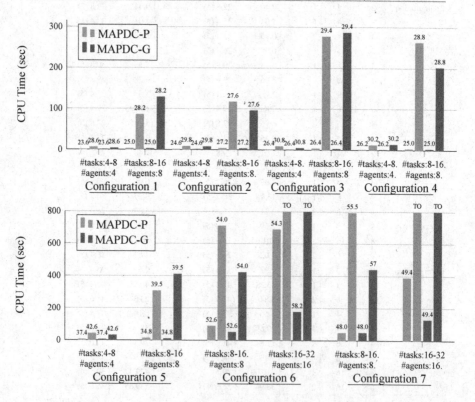

Fig. 4. Scalability as the number of tasks increases when capacity = 1 (Table 2).

For each configuration, we have analysed the effect of changing the number of agents, tasks, and capacity on performances of our solution methods for **MAPDC-P** and **MAPDC-G**. In order to have a controlled comparison, we have doubled a factor while keeping the others fixed, and compared the results for both methods. The results are presented in Table 2.

We have observed (Fig. 3) that increasing the number of agents helps both **MAPDC-P** and **MAPDC-G** in finding solutions more efficiently. This observation makes sense as increasing the number of agents effectively reduces the number of tasks assigned to an agent, and, in turn, reduces the maximum makespan for the problem instance.

We have observed (Fig. 4) that increasing the number of tasks increases the number of tasks that needs to be completed by each agent. Hence, the maximum makespan also increases, and this reduces the efficiency of both **MAPDC-P** and **MAPDC-G**. Note that some of the instances could not be solved within the time limit as the number of tasks increases to 32 for 16 agents.

Similar to increasing the number of agents, increasing the capacity of agents (Fig. 5) leads to a decrease in maximum makespan, and thus reduces the computation time for both **MAPDC-P** and **MAPDC-G**. It is interesting to compare results in Figs. 3 and 5.

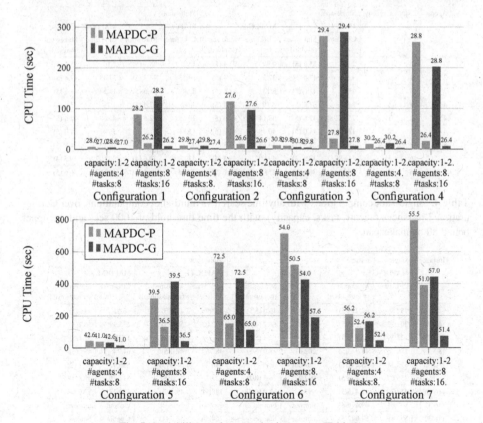

Fig. 5. Scalability as the capacity increases (Table 2).

Even though increasing the number of agents and the capacity both reduce the maximum makespan and improve runtime performance, improvements in Fig. 5 are more visible. This showcases the importance of capacity in the **MAPDC** problem. Increasing the number of agents reduces the maximum makespan, but at the same time strains the solving process due to increased number of possible collisions to avoid.

We have also compared the single-shot and multi-shot computations of CLINGO over some **MAPDC** instances (Table 3). The single-shot ASP formulations of **MAPDC** utilize weak constraints to optimize the maximum makespan, while a sufficiently small upper bound is provided on the makespan for the purpose of grounding. In our experiments with single-shot, we have provided the optimum makespans as upper bounds on makespans. In this way, the single-shot computations do not need to make too many optimizations for large upper bounds but show their best performance alleviating the disadvantage of grounding due to large makespans. It can be seen that even under these ideal conditions, the multi-shot computations perform nearly as good as the singleshot ones for many instances. The run-time of multi-shot computations include the time

Table 3. Comparison of single-shot and multi-shot computations over Configuration 5 instances.

Agents	Tasks	Capacity	Single-shot				Multi-shot			
			MAPDC-G		MAPDC-P		MAPDC-G		MAPDC-P	
			CPU time	Makespan (#solved)	CPU time	Makespan (#solved)	CPU time	Makespan (#solved)	CPU time	Makespan (#solved)
2	2	1	2.98	35.4 (5)	0.99	35.4 (5)	1.92	35.4 (5)	2.16	35.4 (5)
2	4	1	9.52	47.4 (5)	27.59	47.4 (5)	13.23	47.4 (5)	27.48	47.4 (5)
2	4	2	4.63	41.6 (5)	8.13	41.6 (5)	3.84	41.6 (5)	14.54	41.6 (5)
4	4	1	7.51	37.4 (5)	4.49	37.4 (5)	4.66	37.4 (5)	4.79	37.4 (5)
4	8	1	25.11	42.6 (5)	39.14	42.6 (5)	30.69	42.6 (5)	41.68	42.6 (5)
4	8	2	12.62	41.0 (5)	40.48	41.0 (5)	11.81	41.0 (5)	36.41	41.0 (5)
8	8	1	15.49	34.8 (5)	16.63	34.8 (5)	9.73	34.8 (5)	13.15	34.8 (5)
8	16	1	146.90	**39.5 (4)**	493.02	**39.5 (4)**	410.00	**39.5 (4)**	307.07	**39.5 (4)**
8	16	2	29.71	36.6 (5)	255.04	36.6 (5)	38.94	36.6 (5)	128.82	36.6 (5)

Table 4. Single-shot computations with anytime search vs multi-shot computations, over Configuration 7 instances (agents, tasks, capacity), with the time threshold of 1000 secs and the upper bound 80 on makespan.

Instance	Single-shot anytime				Multi-shot			
	MAPDC-G		MAPDC-P		MAPDC-G		MAPDC-P	
	CPU time	Makespan (#opt/#solved)	CPU time	Makespan (#opt/#solved)	CPU time	Makespan (#opt/#solved)	CPU time	Makespan (#opt/#solved)
(4, 4, 1)	95.58	43.0 (5/5)	57.99	43.0 (5/5)	16.99	43.0(5)	16.21	43.0(5)
(4,8,1)	201.12	56.2 (5/5)	794.14	**56.2 (4/5)**	162.02	56.2(5)	233.99	56.2(5)
(4,8,2)	122.59	52.4 (5/5)	710.64	52.4 (5/5)	42.35	52.4(5)	127.96	52.4(5)
(8,8,1)	189.66	48.0 (5/5)	202.67	48.0 (5/5)	48.76	48.0(5)	64.74	48.0(5)
(8,16,1)	855.31	**58.2 (2/5)**	timeout	timeout	440.30	57.0 (3)	816.92	56.5 (2)
(8,16,2)	255.07	51.4 (5/5)	997.27	**76.5 (0/2)**	72.97	51.4(5)	511.79	49.8(4)
(16,16,1)	457.70	49.4 (5/5)	997.23	**67.0 (0/4)**	128.51	49.4 (5)	544.47	47.0 (4)
(16,32,1)	997.61	**69.4 (0/5)**	timeout	timeout	timeout	timeout	timeout	timeout
(16,32,2)	836.89	**54.0 (2/5)**	timeout	timeout	264.36	52.2 (4)	timeout	timeout

required to find the optimum makespan, making them more practical to use, in particular, with **MAPDC-P**.

Furthermore, we have evaluated the single-shot computations with anytime search, with time threshold of 1000 s, over some **MAPDC** instances with an upper bound of 80 on makespan (Table 4). We have observed that anytime search helps with finding a suboptimal solution for all instances, in particular, for **MAPDC-G**, but at the cost of computation time due to grounding with a large makespan. **MAPDC-G** computes optimal solutions for 34 instances (out of 45 instances), using anytime search; and, for some of the remaining instances (e.g., with 8 agents, 16 tasks, 1 capacity), the average suboptimal values are close to the optimal ones.

Finally, our experiments show that using CLINGO with handy configuration (as in [4]) improves the computational performances of **MAPDC-P** and **MAPDC-G** for hard instances (cf. results for Configurations 6 and 7 at Table 5). This suggests the use of CLINGO with a portfolio of different configurations.

Table 5. Results with CLINGO's handy configuration

Configuration	Agents	Tasks	Capacity	MAPDC-G		MAPDC-P	
				CPU time	Makespan (#solved)	CPU time	Makespan (#solved)
Configuration 6	4	4	1	57.50	56.6 (5)	44.43	56.6 (5)
	4	8	1	393.59	72.5 (4)	479.13	72.5 (4)
	4	8	2	75.52	65.0 (5)	212.28	65.0 (5)
	8	8	1	107.17	52.6 (5)	94.21	52.6 (5)
	8	16	1	283.07	54.0 (1)	734.57	54.0 (1)
	8	16	2	184.27	**57.6 (5)**	491.01	**50.5 (2)**
	16	16	1	336.67	**58.2 (5)**	801.47	**54.7 (3)**
	16	32	1	timeout	timeout	timeout	timeout
	16	32	2	414.33	**55.2(5)**	timeout	timeout
Configuration 7	4	4	1	38.92	43.0 (5)	12.92	43.0 (5)
	4	8	1	140.77	56.2 (5)	214.01	56.2 (5)
	4	8	2	61.09	52.4 (5)	91.01	52.4 (5)
	8	8	1	101.25	48.0 (5)	48.13	48.0 (5)
	8	16	1	372.09	**54.8 (4)**	818.10	**57.0 (3)**
	8	16	2	129.54	51.4 (5)	451.97	51.4 (5)
	16	16	1	270.70	**49.4 (5)**	378.01	**47.0 (4)**
	16	32	1	timeout	timeout	timeout	timeout
	16	32	2	328.81	**52.3 (4)**	timeout	timeout

6 Conclusions

We have introduced two novel methods, based on action planning (**MAPDC-P**) and path finding (**MAPDC-G**), to find optimal solutions for the Multi-Agent Pick and Delivery with Capacities problem (**MAPDC**). Both methods rely on formulating the problems in Answer Set Programming, and take advantages of multi-shot computation of the ASP solver CLINGO.

We have experimentally evaluated these two methods on a rich set of benchmark instances that are randomly generated with varying numbers of agents, tasks and capacities, over different warehouses that vary in grid size, shelf width, and horizontal/vertical distances between shelves. We have observed that **MAPDC-P** is more efficient in time in small instances while **MAPDC-G** scales better for larger instances. We have also observed that **MAPDC-P** benefits more from the multi-shot computation.

We have also experimentally evaluated these two methods considering two other computation modes of ASP: single-shot and anytime search. We have observed the advantages of multi-shot computation over single-shot computation, in particular for **MAPDC-P**, in terms of computation time, and the advantages of single-shot anytime computation, in particular for **MAPDC-G**, in terms of the number of problems solved.

In this study, we have evaluated two approaches (i.e., action planning and path finding) in the context of declarative programming. Further evaluations considering non-declarative approaches (e.g., based on search) are part of our ongoing work.

References

1. Bartholdi, J.J., III., Hackman, S.T.: Warehouse and distribution science. Supply Chain and Logistics Institute, Georgia Institute of Technology (2019)
2. Brewka, G., Eiter, T., Truszczynski, M.: Answer set programming: an introduction to the special issue. AI Mag. **37**(3), 5–6 (2016). https://doi.org/10.1609/aimag.v37i3.2669
3. Chen, Z., Alonso-Mora, J., Bai, X., Harabor, D.D., Stuckey, P.J.: Integrated task assignment and path planning for capacitated multi-agent pickup and delivery. IEEE RAL **6**(3), 5816–5823 (2021). https://doi.org/10.1109/LRA.2021.3074883
4. Erdem, E., Kisa, D., Oztok, U., Schüller, P.: A general formal framework for pathfinding problems with multiple agents. In: Proceedings of AAAI (2013)
5. Gebser, M., Kaminski, R., Kaufmann, B., Schaub, T.: Multi-shot ASP solving with clingo. TPLP **19**(1), 27–82 (2019). https://doi.org/10.1017/S1471068418000054
6. Gebser, M., et al.: Experimenting with robotic intra-logistics domains. TPLP **18**(3–4), 502–519 (2018). https://doi.org/10.1017/S1471068418000200
7. Gelfond, M., Lifschitz, V.: Classical negation in logic programs and disjunctive databases. New Gener. Comput. **9**, 365–385 (1991)
8. Grenouilleau, F., van Hoeve, W.J., Hooker, J.N.: A multi-label A* algorithm for multi-agent pathfinding. In: Proceedings of ICAPS, pp. 181–185 (2019)
9. Guthrie, C., Fosso-Wamba, S., Arnaud, J.B.: Online consumer resilience during a pandemic: an exploratory study of e-commerce behavior before, during and after a COVID-19 lockdown. JRCS **61**, 102570 (2021). https://doi.org/10.1016/j.jretconser.2021.102570
10. Hönig, W., Kiesel, S., Tinka, A., Durham, J., Ayanian, N.: Conflict-based search with optimal task assignment. In: Proceedings of AAMAS (2018)
11. Lifschitz, V.: Answer set programming and plan generation. AIJ **138**, 39–54 (2002). https://doi.org/10.1016/S0004-3702(02)00186-8
12. Liu, M., Ma, H., Li, J., Koenig, S.: Task and path planning for multi-agent pickup and delivery. In: Proceedings of AAMAS, pp. 1152–1160 (2019)
13. Ma, H., Koenig, S.: Optimal target assignment and path finding for teams of agents. In: Proceedings of AAMAS, pp. 1144–1152 (2016)

14. Ma, H., Li, J., Kumar, T.K.S., Koenig, S.: Lifelong multi-agent path finding for online pickup and delivery tasks. In: Proceedings of AAMAS, pp. 837–845 (2017)
15. Marek, V.W., Truszczyński, M.: Stable models and an alternative logic programming paradigm. In: Apt, K.R., Marek, V.W., Truszczynski, M., Warren, D.S. (eds.) The Logic Programming Paradigm. Artificial Intelligence. Springer, Heidelberg (1999). https://doi.org/10.1007/978-3-642-60085-2_17
16. Nguyen, V., Obermeier, P., Son, T.C., Schaub, T., Yeoh, W.: Generalized target assignment and path finding using answer set programming. In: Proceedings of IJCAI, pp. 1216–1223 (2017). https://doi.org/10.24963/ijcai.2017/169
17. Niemelä, I.: Logic programs with stable model semantics as a constraint programming paradigm. AMAI **25**, 241–273 (1999)
18. Sharon, G., Stern, R., Felner, A., Sturtevant, N.R.: Conflict-based search for optimal multi-agent pathfinding. AIJ **219**, 40–66 (2015). https://doi.org/10.1016/j.artint.2014.11.006
19. Surynek, P.: On propositional encodings of cooperative path-finding. In: Proceedings of ICTAI, pp. 524–531 (2012). https://doi.org/10.1109/ICTAI.2012.77
20. Vodrázka, J., Barták, R., Svancara, J.: On modelling multi-agent path finding as a classical planning problem. In: Proceedings of ICTAI, pp. 23–28 (2020). https://doi.org/10.1109/ICTAI50040.2020.00014
21. Yu, J., LaValle, S.M.: Optimal multirobot path planning on graphs: complete algorithms and effective heuristics. IEEE TRO **32**(5), 1163–1177 (2016). https://doi.org/10.1109/TRO.2016.2593448

Determining Action Reversibility in STRIPS Using Answer Set Programming with Quantifiers

Wolfgang Faber[1], Michael Morak[1(✉)], and Lukáš Chrpa[2]

[1] University of Klagenfurt, Klagenfurt, Austria
{wolfgang.faber,michael.morak}@aau.at
[2] Czech Technical University in Prague, Prague, Czechia
chrpaluk@fel.cvut.cz

Abstract. In the field of automated planning, an action is called reversible when other actions can be applied in order to revert the effects of this action and return to the original state. In recent years, there has been renewed interest in this topic, which led to novel results in the widely known STRIPS formalism and the PDDL planning language.

In this paper, we aim to solve the computational problem of deciding action reversibility in a practical setting, applying recent advances in the field of logic programming. In particular, a quantified extension of Answer Set Programming (ASP) named ASP with Quantifiers (ASP(Q)) has been proposed by Amendola, Ricca, and Truszczynski, which allows for stacking logic programs by quantifying over answer sets of the previous layer. This language is well-suited to express encodings for the action reversibility problem, since this problem naturally contains a quantifier alternation. In addition, a prototype solver for ASP(Q) is currently developed. We make use of the ASP(Q) language to offer an encoding for action reversibility, and then report on preliminary benchmark results on how well this encoding performs compared to classical ASP.

Keywords: Automated planning · Answer set programming · Reasoning about action and change

1 Introduction

Automated Planning is a field of research that traditionally deals with the problem of generating sequences of actions, called plans, that transform a given initial state of the environment to some goal state [19,20]. An action, simply put, is a modifier that acts upon and changes the environment. An interesting problem in this field is the question whether an action can be reversed by subsequently applying other actions, thus undoing the effects that the action had on the environment. This problem has been investigated on and off throughout the years [10,13], and has recently received renewed interest [6,15,24].

Action reversibility is an important problem with regard to several aspects. Intuitively, actions whose effects cannot be reversed might lead to dead-end states, that is,

© Springer Nature Switzerland AG 2022
J. Cheney and S. Perri (Eds.): PADL 2022, LNCS 13165, pp. 42–56, 2022.
https://doi.org/10.1007/978-3-030-94479-7_4

states from which the goal state can no longer be reached. Early detection of the possibility of dead-end states is beneficial in the plan generation process [23]. Reasoning in more complex structures is even more prone to dead-ends [7]. An example is the concept of Agent Planning Programs [11], which represent networks of planning tasks where the goal state of one task is an initial state of some other task. In the domain of non-deterministic planning, notable Fully Observable Non-Deterministic (FOND) Planning, where actions can have non-deterministic effects, knowledge about reversibility or irreversibility of each set of effects of actions can contribute to early dead-end detection, or to generalise recovery from undesirable action effects, which is important for efficient computation of strong (cyclic) plans [5]. Another aspect is online planning, where we can observe that applying reversible actions is safe and hence explicitly providing information about safe states of the environment could be avoided [9]. Another, although not very obvious, benefit of action reversibility is in plan optimization. If the effects of an action are later reversed by a sequence of other actions in a plan, these actions might be removed from the plan, potentially shortening it significantly. It has been shown that under given circumstances, pairs of inverse actions, which are a special case of action reversibility, can be removed from plans [8].

A general framework for action reversibility that has recently been introduced [24] offers a broad definition of the term, and generalises several existing notions of reversibility, like "undoability" [10], or the concept of "reverse plans" [13]. The concept of reversibility in this general framework directly incorporates the set of states in which a given action is reversible. This notion is called S-reversibility where S is a set of states where an action must be reversible. This is then extended to φ-reversibility, where the set of states is characterized by a formula φ in terms of propositional logic. These notions are then further refined to universal reversibility (referring to the set of all states) and to reversibility w.r.t. some planning task Π (where the action must be reversible in all reachable states w.r.t. the initial state specified in Π). These last two versions match the notion of "undoability" proposed in the literature [10]. Furthermore, the notions can be further restricted to require that some action is reversible by a single "reverse plan" that does not depend on the state in which the action under consideration is applied. For single actions, this matches the concept of the "reverse plan" proposed in the mid-2000s [13].

The complexity analysis of Morak et al. [24] indicates that some of these problems can be addressed by means of Answer Set Programming (ASP) and Epistemic Logic Programs (ELPs). An experimental evaluation of these two languages to compute reverse plans has recently been carried out [15].

In this paper, we leverage the translations implemented in plasp [12], and propose an encoding to solve some of the reversibility problems on PDDL domains, restricted, for now, to the STRIPS fragment [16]. This encoding is written in a recently proposed language extension for ASP, namely, ASP with Quantifiers, or ASP(Q) [1], which introduces an explicit way to express quantifiers and quantifier alternations in ASP. Since deciding ASP(Q) programs is known to be PSPACE-complete in general [1], the same complexity as deciding STRIPS planning problems [3], the language seems well-suited for the task. Our ASP(Q) encoding are arguably simpler than the known ASP and ELP encodings for the problem [15]. Most importantly, though, ASP(Q) allows for a simple modification to decide non-uniform reversibility, for which an ASP or ELP encoding is unlikely to exist under usual complexity assumptions. We also present preliminary experiments that compare our ASP(Q) encoding with the existing ASP and ELP encodings.

2   Background

STRIPS Planning. Let $\mathscr{F}$ be a set of *facts*, that is, propositional variables describing the environment, which can either be true or false. Then, a subset $s \subseteq \mathscr{F}$ is called a *state*, which intuitively represents a set of facts considered to be true. An action is a tuple $a = \langle pre(a), add(a), del(a) \rangle$, where $pre(a) \subseteq \mathscr{F}$ is the set of *preconditions* of a, and $add(a) \subseteq \mathscr{F}$ and $del(a) \subseteq \mathscr{F}$ are the add and delete effects of a, respectively. W.l.o.g., we assume actions to be well-formed, that is, $add(a) \cap del(a) = \emptyset$ and $pre(a) \cap add(a) = \emptyset$. An action a is *applicable* in a state s if $pre(a) \subseteq s$. The result of applying an action a in a state s, given that a is applicable in s, is the state $a[s] = (s \setminus del(a)) \cup add(a)$. A sequence of actions $\pi = \langle a_1, \ldots, a_n \rangle$ is applicable in a state s_0 if there is a sequence of states $\langle s_1, \ldots, s_n \rangle$ such that, for $0 < i \leq n$, it holds that a_i is applicable in s_{i-1} and $a_i[s_{i-1}] = s_i$. Applying the action sequence π on s_0 is denoted $\pi[s_0]$, with $\pi[s_0] = s_n$. The *length* of action sequence π is denoted $|\pi|$.

A *STRIPS planning task* $\Pi = \langle \mathscr{F}, \mathscr{A}, s_0, G \rangle$ is a four-element tuple consisting of a set of *facts* $\mathscr{F} = \{f_1, \ldots, f_n\}$, a set of *actions* $\mathscr{A} = \{a_1, \ldots, a_m\}$, an *initial state* $s_0 \subseteq \mathscr{F}$, and a *goal* $G \subseteq \mathscr{F}$. A state $s \subseteq \mathscr{F}$ is a *goal state (for Π)* if $G \subseteq s$. An action sequence π is called a *plan* if $\pi[s_0] \supseteq G$. We further define several relevant notions w.r.t. a planning task Π. A state s is *reachable from state s'* if there exists an applicable action sequence π such that $\pi[s'] = s$. A state $s \in 2^{\mathscr{F}}$ is simply called *reachable* if it is reachable from the initial state s_0. The set of all reachable states in Π is denoted by $\mathscr{R}_\Pi$. An action a is *reachable* if there is some state $s \in \mathscr{R}_\Pi$ such that a is applicable in s.

Deciding whether a STRIPS planning task has a plan is known to be PSPACE-complete in general and it is NP-complete if the length of the plan is polynomially bounded [3].

Answer Set Programming (ASP). We assume the reader is familiar with ASP and will only give a very brief overview of the core language. For more information, we refer to standard literature [2, 17, 22], and, in our case, the ASP-Core-2 input language format [4].

Briefly, ASP programs consist of sets of *rules* of the form

$$a_1 \mid \cdots \mid a_n \leftarrow b_1, \ldots, b_\ell, \neg b_{\ell+1}, \ldots, \neg b_m.$$

In these rules, all a_i and b_i are *atoms* of the form $p(t_1, \ldots, t_n)$, where p is a predicate name, and $t_1, \ldots, t_n$ are terms, that is, either variables or constants. The domain of constants in an ASP program P is given implicitly by the set of all constants that appear in it. Generally, before evaluating an ASP program, variables are removed by a process called *grounding*, that is, for every rule, each variable is replaced by all possible combination of constants, and appropriate ground copies of the rule are added to the resulting program $ground(P)$. In practice, several optimizations have been implemented in state-of-the-art grounders that try to minimize the size of the grounding.

The result of a (ground) ASP program P is calculated as follows [18]. An *interpretation* I (i.e., a set of ground atoms appearing in P) is called a *model* of P if it satisfies all the rules in P in the sense of classical logic. It is further called an *answer set* of P if there is no proper subset $I' \subset I$ that is a model of the so-called reduct P^I of P w.r.t. I. P^I is defined as the set of rules obtained from P where all negated atoms on the right-hand side of the rules are evaluated over I and replaced by $\top$ or $\bot$ accordingly. The main decision problem for ASP is deciding whether a program has at least one answer set. This has been shown to be Σ^2_P-complete [14].

Answer Set Programming with Quantifiers (ASP(Q)). An extension of ASP, referred to as ASP(Q), has been proposed in [1], providing a formalism reminiscent of Quantified Boolean Formulas, but based on ASP. An ASP(Q) program is of the form

$$\square_1 P_1 \square_2 P_2 \cdots \square_n P_n : C,$$

where, for each $i \in \{1, \dots, n\}$, $\square_i \in \{\exists^{st}, \forall^{st}\}$, P_i is an ASP program, and C is a stratified normal ASP program (this is, as intended by the ASP(Q) authors, a "check" in the sense of constraints). $\exists^{st}$ and $\forall^{st}$ are called *existential* and *universal answer set quantifiers*, respectively.

The intuitive reading of an ASP(Q) program $\exists^{st} P_1 \forall^{st} P_2 \cdots P_n : C$ is that there exists an answer set A_1 of P_1 such that for each answer set A_2 of P_2 extended by A_1 ... such that C extended by A_n is coherent (has an answer set).

Let us be more precise about a program P being extended by an answer set, or rather interpretation I: For an interpretation I, let $f_P(I)$ be the ASP program that contains all true atoms in I as facts and all false atoms in I w.r.t. the Herbrand base of ASP program P as constraints (i.e. rules of the form $\bot \leftarrow a$, for some atom a). Furthermore, for a program P and an interpretation I, let $f_P(\Pi, I)$ be the ASP(Q) program obtained from an ASP(Q) Π by replacing the first program P_1 in Π with $P_1 \cup f_P(I)$. *Coherence* of an ASP(Q) program is then defined inductively:

- $\exists^{st} P : C$ is coherent if there exists an answer set M of P such that $C \cup f_P(M)$ has at least one answer set.
- $\forall^{st} P : C$ is coherent if for all answer sets M of P it holds that $C \cup f_P(M)$ has at least one answer set.
- $\exists^{st} P \Pi$ is coherent if there exists an answer set M of P such that $f_P(\Pi, M)$ is coherent.
- $\forall^{st} P \Pi$ is coherent if for all answer sets M of P it holds that $f_P(\Pi, M)$ is coherent.

In addition, for an existential ASP(Q) program Π (one that starts with $\exists^{st}$), the witnessing answer sets of the first ASP program P_1 are referred to as *quantified answer sets*.

In general, deciding coherence for an ASP(Q) program is known to be PSPACE-complete [1, Theorem 2], and on the n-th level of the polynomial hierarchy for programs with n quantifier alternations [1, Theorem 3].

3   Reversibility of Actions

In this section, we review the notion of uniform reversibility, which is a subclass of action reversibility as explained in detail by Morak et al. [24]. Intuitively, we call an action reversible if there is a way to undo all the effects that this action caused, and we call an action *uniformly reversible* if its effects can be undone by a single sequence of actions irrespective of the state where the action was applied.

While this intuition is fairly straightforward, when formally defining this concept, we also need to take several other factors into account—in particular, the set of possible states where an action is considered plays an important role [24].

Definition 1. *Let $\mathscr{F}$ be a set of facts, $\mathscr{A}$ be a set of actions, $S \subseteq 2^{\mathscr{F}}$ be a set of states, and $a \in \mathscr{A}$ be an action. We call a S-reversible if for each state $s \in S$ wherein a is applicable, there exists a sequence of actions $\pi = \langle a_1, \ldots, a_n \rangle \in \mathscr{A}^n$ such that π is applicable in $a[s]$ and $\pi[a[s]] = s$.*

The notion of reversibility in the most general sense does not depend on a concrete STRIPS planning task, but only on a set of possible actions and states w.r.t. a set of facts. Note that the set of states S is an explicit part of the notion of S-reversibility.

Based on this general notion, it is then possible to define several concrete sets of states S that are useful to consider when considering whether an action is reversible. For instance, S could be defined via a propositional formula over the facts in $\mathscr{F}$. Or we can consider a set of all possible states $(2^{\mathscr{F}})$ which gives us a notion of universal reversibility that applies to all possible planning tasks that share the same set of facts and actions (i.e., the tasks that differ only in the initial state or goals). Or we can move our attention to a specific STRIPS instance and ask whether a certain action is reversible for all states reachable from the initial state.

Definition 2. *Let $\mathscr{F}$, $\mathscr{A}$, S, and a be as in Definition 1. We call the action a*

1. *φ-reversible if a is S-reversible in the set S of models of the propositional formula φ over $\mathscr{F}$;*
2. *reversible in Π if a is $\mathscr{R}_{\Pi}$-reversible for some STRIPS planning task Π; and*
3. *universally reversible, or, simply, reversible, if a is $2^{\mathscr{F}}$-reversible.*

At this point, it is also worth noting that our definition of *reversibility in Π*, for a STRIPS instance Π, coincides with the notion of "undoability" as defined by Daum et al. [10], and our notion of *reversibility* coincides with their notion of "universal undoability."

Given the above definitions, we can already observe some interrelationships. In particular, universal reversibility (that is, reversibility in the set of all possible states) is obviously the strongest notion, implying all the other, weaker notions. It may be particularly important when one wants to establish reversibility irrespective of the concrete STRIPS instance. On the other hand, φ-reversibility may be of particular interest when φ encodes the natural domain constraints for a given planning task. Formally stated in the following proposition, it follows straightforwardly from the definitions of reversibility.

Proposition 1. *Let $\mathscr{F}$, $\mathscr{A}$, and a be as in Definition 1. Then, reversibility of a implies S-reversibility for any set $S \subseteq 2^{\mathscr{F}}$ of states, and further implies reversibility in Π for any STRIPS planning task Π with facts $\mathscr{F}$ and actions $\mathscr{A}$.*

Note that all notions of reversibility of some action a proposed so far simply require that for any state s there exists a sequence of actions that undoes the effects of a after application to s. However, sometimes, it may be useful to look at a set of actions and recognise that some sequence of actions in that set always undoes the effect of some action a, independent of the state s in which a was applied. This leads to the more restrictive notion of *uniform reversibility*.

Definition 3. *Let $\mathscr{F}$, $\mathscr{A}$, S, and a be as in Definition 1. We call a uniformly S-reversible if there exists a sequence of actions $\pi = \langle a_1, \ldots, a_n \rangle \in \mathscr{A}^n$ such that for each $s \in S$ wherein a is applicable it holds that π is applicable in $a[s]$ and $\pi[a[s]] = s$. The more specific notions of reversibility of Definition 2 analogously apply to uniform reversibility.*

The notion of uniform reversibility naturally gives rise to the notion of the reverse plan. We say that some action a has an *(S-)reverse plan π* if a is uniformly (S-)reversible using the sequence of actions π. It is interesting to note that this definition of the reverse plan based on uniform reversibility now coincides with the same notion as defined by Eiter, Erdem, and Faber [13]. Note, however, that in that paper the authors use a much more general planning language.

Even if the length of the reverse plan is polynomially bounded, the problem of deciding whether an action is uniformly (φ-)reversible is intractable. In particular, deciding whether an action is universally uniformly reversible (resp. uniformly φ-reversible) by a polynomial length reverse plan is NP-complete (resp. in Σ_2^P) [24].

4 ASP(Q) Encodings of Reversibility

After reviewing the relevant features of *plasp*, described by [12], in Sect. 4.1, we first present an ASP(Q) encoding for determining uniform reversibility in Sect. 4.2 and then an encoding for non-uniform reversibility in Sect. 4.3.

4.1 the *plasp* Format

The system *plasp*, described by Dimopoulos et al. [12], transforms PDDL domains and problems into facts. Together with suitable programs, plans can then be computed by ASP solvers—and hence also by ELP solvers, since ELPs are a superset of ASP programs. Given a STRIPS domain with facts $\mathscr{F}$ and actions $\mathscr{A}$, the following relevant facts and rules will be created by *plasp*:

```
variable(variable("f")). for all f ∈ 𝓕
action(action("a")). for all a ∈ 𝓐
precondition(action("a"),variable("f"),value(variable("f"),true))
  :- action(action("a")).
  for each a ∈ 𝓐 and f ∈ pre(a)
```

```
postcondition(action("a"),effect(unconditional),variable("f"),
             value(variable("f"),true)) :- action(action("a")).
   for each a ∈ 𝒜 and f ∈ add(a)
postcondition(action("a"),effect(unconditional),variable("f"),
             value(variable("f"),false)) :- action(action("a")).
   for each a ∈ 𝒜 and f ∈ del(a)
```

In addition, a predicate contains encodes all possible values for a given variable (for STRIPS, this is either true or false).

Example 1. The STRIPS domain with $\mathscr{F} = \{f\}$ and actions $del\text{-}f = \langle\{f\},\emptyset,\{f\}\rangle$ and $add\text{-}f = \langle\emptyset,\{f\},\emptyset\rangle$ is written in PDDL as follows:

```
(define (domain example1)
(:requirements :strips)
(:predicates (f) )
(:action del-f
 :precondition (f)
 :effect (not (f)))
(:action add-f
 :effect (f)))
```

plasp translates this domain to the following rules (plus a few technical facts and rules):

```
variable(variable("f")).
action(action("del-f")).
precondition(action("del-f"),variable("f"),value(variable("f"),true))
          :- action(action("del-f")).
postcondition(action("del-f"),effect(unconditional),variable("f"),
             value(variable("f"),false)) :- action(action("del-f")).
action(action("add-f")).
postcondition(action("add-f"),effect(unconditional),variable("f"),
             value(variable("f"),true)) :- action(action("add-f")).
```

4.2   a Uniform Reversibility Encoding Using ASP(Q)

In this section, we present our ASP(Q) encoding for checking whether, in a given domain, there is an action that is uniformly reversible. As we have seen in Sect. 4.1, the *plasp* tool is able to rewrite STRIPS domains into ASP rules even when no concrete planning instance for that domain is given. We present an encoding for (universal) uniform reversibility, which can, however, easily be extended to uniform φ-reversibility. To a degree, our encoding is based on the sequential-horizon.lp encoding for solving planning tasks in the *plasp* distribution.

Note that *universal* uniform reversibility is computationally easier than φ-uniform reversibility (under standard complexity-theoretic assumptions). For a given action (and polynomial-length reverse plans), the former can be decided in NP, while the latter is harder [24, Theorem 18 and 20]. Our encoding has the power to solve the latter problem.

The basic idea of the encoding is to have an existentially quantified program first, which guesses the reverse plan, followed by a universally quantified one, which creates the trajectories from any choice of the initial state, and the check program will establish whether the trajectory leads back to the initial state, yielding $\Pi^u = \exists^{st} P_1^u \forall^{st} P_2^u : C^u$.

The ASP(Q) encoding makes use of the following main predicates (in addition to several auxiliary predicates, as well as those imported from *plasp*):

- chosen/1 encodes the action to be tested for reversibility.
- holds/3 encodes that some fact (or variable, as they are called in *plasp* parlance) is set to a certain value at a given time step.
- occurs/2 encodes the candidate reverse plan, saying which action occurs at which time step.

Let us now describe P_1^u first. It will contain the plasp output for the domain, a fact chosen(a) for the action a to be checked for reversibility, a fact horizon(k) and a range of facts time(0..k+1) for reverse plan lengths k. Moreover, P_1^u contains:

```
occurs(A, 1) :- chosen(A).
occurs(A, T) | -occurs(A, T) :- action(action(A)), time(T), T > 1.
:- occurs(A,T), occurs(B,T), A!=B.
oneoccurs(T) :- occurs(A,T), time(T), T > 0.
:- time(T), T>0, not oneoccurs(T).
plan(A, T - 1) :- occurs(A, T), T > 1.
```

The first rule fixes the chosen action at time 1, while the following four lines choose exactly one of the available actions at times 2 to k+1. The last line just isolates the reverse plan. Using choice rules and aggregates, presuming that it is guaranteed that only one action is chosen, this can alternatively be written as:

```
occurs(A, 1) :- chosen(A).
{occurs(A, T)} :- action(action(A)), time(T), T > 1.
:- #count{A:occurs(A, T)}!=1,time(T), T > 1.
plan(A, T - 1) :- occurs(A, T), T > 1.
```

It is easy to see that there is a one-to-one correspondence between action sequences of length k and answer sets of P_1^u.

Now let us turn to P_2^u, it contains the following rules:

```
holds(V, Val, 0) :- chosen(A),
  precondition(action(A), variable(V), value(variable(V), Val)).

holds(V,Val,0) | -holds(V,Val,0) :- variable(variable(V)),
  contains(variable(V),value(variable(V),Val)).
oneholds(V,0) :- holds(V,Val,0).
:- variable(variable(V)), not oneholds(V,0).
:- holds(V,Val,0), holds(V,Val1,0), Val != Val1.

caused(V, Val, T) :- occurs(A, T),
  postcondition(action(A), E, variable(V), value(variable(V), Val)).
```

```
modified(V, T) :- caused(V, _, T).
holds(V, Val, T) :- caused(V, Val, T).
holds(V, Val, T) :- holds(V, Val, T - 1), not modified(V, T), time(T).
```

The first rule sets some fluent values that are necessary for executability of the action to be reversed. The following four rules then guess an initial state, in which the action to be reversed is executable. The last four rules create the trajectories along the actions that will be fixed by the answer set of P_1^u. In particular, the first of the rules deals with direct action effects, while the remaining ones handle inertia (fluents that are untouched by the action in question and therefore remain as they are).

Rules 2 to 5 can again be written more compactly using choice rules and an aggregate:

```
{holds(V,Val,0)} :- contains(variable(V),value(variable(V),Val)).
:- #count{Val:holds(V,Val,0)} != 1, variable(variable(V)).
```

The last portion of the program, C, checks whether the state at time k+1 is the same as the initial state and whether the preconditions of all actions is met. Only then the plan is a reverse plan. This is done using three constraints:

```
:- holds(V, Val, 0), not holds(V, Val, H+1), horizon(H).
:- holds(V, Val, H+1), not holds(V, Val, 0), horizon(H).
:- precondition(action(A), variable(V), value(variable(V), Val)),
   occurs(A, T),  not holds(V, Val, T - 1).
```

It is not hard to check that each quantified answer set of Π^u corresponds to a universal uniform reverse plan of the chosen action. If one wishes to test all actions in the domain for universal uniform reversibility, one can simply add the following rules to P_1^u, which guess an action to be tested for reversibility:

```
chosen(A) | -chosen(A) :- action(action(A)).
:- chosen(A), chosen(B), A!=B.
onechosen :- chosen(A).
:- not onechosen.
```

Alternatively, using choice rule and aggregate:

```
{ chosen(A) } :- action(action(A)).
:- #count{A:chosen(A)} != 1.
```

This is what we will do in our experiments.

Theorem 1. *Given a STRIPS planning task* $\langle \mathscr{F}, \mathscr{A}, s_0, G \rangle$*, the ASP(Q) encoding in this section produces exactly one quantified answer set for each universally uniformly reversible action* $a \in \mathscr{A}$ *and a reverse plan* π *of length* k *for a, if it exists.*

It is also easy to see that our encoding can be modified for non-universal uniform reversibility without efforts, it is enough to constrain the initial state in P_2^u to the set of states S in question. For instance, if S is encoded via a formula φ it is easy remove initial states that do not satisfy φ.

4.3 A Non-uniform Reversibility Encoding Using ASP(Q)

Let us turn to non-uniform reversibility and modify the encoding of the previous section. Intuitively, instead of encoding "there exists a plan such that for all initial states it leads back" here we need an inversion to "for all initial states there exists a plan that leads back". But this is fairly straightforward in ASP(Q). For a pre-chosen action to be reversed this gives rise to $\Pi^n = \forall^{st} P_1^n \exists^s P_2^n : C^n$.

Similar to P_1^u, P_1^n will contain the plasp output for the domain, a fact chosen(a) for the action to be checked for reversibility, a fact horizon(k) and a range of facts time(0..k+1) for reverse plan lengths k. In addition, it will only contain a guess for all initial states, in which the action to be reversed is executable. We use a separate predicate holds0 just to avoid sharing predicate names over different programs (the prototype tool that we experimented with does not support this either).

```
holds0(V, Val, 0) :- chosen(A),
  precondition(action(A), variable(V), value(variable(V), Val)).

holds0(V,Val,0) | -holds0(V,Val,0) :- variable(variable(V)),
  contains(variable(V),value(variable(V),Val)).
oneholds0(V,0) :- holds0(V,Val,0).
:- variable(variable(V)), not oneholds0(V,0).
:- holds0(V,Val,0), holds0(V,Val1,0), Val != Val1.
```

P_2^n then contains essentially the remaining rules of Π^u plus one rule that interfaces holds0 with holds:

```
holds(V,Val,0) :- holds0(V,Val,0).

occurs(A, 1) :- chosen(A).
occurs(A, T) | -occurs(A, T) :- action(action(A)), time(T), T > 1.
:- occurs(A,T), occurs(B,T), A!=B.
oneoccurs(T) :- occurs(A,T), time(T), T > 0.
:- time(T), T>0, not oneoccurs(T).
plan(A, T - 1) :- occurs(A, T), T > 1.

caused(V, Val, T) :- occurs(A, T),
  postcondition(action(A), E, variable(V), value(variable(V), Val)).

modified(V, T) :- caused(V, _, T).
holds(V, Val, T) :- caused(V, Val, T).
holds(V, Val, T) :- holds(V, Val, T - 1), not modified(V, T), time(T).
```

Finally, C^n is unchanged, i.e., $C^n \equiv C^u$.

It is easy to see that Π^n encodes universal non-uniform reversibility, and again a modification to non-universal non-uniform reversibility is straightforward.

For testing all actions in the domain for non-uniform reversibility, one needs to add an extra existential program that guesses the action to be reversed, say P_0^n:

```
chosen(A) | -chosen(A) :- action(action(A)).
```

```
:- chosen(A), chosen(B), A!=B.
onechosen :- chosen(A).
:- not onechosen.
```

$\exists^{st} P_0^n \Pi^n$ will then produce a quantified answer set for all non-uniformly reversible actions in the domain.

5   Experiments

We have conducted preliminary experiments on universal uniform reversibility, as it allows for comparison to existing ASP-related solving methods. We have obtained an as-yet-unpublished prototype implementation for ASP(Q) from Francisco Ricca, called qasp version 0.1.2, and implemented a tool for generating Π^u as presented in Sect. 4.2. All our benchmark files, including generator scripts, are available at https://seafile.aau. at/d/eb22aab5223f4e8abfcc/.

The domains of our generated benchmarks are reused from [15] and look as follows:

```
(define (domain rev-i)
(:requirements :strips)
(:predicates (f0) ... (fi))
(:action del-all
 :precondition (and  (f0) ... (fi) )
 :effect (and  (not (f0)) ... (not (fi))))
(:action add-f0
 :effect (f0))
...
(:action add-fi
 :precondition (fi-1)
 :effect (fi)))
```

The action del-all has a universal uniform reverse plan ⟨ add-f0, ..., add-fi ⟩. We have generated instances from i = 1 to i = 6 and from i = 10 to i = 200 with step 10. We have analyzed runtime and memory consumption of two problems: (a) finding the unique reverse plan of size i (by setting the constant horizon to i) and proving that no other reverse plan exists, and (b) showing that no reverse plan of length i-1 exists (by setting the constant horizon to i-1). We compare our encoding, described in Sect. 4.2, to the "general" ASP and ELP encodings presented by Faber, Morak, and Chrpa [15]. We omit the "simple" ASP and ELP encodings presented therein, since they make use of a complexity-theoretic shortcut (and hence are only able to solve universal uniform reversibility), which cannot be exploited with our ASP(Q) encoding. Hence, to get comparative benchmarks, all three encodings that we benchmark here are able to solve the exact same problem: uniform φ-reversibility.

We used plasp 3.1.1 (https://potassco.org/labs/plasp/), as well as eclingo 0.2.0 (https://github.com/potassco/eclingo) and built on top of clingo 5.4.1 (https://potassco. org/clingo/), and clingo itself, for the ASP and ELP benchmark set, and the preliminary ASP(Q) solving tool *qasp*, version 0.1.2, which rewrites ASP(Q) programs to Quantified Boolean Formulas (QBFs) and then use the well-known QuAbS QBF solver [21]

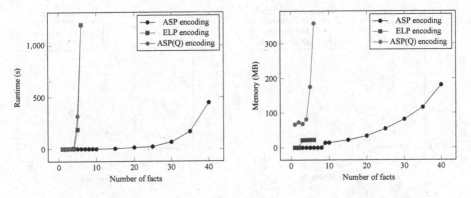

Fig. 1. Calculating the unique reverse plan (plan length equals number of facts)

(see the benchmark archive for qasp), on a computer with a 2.3 GHz AMD EPYC 7601 CPU with 32 cores and 500 GB RAM running CentOS 8. We have set a timeout of 20 min and a memory limit of 16 GB (which was never exceeded).

The results for problem (a) are plotted in Fig. 1, requiring that solvers output all models that they find (i.e. after finding the first and only model containing a reverse plan, they have to prove that this is also the last model). As expected, and as already known [15], the plain ASP encoding performs best, given the extensive optimizations that have gone into ASP solvers over the years. Both the ELP encoding and the ASP(Q) encoding offer similar benchmark performance, which is, however, much worse than for the ASP encoding. This is not surprising, given the fact that neither ELP nor ASP(Q) solvers are optimized. In fact, both are preliminary system prototypes that need further optimization to realize their performance potential. However, clearly, both systems are able to solve a portion of the provided benchmarks within the 20 min time window given. The much more elegant and readable language that is offered by ASP(Q), when compared to encoding Σ_2^P-level problems in ASP, is a tradeoff that may be worth considering. For the qasp system, memory consumption is higher than for the ASP and ELP solvers as well. This was, again, expected, as the qasp system is written in Java, where as eclingo and clingo are written in the leaner C++ programming language (interfacing via python).

The results for problem (b) are plotted in Fig. 2. Interestingly, compared to (a), all the encodings performed significantly better, but overall offer a similar picture.

In total, the ELP and ASP(Q) encodings scale worse than the ASP encoding. However, since these systems solve the same problem from a complexity-theoretic perspective, we see this as an indicator of how much optimization potential is still "hidden" for qasp, or any solver for the ASP(Q) language. Due to the elegance of the modeling language, however, we hope that our paper will encourage further development and improvements in the young field of ASP(Q) solvers.

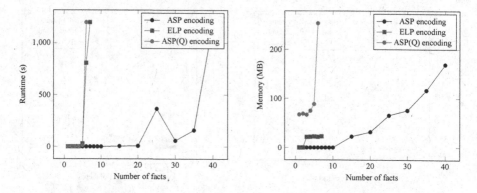

Fig. 2. Determining nonexistence of a reverse plan (plan length one step too short)

6 Conclusions

In this paper, we have given a review of several notions of action reversibility in STRIPS planning, as originally presented by Morak et al. [24]. We then proceeded, on the basis of the PDDL-to-ASP translation tool *plasp* [12], using the relatively novel language of ASP with Quantifiers, ASP(Q), to offer an encoding to solve the task of uniform φ-reversibility of STRIPS actions, given a corresponding planning domain. When given to an appropriate solving system, this encoding, combined with the ASP translation of STRIPS planning domains produced by *plasp*, then yields a set of models, each one representing a (universal) uniform φ-reverse plan for each action in the domain, for which such a reverse plan could be found. This encoding appears much more natural than the saturation-based ASP encoding, but arguably also more natural than the ELP encoding in [24]. Importantly, we were also able to provide a similar encoding for non-uniform φ-reversibility of STRIPS actions, which (under usual complexity assumptions) is impossible to achieve using ASP and ELP.

In order to test whether our encodings can be used in practice, we performed a set of benchmarks on artificially generated instances by checking whether there is an action that is universally uniformly reversible. We compared our ASP(Q) encoding to two existing encodings presented by Faber, Morak, and Chrpa [15], which make use of the power of world views containing multiple answer sets in ELP, and the encoding technique of saturation as of [14] in ASP, respectively, to encode universal quantifiers. This feature, of course, is present directly in the language of ASP(Q). All of the encodings we compared try to directly encode the definition of uniform reversibility: for an action to be uniformly reversible, there must exist a plan, and this plan must revert the action in all possible starting states (where it is applicable). Hence all of the encodings in our benchmark set are powerful enough to test for uniform φ-reversibility.

For the ELP and ASP communities, it will probably not come as a surprise that our ASP(Q) encoding, using a prototype solving system, perform worse than the ASP encoding, using a heavily optimized solver. We see this as a call-to-action to further optimize and improve the qasp system we tested, or, indeed, any other ASP(Q) solver in development. From our experiments, it seems that the performance of ASP solvers, while significantly better, may not be completely out of reach.

For future work, we intend to optimize our encoding further, and test them with optimized versions of ASP(Q) solvers, as they become available. Also, since qasp uses a rewriting to QBF, different backend QBF solvers should be tested. It would also be interesting to see how the encodings perform when compared to a procedural implementation of the algorithms proposed for reversibility checking by [24]. We would also like to compare our approach to existing reversibility tools proposed in the literature, like *RevPlan*[1] (implementing techniques of [13]) and *undoability* (implementing techniques of [10]). However, this requires matching the version (uniform, non-uniform, universal, etc.) and setting (STRIPS, ADL, other planning languages) of reversibility that these tools solve. Furthermore, we aim to explore how our techniques can be extended to planning languages more expressive than STRIPS. We envision various avenues for that, one is to deal with "lifted representations" (going beyond propositional atoms), another one is to allow for non-deterministic action effects. With the power of the quantifier operators in ASP(Q), such extensions to our encoding should be doable in an elegant, readable way, whereas plain ASP soon reaches the limits of its expressive power.

Acknowledgments. Supported by the S&T Cooperation CZ 05/2019 "Identifying Undoable Actions and Events in Automated Planning by Means of Answer Set Programming", by the Czech Ministry of Education, Youth and Sports under the Czech-Austrian Mobility program (project no. 8J19AT025) and by the OP VVV funded project "Research Center for Informatics", number CZ.02.1.01/0.0/0.0/16_019/0000765.

References

1. Amendola, G., Ricca, F., Truszczynski, M.: Beyond NP: quantifying over answer sets. Theory Pract. Log. Program. **19**(5–6), 705–721 (2019). https://doi.org/10.1017/S1471068419000140
2. Brewka, G., Eiter, T., Truszczynski, M.: Answer set programming at a glance. Commun. ACM **54**(12), 92–103 (2011). https://doi.org/10.1145/2043174.2043195
3. Bylander, T.: The computational complexity of propositional STRIPS planning. Artif. Intell. **69**(1–2), 165–204 (1994). https://doi.org/10.1016/0004-3702(94)90081-7
4. Calimeri, F., et al.: Asp-core-2 input language format. Theory Pract. Log. Program. **20**(2), 294–309 (2020). https://doi.org/10.1017/S1471068419000450
5. Camacho, A., Muise, C.J., McIlraith, S.A.: From FOND to robust probabilistic planning: computing compact policies that bypass avoidable deadends. In: Proceedings ICAPS, pp. 65–69 (2016). http://www.aaai.org/ocs/index.php/ICAPS/ICAPS16/paper/view/13188
6. Chrpa, L., Faber, W., Morak, M.: Universal and uniform action reversibility. In: Proceedings KR (2021)
7. Chrpa, L., Lipovetzky, N., Sardiña, S.: Handling non-local dead-ends in agent planning programs. In: Proceedings IJCAI, pp. 971–978 (2017). https://doi.org/10.24963/ijcai.2017/135
8. Chrpa, L., McCluskey, T.L., Osborne, H.: Optimizing plans through analysis of action dependencies and independencies. In: Proceedings ICAPS (2012). http://www.aaai.org/ocs/index.php/ICAPS/ICAPS12/paper/view/4712

---

[1] http://www.kr.tuwien.ac.at/research/systems/revplan/index.html.

9. Cserna, B., Doyle, W.J., Ramsdell, J.S., Ruml, W.: Avoiding dead ends in real-time heuristic search. In: Proceedings of the Thirty-Second AAAI Conference on Artificial Intelligence, (AAAI-18), pp. 1306–1313 (2018)

10. Daum, J., Torralba, Á., Hoffmann, J., Haslum, P., Weber, I.: Practical undoability checking via contingent planning. In: Proceedings ICAPS, pp. 106–114 (2016). http://www.aaai.org/ocs/index.php/ICAPS/ICAPS16/paper/view/13091

11. De Giacomo, G., Gerevini, A.E., Patrizi, F., Saetti, A., Sardiña, S.: Agent planning programs. Artif. Intell. **231**, 64–106 (2016). https://doi.org/10.1016/j.artint.2015.10.001

12. Dimopoulos, Y., Gebser, M., Lühne, P., Romero, J., Schaub, T.: plasp 3: towards effective ASP planning. Theory Pract. Logic Program. **19**(3), 477–504 (2019). https://doi.org/10.1017/S1471068418000583

13. Eiter, T., Erdem, E., Faber, W.: Undoing the effects of action sequences. J. Appl. Logic **6**(3), 380–415 (2008). https://doi.org/10.1016/j.jal.2007.05.002

14. Eiter, T., Gottlob, G.: On the computational cost of disjunctive logic programming: propositional case. Ann. Math. Artif. Intell. **15**(3–4), 289–323 (1995)

15. Faber, W., Morak, M., Chrpa, L.: Determining action reversibility in strips using answer set and epistemic logic programming. Theory Pract. Log. Program. **21**(5), 646–662 (2021)

16. Fikes, R., Nilsson, N.J.: STRIPS: a new approach to the application of theorem proving to problem solving. Artif. Intell. **2**(3/4), 189–208 (1971)

17. Gebser, M., Kaminski, R., Kaufmann, B., Schaub, T.: Answer set solving in practice. Synth. Lect. Artif. Intell. Mach. Learn. **6**(3), 1–238 (2012). https://doi.org/10.2200/S00457ED1V01Y201211AIM019

18. Gelfond, M., Lifschitz, V.: Classical negation in logic programs and disjunctive databases. New Gener. Comput. **9**(3/4), 365–386 (1991). https://doi.org/10.1007/BF03037169

19. Ghallab, M., Nau, D.S., Traverso, P.: Automated planning - theory and practice. Elsevier, Amsterdam (2004)

20. Ghallab, M., Nau, D.S., Traverso, P.: Automated Planning and Acting. Cambridge University Press (2016). http://www.cambridge.org/de/academic/subjects/computer-science/artificial-intelligence-and-natural-language-processing/automated-planning-and-acting?format=HB

21. Hecking-Harbusch, J., Tentrup, L.: Solving QBF by abstraction. In: Orlandini, A., Zimmermann, M. (eds.) Proceedings Ninth International Symposium on Games, Automata, Logics, and Formal Verification, GandALF 2018, Saarbrücken, Germany, 26–28th September 2018, EPTCS, vol. 277, pp. 88–102 (2018). https://doi.org/10.4204/EPTCS.277.7

22. Lifschitz, V.: Answer Set Programming. Springer, Heidelberg (2019)

23. Lipovetzky, N., Muise, C.J., Geffner, H.: Traps, invariants, and dead-ends. In: Proceedings ICAPS, pp. 211–215 (2016). http://www.aaai.org/ocs/index.php/ICAPS/ICAPS16/paper/view/13190

24. Morak, M., Chrpa, L., Faber, W., Fišer, D.: On the reversibility of actions in planning. In: Proceedings KR, pp. 652–661 (2020). https://doi.org/10.24963/kr.2020/65

Functional Programming

Functional Programming
on Top of SQL Engines

Tobias Burghardt⬤, Denis Hirn⬤, and Torsten Grust(✉)⬤

Department of Computer Science, Database Research Group, University of Tübingen,
Tübingen, Germany
tobias.burghardt@student.uni-tuebingen.de,
{denis.hirn,torsten.grust}@uni-tuebingen.de

Abstract. SQL database systems support user-defined functions (UDFs),
but they hardly encourage *programming* with these functions. Quite the
contrary: the systems' focus on plan-based query evaluation penalizes
every function call at runtime, rendering programming with UDFs—
especially if these are recursive—largely impractical. We propose to take
UDFs for what they are (namely functions) and subject UDFs to a
pipeline of function compilation techniques well-established by the FP
community (CPS conversion, defunctionalization, and translation into
trampolined style, in particular). The result is a non-invasive SQL-level
compiler for recursive UDFs that naturally supports memoization and
emits iterative CTEs which contemporary SQL engines evaluate efficiently. Functions may not be first class in SQL, but functional programming close to the data can still be efficient.

Keywords: SQL · Recursive UDFs · CPS · Defunctionalization ·
Trampolined style

1 Recursive SQL UDFs: From 1000s of Plans to One Plan

SQL database engines are experts in the plan-based execution of *queries*. Engine
internals are specifically designed to support query-to-plan compilation, optimization through plan rewriting, and the—often interpreted—evaluation of the
resulting plans.

"If all you have is a hammer, everything looks like a nail." SQL user-defined
functions (UDFs) receive this plan-centric treatment, too, but in their case the
results can only be described as sobering: UDF runtime performance often is
disappointing and it is established lore among SQL developers that UDFs are
thus best avoided [12,24,34]. Indeed, SQL applications pay for the engines' plan-
based approach to UDF evaluation literally with every function call.

To make this concrete, consider UDF floyd(n,s,e) of Fig. 1 which implements
Floyd & Warshall's algorithm [16] to find the length of the shortest path between
nodes s and e in a directed graph. The function operates over table edges in which

© Springer Nature Switzerland AG 2022
J. Cheney and S. Perri (Eds.): PADL 2022, LNCS 13165, pp. 59–78, 2022.
https://doi.org/10.1007/978-3-030-94479-7_5

```
1  -- length of shortest path (via nodes 1...n) from node s to e
2  CREATE FUNCTION floyd(n int, s int, e int) RETURNS int AS
3  $$
4   SELECT CASE WHEN n = 0 THEN (SELECT edge.w
5                                  FROM   edges AS edge
6                                  WHERE  (edge.here, edge.there) = (s, e))
7               ELSE LEAST(floyd(n-1, s, e), floyd(n-1, s, n) + floyd(n-1, n, e))
8          END;
9  $$ LANGUAGE SQL STABLE;
```

Fig. 1. Recursive UDF floyd, a SQL transcription of function *floyd* of Fig. 2b. Yields NULL if there is no path from nodes s to e via nodes $1\dots n$.

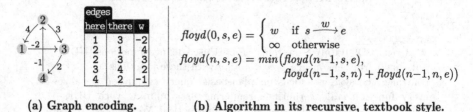

$$floyd(0,s,e) = \begin{cases} w & \text{if } s \xrightarrow{w} e \\ \infty & \text{otherwise} \end{cases}$$
$$floyd(n,s,e) = min\big(floyd(n-1,s,e),$$
$$floyd(n-1,s,n) + floyd(n-1,n,e)\big)$$

(a) Graph encoding. | **(b) Algorithm in its recursive, textbook style.**

Fig. 2. Floyd & Warshall's algorithm over a directed graph (no negative cycles). We have $floyd(4,2,3) = 2$ and $floyd(3,3,2) = \infty$, for example.

a row $\langle h,t,w \rangle$ represents the directed edge $h \xrightarrow{w} t$ of length w (Fig. 2a shows a sample graph and its encoding in table edges).

Note that the code of Fig. 1 constitutes a direct transcription of recursive function *floyd* (see Fig. 2b) into SQL. This formulation in *functional style* [11] leads to a compact and readable SQL implementation of floyd(n,s,e), yet incurs a flood of recursive UDF calls during evaluation (the UDF of Fig. 1 performs $\sum_{i=1}^{n} 3^i = (3^{n+1}-3)/2$ such calls in the absence of memoization). On each top-level or recursive call, the SQL engine creates a new plan context for callee floyd to

(P1) compile the SELECT block comprising the function's body into a plan,
(P2) improve this initial plan through optimizing plan rewrites,
(P3) instantiate the resulting plan given the current arguments n, s, and e,
(P4) evaluate the plan using a Volcano-style interpreter [19], and finally
(P5) tear down plan data structures before the result is returned and the evaluation of the calling query's plan can resume.

Since the engine needs to keep the plans for callers and callees around, the evaluation of any recursive UDF f leads to a nesting of plan contexts $c_0, c_1, \dots$ as depicted in Fig. 3. The repeated effort for plan generation and instantiation (steps P1 and P2, denoted *call* in Fig. 3) plus teardown and caller plan resumption (P5, denoted *ret*) adds up to a significant runtime toll which can easily dwarf the productive time spent evaluating the plan for f's body (steps P3 and P4, denoted *eval*). Plans are rich data structures and, in a sense, the engine finds itself creating and destroying *"super-heavy stack frames"* to drive the evaluation of recursive UDFs.

If we profile the query engine of PostgreSQL (version 13) during the evaluation of a call to floyd—which, in this particular case, leads to 88,573 recursive invocations—we find that the system spends 96% of the overall runtime for function body analysis, query compilation, and plan handling. PostgreSQL implements function inlining (albeit to depth 1 only which thus is of limited use for recursive UDFs) and plan caching: steps P1 and P2 are performed only on the first encounter of a UDF f and the resulting plan is saved for reuse during future invocations of f. This plan caching, however, does not apply to self-invocations and we observe that PostgreSQL performs steps P1–P5 over and over for every recursive call.

SQL plan contexts

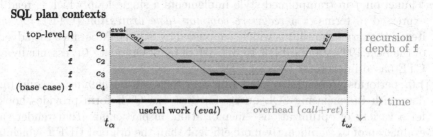

Fig. 3. Nested plan contexts built to evaluate a top-level SQL query Q that contains a call to a linear-recursive UDF f. Overall evaluation time for Q is $t_\omega - t_\alpha$.

The situation certainly is dire, but PostgreSQL indeed fares well if compared to other off-the-shelf SQL DBMSs: MySQL forbids the use of recursion in SQL UDFs (or *stored functions*) in the first place [28, § 25.8], while Oracle and Microsoft SQL Server impose restrictions like recursion-depth limits on UDFs (50 and 32, respectively). PostgreSQL will bail out once the stacked plan contexts exhaust the DBMS server's available process memory [27,29,31]. At the bottom line, UDFs appear to be more of an afterthought in SQL engine design than anything else.

Goal: Treating SQL UDFs Like Functions (Not Queries). Does the associated runtime penalty thus render the use of function-centric SQL code—and recursion, in particular—impractical? Since UDFs in functional style are one elegant way to express and perform *complex computation close to the data* [11,36], we would consider this a true loss.

The present work proposes to abstain from immediate (re-)planning on every call and instead take recursive UDFs for what they are: *functions*. This opens up a box that contains tools other than the plan hammer:

(F1) We view a UDF f as a plain function f in the sense of functional programming (FP). Function f operates over values of the SQL data model and embeds scalar SQL expressions but otherwise is a vanilla function (Sect. 2.1).

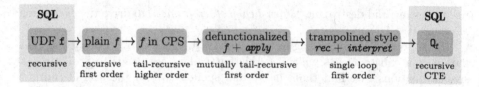

Fig. 4. Using the FP toolbox to compile recursive SQL UDFs into CTEs.

(F2) To f we then apply a pipeline of established function compilation techniques, see Fig. 4. Specifically, we translate f into continuation-passing style (CPS) [2,38], defunctionalize [35], and finally transform f into trampolined style [17] (Sect. 2.2 and 2.3).

(F3) Function f in trampolined style implements a single loop which is readily expressed in terms of a *recursive common table expression* (CTE), *i.e.*, an iterative query form that is widely supported by SQL DBMSs since the advent of the SQL:1999 standard [13,15,37]. We obtain SQL query Q_f, essentially an CTE-based interpreter loop for UDF f.

(F4) Q_f performs no recursive UDF calls and thus will be *planned once* in tandem with its enclosing SQL query. Further, the CTE form provides hooks for a variety of optimizations—memoization, in particular—that render the evaluation of Q_f significantly more efficient than the original UDF f which Q_f can replace entirely (Sect. 3).

The above implements a SQL-level compilation from recursive UDFs to CTEs that is non-invasive and applicable to any DBMS that adheres to SQL:1999—note that this even includes systems that do not natively support recursive UDFs (like MySQL). Section 4 applies this new approach to UDF compilation to a set of recursive functions of varying complexity to demonstrate that function-centric SQL code indeed is one viable way to efficiently compute close to database-resident data.

2   Treating SQL UDFs Like Functions (Not Queries)

The following sketches the SQL-to-SQL compilation of recursive UDFs into CTEs. While we cannot unfold all details, we shine a light on all essential stages of the pipeline in Fig. 4.

Boxing SQL Subexpressions. We prepare the compilation of UDF f by focusing on the essence of the recursive computation that f performs, *i.e.*, (1) conditionals that separate base from recursive cases and (2) the sites of recursive calls. These essentials are preserved while all other SQL expressions are wrapped in "black boxes." The contents of these boxes do not affect the subsequent UDF compilation steps and the contained SQL fragments only reappear once the final CTE Q_f is emitted.

Figure 5 shows the boxes **1**, ... , **4** and their contained scalar SQL expressions (in $\lceil \cdot \rceil$) for UDF floyd of Fig. 1. Free variables and recursive call sites inside a box $\lceil b \rceil [e_0, \dots, e_n]$ are exposed in terms of box parameters e_i: replacing v_i by e_i in b yields the original SQL expression. (We abbreviate both $\lceil v_0 \rceil [e]$ and $\lceil e \rceil [\,]$ by e to aid readability.) Besides the boxes, we are left with the top-level SELECT block whose CASE-WHEN-ELSE-END conditional identifies the base and recursive cases in floyd.

```
1  -- length of shortest path (via nodes 0...n) from node s to e
2  CREATE FUNCTION floyd(n int, s int, e int) RETURNS int AS
3  $$                                                              2
4      SELECT CASE WHEN ⌈v₀ = 0⌉[n] THEN ( SELECT edge.w
                        1                  FROM   edges AS edge
5                                          WHERE  (edge.here, edge.there) = (v₀, v₁)⌋[s,e])
6
7            ELSE ⌈LEAST(v₀, v₁ + v₂)⌋[floyd(⌈v₀-1⌉[n], s, e),
8                  3                    floyd(⌈v₀-1⌉[n], s, n),
9                                        floyd(⌈v₀-1⌉[n], n, e)]
10     END;                                          4 ×3
11 $$ LANGUAGE SQL STABLE;
```

Fig. 5. UDF floyd and SQL subexpression boxes. (Box 4 occurs three times.)

As discussed here, the compilation scheme applies to recursive SQL UDFs defined via CREATE FUNCTION $f(x_1\ \tau_1, \dots, x_n\ \tau_n)$ RETURNS τ AS ... that adhere to the following syntactic constraints:

1. Return type τ is a scalar SQL type (*i.e.*, f may not be a table-valued function), and
2. in a recursive call $f(e_1, \dots, e_n)$, only the $x_1, \dots, x_n$ may occur free in the arguments e_i. This restriction ensures that we can lift the call out of its enclosing SQL expression b and place it in the parameter list of box $\lceil b \rceil$.

2.1 Transition from SQL to FP

Input UDF f is now recast as a first-order function f expressed in a simple ML-style language. Importantly, since SQL subexpression boxing has left us with the recursive backbone of the UDF, a (1) CASE-OF conditional, (2) function invocation, and (3) the boxed expressions themselves already make a complete FP target language. In consequence, the atomic types of this language are just the scalar SQL types. For UDF floyd, the resulting function *floyd* is reproduced in Fig. 6.

Let us stress once more that this and all following compilation steps leave the boxes ■ intact: in particular, we are never concerned with the FP-equivalent of the rich semantics of SQL's SELECT-FROM-WHERE blocks (as contained in box 2, for example). The boxes are not unpacked before we reach the end of the translation pipeline and are ready to assemble the recursive CTE.

```
1  floyd : (int,int,int) → int
2  floyd(n,s,e) =
3  CASE 1[n] OF
4    true:  2[s,e]
5    false: 3[ floyd(4[n],s,e),
6              floyd(4[n],s,n),
7              floyd(4[n],n,e)]
8
```

Fig. 6. FP-equivalent of UDF floyd. The boxes ■ remain opaque.

2.2   From Recursion Towards Iteration: CPS and Defunctionalization

Since we are heading towards a single-loop interpreter for UDF f that does not perform any recursive calls, we proceed by rewriting f's FP-equivalent f into

```
1  floyd : (int,int,int,int → int) → int
2  floyd(n,s,e,k) =
3    CASE 1[n] OF
4    true:  k(2[s,e])
5    false: floyd(4[n],s,e,
6              ⎧    λs₁.floyd(4[n],s,n,
7          A ⎨  B    λs₂.floyd(4[n],n,e,
8              ⎩  C    λs₃.k(3[s₁,s₂,s₃]))))
```

Fig. 7. *floyd* in CPS. Invocation via *floyd*(n,s,e,λx.x).

continuation-passing style (CPS) [1,38]. f in CPS exclusively performs tail calls (which directly translate into iteration later on). Further, CPS explicitly orders the evaluation of function arguments—the CTE-based interpreter, too, will implement just this ordering. *floyd* in CPS (Fig. 7) computes intermediate results s_1, s_2, s_3 (in this order) and passes these to the continuations A, B, C, respectively.

Application of the well-established CPS conversion is the first time that we benefit from entering the FP domain. Here, we are free to build on language features like the higher-order continuation arguments k, provided that we ensure that such features can be compiled away before we transition back to SQL.

Continuations as Data: Defunctionalization. In preparation for this back-transition to the SQL domain in which functions are not first class, we opt to represent the continuations in terms of data. See Fig. 8 for *floyd*'s form after this step.

```
1  floyd : (int,int,int,stack) → int
2  floyd(n,s,e,ks) =
3    CASE 1[n] OF
4    true:  apply(2[s,e],ks)
5    false: floyd(4[n],s,e,PUSH(⟨A,n,s,e,□,□⟩,ks))

6  apply : (int, stack) → int
7  apply(x,ks) = LET ⟨k,n,s,e,s₁,s₂⟩ = TOP(ks) IN
8    CASE k OF
9    Z: x
10   A: floyd(4[n],s,n,PUSH(⟨B,n,□,e,x,□⟩,POP(ks)))
11   B: floyd(4[n],n,e,PUSH(⟨C,□,□,□,s₁,x⟩,POP(ks)))
12   C: apply(3[s₁,s₂,x],POP(ks))
```

Fig. 8. *floyd* after defunctionalization. LET in Line 7 matches on closure records.

Defunctionalization [35] introduces closure records $\langle k, env \rangle$ in which tag k identifies the continuation (for *floyd*, $k \in \{A, B, C\}$) and *env* holds the environment of free variables. For *floyd*, $env \equiv n, s, e, s_1, s_2$; we replace variable v by $\square$ if v is undefined in *env* and thus obtain closure records of fixed width ($1 + 5 = 6$ in the case of *floyd*). The nesting of continuations is encoded in terms of a stack of closure records (see argument ks of type stack with operations EMPTY, PUSH, POP, TOP in Fig. 8). Auxiliary function *apply*(x,ks) inspects tag k of the topmost closure record on stack ks and invokes the associated continuation on argument x. When *apply* recognizes continuation tag k = z, the final result x is returned (see Line 9 in Fig. 8). We can thus start the computation via *floyd*(n,s,e,PUSH(⟨z,□,□,□,□,□⟩,EMPTY)).

2.3   Trampolined Style: Single Loop Replaces Mutual Recursion

We have arrived at the pair $f/apply$ of functions which mutually recurse. (Note: an input of n mutually recursive SQL UDFs $f_1, \ldots, f_n$ would lead us to a family $f_1/\cdots/f_n/apply$ of $n+1$ FP functions at this point.) For the defunctionalized $floyd$, the resulting call graph is depicted in Fig. 9a.

The complexity of this call graph is at odds with the single-loop iteration that SQL's recursive common table expressions can express (Sect. 3 below elaborates on the semantics of recursive CTEs). A better match is offered by *trampolined style* [17] in which a designated *trampoline* function is in charge of dispatching *all* function calls in a given program: to invoke g from f, (1) f tail calls *trampoline*, providing the arguments to be passed on to g along with function label $fn = \textcircled{g}$, (2) then *trampoline* invokes g as directed by fn. *trampoline*'s full control of whether and how the computation proceeds enables a wide variety of applications of trampolined style [17]—here, we are primarily interested in the inherent call graph simplification it provides (see Fig. 9b). From here, inlining the bodies of $floyd$ and $apply$ into *trampoline* yields the single loop we were after (Fig. 9c): the evaluation of *trampoline* is iterated until function label argument $fn = \textcircled{x}$ directs the program to exit.

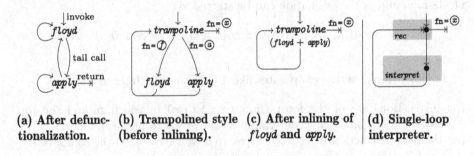

(a) After defunc- (b) Trampolined style (c) After inlining of (d) Single-loop
tionalization.   **(before inlining).** $floyd$ **and** $apply$.   **interpreter.**

Fig. 9. Call graphs before and after transformation into trampolined style.

We break the trampolined-style program into two functions: *rec* implements the single-loop iteration and is invariably required to compile any recursive UDF. (Section 3 will show that *rec* embodies SQL's recursive CTE construct.) *rec* iteratively invokes work horse *interpret* which performs the UDF-specific computation, also see Fig. 9d.

interpret systematically derives from the $f/apply$ pair; Fig. 10 shows the instance originating from $floyd/apply$ of Fig. 8. After inlining, *interpret* incorporates both functions and the outermost CASE of Line 7 inspects label fn (of type $fun = \{\textcircled{f}, \textcircled{a}\}$) to proceed either like $floyd$ ($\textcircled{f}$) or $apply$ ($\textcircled{a}$). By construction, both $floyd$ and $apply$ exclusively advance computation through mutual invocation (unless they return result x). Thus, following trampolined style, in *interpret* we encode a call $floyd(n,s,e,ks)$ by returning tuple $(\textcircled{f},n,s,e,\square,ks,\square)$ to *rec*. On the next iteration, *interpret* will proceed like $floyd$ as required. Likewise, tuple

```
1  rec : (fun,int,int,int,int,stack,int) → int
2  rec(fn,n,s,e,x,ks,res) = CASE fn OF
3                             ⓐ:  res
4                             ELSE rec(interpret(fn,n,s,e,x,ks,res))

5  interpret : (fun,int,int,int,int,stack,int) → (fun,int,int,int,int,stack,int)
6  interpret(fn,n,s,e,x,ks,res) =
7    CASE fn OF
8      ⓘ: CASE 𝟏[n] OF
9          true:  (ⓐ,□  ,□,□,𝟐[s,e]    ,ks                        ,□)
10         false: (ⓘ,𝟒[n],s,e,□         ,PUSH(⟨A,n,s,e,□,□⟩,ks)    ,□)
11     ⓐ: LET ⟨k,n,s,e,s₁,s₂⟩ = TOP(ks) IN
12         CASE k OF
13           Z:  (ⓐ,□  ,□,□,□          ,□                         ,x )
14           A:  (ⓘ,𝟒[n],s,n,□         ,PUSH(⟨B,n,□,e,x,□⟩,POP(ks)) ,□)
15           B:  (ⓘ,𝟒[n],n,e,□         ,PUSH(⟨C,□,□,□,s₁,x⟩,POP(ks)),□)
16           C:  (ⓐ,□  ,□,□,𝟑[s₁,s₂,x] ,POP(ks)                    ,□)
                 fn  n   s e   x                    ks               res
```

Fig. 10. Trampolined-style interpreter (*floyd* and *apply* inlined into *interpret*).

(ⓐ,□,□,□,x,ks,□) encodes a call *apply*(x,ks). Returning (ⓐ,□,□,□,□,□,x) from *interpret* directs *rec* to finish the computation with result x. Given arguments n, s, and e, the evaluation can be started via

$$rec(ⓘ,n,s,e,□,PUSH(⟨Z,□,□,□,□,□⟩,EMPTY),□) \ . \qquad (*)$$

Looking closer, *interpret* operates like a UDF-specific *interpreter*:

(i1) instructions are of the form (fn,n,s,e,x,ks,res) in which fn and the top continuation k on stack ks determine which action to perform, before

(i2) the next instruction is returned to *rec* to advance (or halt) the computation.

This interpreter consumes and produces tuple-shaped instructions (whose regular format we have tried to indicate via (   ) in Fig. 10). We benefit from this regularity when we transcribe the interpreter into its equivalent SQL form in the subsequent section.

3   An Iterative SQL-Based Interpreter for Recursive UDFs

A SQL:1999 *recursive common table expression* [4,37] takes the syntactic form WITH RECURSIVE $W(\cdots)$ AS (Q_{init} UNION ALL $Q_{interpret}$). It expresses a computation that directly fits the single-loop iteration pattern (and one could argue that *recursive* CTE is a misnomer). The diagram on the following page explains this iterative computation, compare it with Fig. 9d:

```
1  CREATE FUNCTION floyd(n int, s int, e int) RETURNS int AS
2  $$
3  WITH RECURSIVE rec(fn,n,s,e,x,ks,res) AS (
4    SELECT    ⑦,n      ,s  ,e  ,□            ,PUSH((Z,□,□,□,□,□),EMPTY)          ,□
5    UNION ALL -- recursive union
6    SELECT  interpret.*
7    FROM    rec AS r,
8    LATERAL (SELECT (TOP(r.ks)).*) AS k(k,n,s,e,s₁,s₂),
10   LATERAL (
14     SELECT  ⓐ,□       ,□  ,□  ,❷[r.s,r.e]   ,r.ks                              ,□
15     WHERE  r.fn = ⑦ AND ❶[r.n]
16     UNION ALL
17     SELECT  ⑦,❹[r.n],r.s,r.e,□            ,PUSH((A,r.n,r.s,r.e,□,□),r.ks)     ,□
18     WHERE  r.fn = ⑦ AND NOT ❶[r.n]
19     UNION ALL
20     SELECT  ⓐ,□       ,□  ,□  ,□            ,□                                 ,r.res
21     WHERE  r.fn = ⓐ AND k.k = Z
22     UNION ALL
23     SELECT  ⑦,❹[k.n],k.s,k.n,□            ,PUSH((B,k.n,□,k.e,r.x,□),POP(r.ks)),□
24     WHERE  r.fn = ⓐ AND k.k = A
25     UNION ALL
26     SELECT  ⑦,❹[k.n],k.n,k.e,□            ,PUSH((C,□,□,□,k.s₁,r.x),POP(r.ks)) ,□
27     WHERE  r.fn = ⓐ AND k.k = B
28     UNION ALL
29     SELECT  ⓐ,□       ,□  ,□  ,❸[k.s₁,k.s₂,r.x],POP(r.ks)                     ,□
30     WHERE  r.fn = ⓐ AND k.k = C
31   ) AS interpret(fn,n,s,e,x,ks,res)
32 )            fn  n    s   e          x                    ks              res
33 SELECT r.res
34 FROM   rec AS r
35 WHERE  r.fn = ⓐ;
36 $$ LANGUAGE SQL STABLE;
```

Fig. 11. Iterative CTE-based interpreter replacing the UDF floyd of Fig. 1.

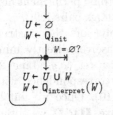

(CTE1) Empty *union table* U which will hold the overall result. Evaluate SQL query Q_{init} and place its rows in *working table* W.

(CTE2) If W is empty, return U as the final result. Otherwise, add the rows of W to U.

(CTE3) Evaluate query $Q_{interpret}$ over the current table W and replace the contents of W with the resulting rows. Go to CTE2.

We build on these CTEs to construct a SQL formulation of the single-loop UDF interpreter. Figure 11 shows the CTE we obtain from a straightforward transcription of the function pair *rec* + *interpret* of Fig. 10 into SQL. (In the SQL code and tables below, □ abbreviates the NULL value.) Here, the CTE is wrapped in a SQL UDF floyd that could replace the original of Fig. 1. The CTE body in Lines 3 to 35, however, can also stand on its own: it contains *no recursive calls* and thus could be inlined at the call sites of floyd.

Just like *rec* and *interpret*, the CTE works over tuples (fn,n,s,e,x,ks,res). To kickstart interpretation, Q_{init} (*i.e.*, the SELECT of Line 4) places an appropriate tuple—or: "instruction", see (*) above—in working table W (named rec in Fig. 11). The iterated $Q_{interpret}$ in Lines 6 to 31 reads the current instruction tuple r off table **rec**, processes it, and emits the subsequent instruction that (1) replaces the current tuple in **rec** and (2) also is added to overall result table U. Instruction processing entails

(IP1) accessing the topmost continuation on stack **ks**. Much like the **LET** in Line 7 of Fig. 10, we use **LATERAL** [37] to bind this continuation to k and make it available to the rest of the query. There is a variety of SQL-side implementation alternatives for stack **ks** and its **PUSH, POP, TOP** operations. We return to these below.

(IP2) Then, inspection of the function label $r.fn \in \{\textcircled{a}, \textcircled{f}, \textcircled{e}\}$ and closure tag $k.k \in \{\text{A}, \text{B}, \text{C}, \text{Z}\}$ is used to select the proper subsequent instruction.

APPEND
⊢RESULT $[p_1]$
└⟨plan for Q_1⟩
⊢RESULT $[p_2]$
└⟨plan for Q_2⟩

Function *interpret* of Fig. 10 implements step IP2 in terms of **CASE-OF** multi-way conditionals. Here, we use a tower of predicated **SELECT-WHERE** query blocks chained together via **UNION ALL** (Lines 14 to 30 in Fig. 11). Note that the **WHERE** predicates are mutually exclusive such that at most one block can emit an instruction tuple per iteration. In particular, no tuple is produced if $r.fn = \textcircled{e}$: working table **rec** will be empty and the recursive CTE will finish as required (see CTE2 above). Contemporary RDBMSs implement this form of multi-way dispatch efficiently. Consider Q_1 **UNION ALL** Q_2 in which the Q_i contain **WHERE** predicates p_i that are *independent* of the outcome of their Q_i. On PostgreSQL, this translates into the plan shown on the left. In such a plan, operators **RESULT** evaluate the p_i *before* the sub-plans for the Q_i are processed [23,31]. Should p_i turn out **false**, the plan for Q_i is never entered. This exhibits the expected characteristic of multi-way branching and proves to be performant also on other RDBMSs (*e.g.* on Oracle 19c with its **UNION-ALL**/**FILTER** pairs [29]).

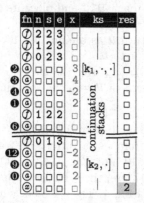

Fig. 12. CTE union table result for floyd(2,2,3).

The assembly of the instruction tuples themselves directly mimics function *interpret* (*e.g.*, Line 23 of Fig. 11 is in correspondence with Line 10 of Fig. 10). Once we unfold the contained boxes **1** to **4**, we obtain a syntactically complete CTE that can replace the original UDF of Fig. 1.

Union Table = Instruction Trace. Given the semantics of the recursive CTE, any invocation of this SQL-based interpreter will yield a union table U that collects *a trace of all instructions evaluated by the interpreter*. Each iteration contributes one row to U. To illustrate, Fig. 12 contains an excerpt of the table resulting from a call floyd(2,2,3) (disregard the annotations in ● for now). As expected, we find rows with $fn = \textcircled{f}$ which represent the recursive calls to *floyd* (cf. Fig. 8), including the top-level call floyd(2,2,3). Rows with fn = ⓐ correspond to the application of the current top continuation on stack ks to intermediate result x (again, recall the invocations of *apply* in Fig. 8). The single row with fn = ⓔ holds the overall result value in column res. Exactly this (grey) table cell is extracted and returned by the final SELECT block in Lines 33 to 35 of Fig. 11.

3.1 Memoizing the Results of Recursive Calls

A reduction of function call overhead is welcome and Sect. 4 will assess the performance advantage that the iterative interpreter has over recursive UDF evaluation. Avoiding the (re-)evaluation of functions altogether, however, certainly beats any execution strategy. This is the promise of *memoization* [6, 26]: once we have spent the effort to evaluate $f(args)$ to value *res*, memoize the pair $(args, res)$ and immediately respond with *res* on subsequent calls with arguments *args*. For UDFs like floyd(n,s,e) which otherwise performs $O(3^n)$ recursive calls, memoization can be absolutely vital.

The SQL-based interpreter can provide memoization for any UDF f. No change to f is required. To this end, we associate n-ary UDF f with a table memo($args$, res) of $n+1$ columns (for floyd, this memo table has columns $|\underline{n}|\underline{s}|\underline{e}|res|$ with key (n,s,e)). The following lines augment floyd's interpreter of Fig. 11 to perform a lookup in memo for the current arguments (r.n,r.s,r.e):

```
 9  LATERAL ( ⟨lookup in table memo for arguments (r.n,r.s,r.e)⟩ ) AS m("memo?",res),
10  LATERAL (
11      SELECT ⓐ AS fn,r.n,r.s,r.e,m.res AS x,r.ks,□ AS res
12      WHERE  r.fn = ⑦ AND m."memo?"
13      UNION ALL
```

On a successful lookup indicated by m."memo?" = true, the memoized value m.res is passed directly to the current continuation on top of stack r.ks (Line 11). Effectively, the entire subtree of recursive invocations below call floyd(r.n,r.s,r.e) is cut short, regardless of whether the call occurs at the top level or deep in the recursion.

How do we populate table memo? For one answer, inspect the call tree for top-level invocation *floyd*(2,2,3) in Fig. 13. When recursive call ❷ to *floyd*(0,2,3) has computed intermediate result 3, it passes value x = 3 to the top continuation on stack ks (which will proceed with call ❸ as determined by CPS). Since union table U collects a *log of all such continuation invocations* in rows with fn = ⓐ (see column x in the row annotated with ❷ in Fig. 12), it is a viable source for memo entries:

(M1) Run the CTE-based interpreter, obtain union table U.

(M2) In U, find all rows u with u.fn = ⓐ. If not already present, insert row $(args$,u.x) into memo where *args* denotes the arguments of the current call.[1] (We find 13 such rows if the interpreter has evaluated floyd(2,2,3),

---

[1] To facilitate M2, we assume that the closure records in u.ks additionally provide *args*. In Fig. 12, for call ❷, the topmost closure record k_1 would hold the arguments (n,s,e) = (0,2,3). Likewise, k_2 would hold (1,2,3) for call ❾.

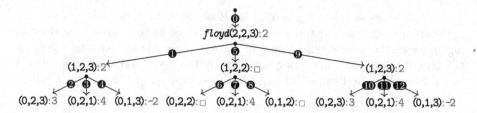

Fig. 13. Call tree for top-level call *floyd*(2,2,3). Edge indicates the ith call performed by the interpreter. Grey •—❻—→ denote the results of the calls.

corresponding to the 13 nodes in the call tree of Fig. 13. The lookup in the added Line 9 above will find these entries during subsequent interpreter runs.)

Once completely filled, floyd's memo table contains n^3 rows for a graph of n nodes. Builtin index support for the key lookups performed by Line 9 render this form of memoization highly efficient—Sect. 4 shines a light on this.

Note that the applicability of memoization hinges on UDF f being referentially transparent, either generally (IMMUTABLE functions [31, §37.7]) or at least within a transaction context (STABLE functions like floyd due to its access to table edges, see Line 9 in Fig. 1). These degrees of referential transparency also define the lifetime of table memo.

3.2 Optimizations: Slimmer/Shorter Working and Union Tables

The UDF compiler described so far is already fully workable, yet lends itself to a variety of optimizations that help to reduce space usage and runtime. Below, we touch on three improvements that aim to cut down CTE working and union table sizes. The space savings effects increase as we go.

Sharing Argument Columns. The tuple-shaped instructions reserve separate slots for (1) the arguments of the functions f and *apply* (recall Sect. 2.3) and (2) result value res. This defines the width of the rows that we store in the CTE's working and union tables W and U. The narrower these rows, the less space is needed to hold the instruction log in table U.

Since each instruction *either* invokes f *or* *apply* *or* returns res, these argument tuple slots can be shared between the functions and res, provided their types coincide. In the case of UDF floyd, *floyd*(n,s,e,ks) and *apply*(x,ks) currently only share common argument ks, leading to a tuple width of $1\,(\text{fn}) + 4 + 2 + 1\,(\text{res}) - 1\,(shared\ \text{ks}) = 7$. Given the int-typed arguments and res, this can be brought down to $1\,(\text{fn}) + 1\,(\text{n}|\text{x}) + 1\,(\text{s}|\text{res}) + 1\,(\text{e}) + 1\,(\text{ks}) = 5$. In particular, when multiple mutually recursive UDFs $f_1, \ldots, f_n$ are compiled jointly, argument sharing can drastically reduce the number of NULL (□) cells in table U.

Continuation Stacks Outside Tables W and U. The SQL array type is one possible SQL-side implementation of the continuation stack in column ks. TOP, POP, and

PUSH then efficiently operate on the array head element. Still, the array's length is determined by recursion depth—if we recurse deeply, sizable ks entries lead to measurable effort when the CTE assembles instruction tuples to be placed in table W or appended to U.

We have thus experimented with a PostgreSQL extension that hosts the continuation stack *outside* of tables W and U. Here, column ks merely refers to a table-like structure of closure records living in a separate memory region that is private to the SQL query that runs the interpreter. Section 4 reports on the runtime advantages of replacing array-based stacks with this tabular representation.

Avoid Building the Instruction Log. The semantics of WITH RECURSIVE entail the construction of union table U (see CTE1–CTE3 at the beginning of this section). This instruction log has enabled memoization but, indeed, only the single row with fn = ⓐ is essential to return result res to the caller. If we opt to forego memoization, we can reach for WITH ITERATE [12,30]. This non-standard variant of SQL's CTE only ever remembers the rows *added last* to working table W. No union table U is involved at all. Instead, the last non-empty W is returned as the final result.

A WITH ITERATE-based interpreter only holds the current instruction tuple in memory, the last of which will have fn = ⓐ. Should memoization be of no concern for a particular UDF, this optimization promises significant space and runtime savings. We have documented both in the context of earlier related work [12,22] and also assess the effect of WITH ITERATE in Sect. 4.

4 Experiments: Functional Programming on Top of PostgreSQL

Recursive UDF processing through the repeated unfolding and planning of function bodies renders relational DBMSs as poor *programming* environments [3,11]. We argue that it does not have to be this way: the SQL UDF compilation strategy of Fig. 4 can turn PostgreSQL into a viable functional programming platform on which complex computation is performed with and *right next to* the tabular data [36].

To make this point, the 10 recursive UDFs of Table 1 address algorithmic problems that would typically not be considered database-resident computations due to (1) their inefficiency when expressed as SQL functions or (2) the forbidding complexity of their manual formulation in terms of a recursive CTE. The UDFs provide implementations of recursive algorithms taken from a variety of domains, ranging from typical database workloads (*e.g.*, over time series or graphs) to more exotic applications. Here, we implement these functions as recursive UDFs in the compact and readable functional style of floyd (Fig. 1):

- comps, like floyd, operates over relational adjacency encodings of directed graphs.
- dtw stretches (or shrinks) tabular time series to find minimum-distance matchings between two such series, applications of which are found in machine learning or signal processing.

Table 1. Impact of compilation and memoization for 10 recursive SQL UDFs.

UDF Description		Recursion	Overhead [%]		Time/Call [ms]		Memoize
			UDF	CTE	UDF	CTE	15 000 calls
comps	Find connected DAG components	2-way	90.64	6.79	3.91	0.48	
dtw	Dynamic Time Warping distance	3-way	97.59	1.82	196.96	12.57	
eval	Evaluate arithmetic expressions	2-way	96.00	3.21	22.45	1.04	
floyd	Find lengths of shortest paths	3-way	96.74	1.88	9605.80	652.40	
fsm	Parse with a finite state machine	Linear	94.08	15.24	0.92	0.10	
lcs	Find longest common substring	2-way	98.43	0.67	140.88	11.04	
mbrot	Compute Mandelbrot set	Tail	97.43	29.44	129.58	6.74	
march	Trace border of 2D object	Linear	89.37	3.47	39.13	5.76	
paths	Construct file system path names	Tail	92.27	19.75	0.60	0.06	
vm	Run program on a virtual machine	Tail	98.17	1.61	401.00	2.19	

- eval, vm implement a simple interpreter and virtual machine which enable database applications to regard table-resident data as code.
- fsm and lcs are representatives of string-based algorithms, a plethora of which are found in the data-intensive bioinformatics domain, for example.
- paths realizes a typical bottom-up traversal over hierarchical data (here: a file system directory tree).
- march implements *Marching Squares* [25], a classic algorithm in computer graphics that also applies to geographical and map data.
- mbrot, finally, constitutes a compute-intensive but data-agnostic algorithm, certainly at the exotic end of the UDF spectrum.

We have also chosen these UDFs to exhibit different recursion patterns (see column **Recursion** in Table 1). Interested readers may evaluate the original as well as compiled UDFs on their local PostgreSQL instances. All required SQL source files are available for download.[2]

For reference: the measurements below report the average of multiple runs, performed on PostgreSQL v13.0. We rely on the vanilla system except where we explicitly mention the use of the query-private table storage extension, recall Sect. 3.2. The database system was hosted on a 64-bit Linux machine (two AMD EPYC™ 7402 CPUs at 2.8 GHz and 512 GB of RAM, 128 GB of which were assigned to hold the database buffer). The database server's execution stack was set to 6 MB, sufficient to hold the frames of all recursive UDFs in our experiments.

Reducing Function Call Overhead (No Memoization). Compilation into CTE form yields iterative SQL queries that do not perform recursive UDF invocations. The saved function call overhead (see Fig. 3) is the runtime reduction we are after. Indeed, we find this overhead to account for 95% of the overall runtime of SQL queries Q that invoke the UDFs repeatedly with random arguments (averaged across all UDFs, see column **Overhead**). It is now apparent that Fig. 3 painted

---

[2] https://github.com/FP-on-Top-of-SQL-Engines/Code.

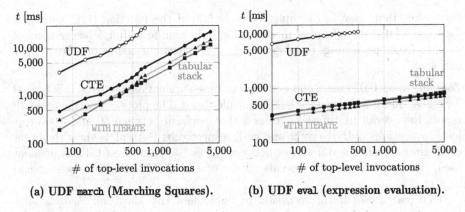

(a) UDF march (Marching Squares).   (b) UDF eval (expression evaluation).

Fig. 14. Runtime of SQL query Q before and after UDF compilation, impact of CTE optimizations.

an optimistic picture: the *eval* phases of useful work tend to make up no more than $1/20$ of Q's overall timespan $t_\omega - t_\alpha$.

Even without memoization or the optimizations of Sect. 3.2 enabled, UDF compilation brings this overhead down to an average of about 8%. The remaining overhead is to be attributed to Q's invocation of the non-recursive UDF that wraps the CTE (see Fig. 11). If this residual overhead is noticeable—*e.g.*, for computationally lightweight functions like fsm and paths or frequently-invoked UDFs (mbrot is called 16 950 times by Q)—it may be advisable to inline the CTE at the UDF call site(s) in Q. This significant reduction of the call overhead is reflected by column **Time/Call** which reports on the average runtime per top-level function call before and after compilation. Call time reductions by a factor of 10 are typical. For UDF vm, we even measure an improvement by factor 180: vm is structured in terms of 9 conditional branches each of which handles one kind of VM instruction. While the branches are mutually exclusive, all 9 contain recursive calls to vm which are unfolded (once) and then planned during each invocation. Post compilation, none of this effort remains.

Impact of Memoization. CTEs require time and space to construct union table U and our approach to memoization (Sect. 3.1) aims to exploit this effort. (Aside: tail-recursive functions need no stack and this also applies to their CTE form. Regardless of recursion depth, UDFs mbrot, path, and vm only ever store the initial closure record $\langle z, \square, \square, \square, \square, \square \rangle$ of $(*)$ in column ks of tables W and U, keeping table size and maintenance costs low.) Column **memoize** of Table 1 documents the runtime impact of memoization once we enable it for a sequence of 15 000 calls to the compiled UDFs. Over time (from left to right), recursive invocations find their random arguments in table memo with increasing probability and, as expected, call times go down. Memoization effects are beneficial across all 10 UDFs of Table 1. The behavior of dtw reflects our choice of arguments in this particular case: the function is evaluated over time series of increasing length and timings ramp up until the maximum sequence length has been reached—at this point, table memo has completely materialized the function [11]. Note that for some UDFs, the effects of memoization only manifest after a larger number of calls: for comps, timings develop like ⌞＿＿＿＿ over the course of 150 000 invocations.

Zooming in on UDFs march and eval. In database application contexts, it is typical for a SQL query Q to invoke a UDF multiple times. The plots of Fig. 14a and 14b report the overall runtime of queries Q that perform between 50 and 5 000 top-level invocations of UDFs march and eval, respectively. Both plots show the order of magnitude runtime differences between UDFs (∘∘) and their CTE equivalent (•—•). The experiment also reveals effects of the CTE optimizations sketched in Sect. 3.2.

UDF march uses linear recursion to implement the *Marching Squares* algorithm that traces the border of an object in the 2D plane [25]. Each step of the recursion adds one point to the border, leading to recursion depths of up to 480 in our experiments (way beyond the depth limits that engines like Oracle or SQL Server enforce). Once march is compiled into and evaluated as a CTE, we thus find array-encoded continuation stacks of that same length in column ks of tables W and U. When the CTE-based interpreter pushes onto those stacks and embeds them in the next instruction to execute, PostgreSQL performs costly array copy operations. The tabular continuation stack representation outside W and U described in Sect. 3.2 avoids these copy costs and admits constant-time PUSH and POP. The runtime measurements •■• in Fig. 14a manifest these savings. In addition to sizable stacks, march has to cope with the construction of a potentially large function result: ever longer arrays of border points accumulate in column res of the rows in union table U. The switch from WITH RECURSIVE to WITH ITERATE can avoid the associated row construction and table maintenance effort (at the cost of disabling memoization), see ▲▲▲ in Fig. 14a.

Both optimizations only show negligble effects for eval, however. The UDF performs bottom-up evaluation of subexpressions in a large arithmetic expression tree. Here, the tree depth of 16 defines the maximum recursion depth. This leads to short continuation stacks in column ks which are handled efficiently even in their vanilla array representation: the tabular stack optimization does not pay off (•■• and •—• overlap in Fig. 14b). Further, the CTE for eval holds comparatively compact results of type numeric in column res of table U. The use of WITH ITERATE thus, too, only has marginally impact (▲▲▲) and the system fares just fine with the standard WITH RECURSIVE construct.

5   More Related Work

The tension between the sobering performance of UDFs and the growing need to move computation closer to high-volume data [7,9], has led the DB community to double down on its efforts to improve the runtime behavior of procedural SQL code [5,14,18,33].

Recursive UDFs. The massive function call overhead in database engines has prompted earlier work in which we pursued an (arguably more complex) two-phase compilation of recursive SQL UDFs [11]. This approach (1) slices the UDF body to build a call graph (cf. Fig. 13) as an explicit tabular data structure, before (2) it uses a recursive CTE to schedule the bottom-up evaluation of that graph. Access to the graph enabled optimizations like the sharing of common subcomputations, but graph construction and maintenance resulted in CTEs that are complex when compared to the simple interpreters emitted by the present CPS-inspired compilation strategy.

R-SQL [3] divides recursive SQL functions into a pure-SQL core and an database-external driver program (*e.g.*, Python code). The latter then controls the iterative in-database evaluation of the core, requiring repeated crossings of the DB/PL border during query execution. Our SQL-to-SQL compilation scheme exactly aims to avoid any passes through the infamous bottleneck between the database engine and external language processors [32].

We argue that UDFs in functional style lead to compact and idiomatic formulations of in-database computation. *RaSQL* [20] asks developers to express algorithms directly in terms of generalized recursive CTEs that can be evaluated efficiently provided that the resulting queries have the *PreM* property [39]. Recursive CTEs are expressive but their fixpoint semantics [4] and syntactic complexity render them unapproachable for many developers. We would rather bank on a compiler that generates CTEs for us.

Our focus has been on UDFs expressed in SQL, but the chain of compilation steps (starting from "plain f", recall Fig. 4) is agnostic about the actual source language. f could be formulated in *Links* [10], for example. In this case, boxes ■ would contain *Links* code which—once translated into SQL using the techniques described by Cheney et al. in [8]—could be placed inside the generated recursive CTE to emit a pure SQL equivalent of recursive *Links* functions (which were not considered to be *shreddable* up to now).

Imperative SQL (PL/SQL, T-SQL). Evaluation of imperative code in PL/SQL procedures (or its PL/pgSQL and T-SQL dialects) involves frequent switches between plan-based query processing and statement-by-statement code interpretation [12]. The resulting friction at runtime motivated work that transforms PL/SQL procedures into pure SQL expressions that can be inlined with the calling SQL query. *Froid* (and its successor *Aggify*) spearheaded research that aims to compile PL/SQL away entirely [21,22,34]. Branching off the *Froid* work, we devised a PL/SQL-to-SQL compiler that significantly extends the admissable language constructs, arbitrarily nested iterative control flow, in particular [23]. The compiler emits CTE-based interpreters that resemble those of Sect. 3 and improves PL/SQL runtime performance significantly.

6 Wrap-Up

We are positive that this SQL UDF compiler is more than a curious ramble through FP land. The runtime savings of about 90% are significant. Applicability is immediate since we pursue a non-invasive, source-level transformation that can be implemented on top of any database engine with SQL:1999 support.

This is work in flux and a variety of knobs remain to be tuned and turned. Among these, we currently study *batching* which evaluates a UDF f for a set of n arguments. Batching can be implemented by providing n initial instructions (recall $(*)$), one for each argument. Table W will then hold n (not 1) rows during CTE processing such that, effectively, n calls to f are evaluated in tandem. Batching will bring down the number of plan context switches between calling query Q and f once more and also opens up opportunities for parallel function call evaluation.

References

1. Appel, A.: Compiling with Continuations. Cambridge University Press (1992). https://doi.org/10.1017/CBO9780511609619
2. Appel, A.: SSA is functional programming. ACM SIGPLAN Not. **33**(4) (1998). https://doi.org/10.1145/278283.278285
3. Aranda, G., Nieva, S., Sáenz-Pérez, F., Sánchez-Hernández, J.: R-SQL: an SQL database system with extended recursion. Electron. Commun. EASST **64** (2013)
4. Bancilhon, F.: Naive evaluation of recursively defined relations. In: Brodie, M.L., Mylopoulos, J. (eds.) On Knowledge Base Management Systems, pp. 165–178. Springer, New York (1986). https://doi.org/10.1007/978-1-4612-4980-1_17
5. Binnig, C., Behrmann, R., Faerber, F., Riewe, R.: FunSQL: it is time to make SQL functional. In: Proceedings of the EDBT/ICDT DanaC, Berlin, Germany, March 2012. https://doi.org/10.1145/2320765.2320786
6. Bird, R.: Tabulation techniques for recursive programs. ACM Comput. Surv. **12**(4) (1980). https://doi.org/10.1145/356827.356831
7. Boehm, M., Kumar, A., Yang, J.: Data Management in Machine Learning Systems. Synthesis Lectures on Data Management, Morgan & Claypool (2019). https://doi.org/10.2200/S00895ED1V01Y201901DTM057
8. Cheney, J., Lindley, S., Wadler, P.: Query shredding: efficient relational evaluation of queries over nested multisets. In: Proceedings of the SIGMOD (2014). https://doi.org/10.1145/2588555.2612186
9. Cohen, J., Dolan, B., Dunlap, M., Hellerstein, J., Welton, C.: MAD skills: new analysis practices for big data. Proc. VLDB **2**(2) (2009). https://doi.org/10.14778/1687553.1687576
10. Cooper, E., Lindley, S., Wadler, P., Yallop, J.: Links: web programming without tiers. In: Proceedings of the FMCO, Amsterdam, The Netherlands (2006). https://doi.org/10.1007/978-3-540-74792-5_12
11. Duta, C., Grust, T.: Functional-style SQL UDFs with a capital 'F'. In: Proceedings of the SIGMOD (2020). https://doi.org/10.1145/3318464.3389707
12. Duta, C., Hirn, D., Grust, T.: Compiling PL/SQL away. In: Proceedings of the CIDR (2020)
13. Eisenberg, A., Melton, J.: SQL:1999, formerly known as SQL3. ACM SIGMOD Rec. **28**(1) (1999). https://doi.org/10.1145/309844.310075
14. Emani, K., Ramachandra, K., Bhattacharya, S., Sudarshan, S.: Extracting equivalent SQL from imperative code in database applications. In: Proceedings of the SIGMOD, San Francisco, CA, USA, June 2016. https://doi.org/10.1145/2882903.2882926

15. Finkelstein, S., Mattos, N., Mumick, I., Pirahesh, H.: Expressive Recursive Queries in SQL. Joint Technical Committee ISO/IEC JTC 1/SC 21 WG 3, Document X3H2-96-075r1, March 1996
16. Floyd, R.: Algorithm 97: shortest path. Commun. ACM **5**(6) (1962). https://doi.org/10.1145/367766.368168
17. Ganz, S., Friedman, D., Wand, M.: Trampolined style. In: Proceedings of the ICFP, Paris, France, September 1999. https://doi.org/10.1145/317636.317779
18. Gévay, G., Quiané-Ruiz, J.A., Markl, V.: The power of nested parallelism in big data processing: hitting three flies with one slap. In: Proceedings of the SIGMOD, Xi'an, Shaanxi, China, June 2021. https://doi.org/10.1145/3448016.3457287
19. Graefe, G.: Volcano–an extensible and parallel query evaluation system. IEEE TKDE **6**(1) (1994). https://doi.org/10.1109/69.273032
20. Gu, J., et al.: RaSQL: greater power and performance for big data analytics with recursive-aggregate-SQL on spark. In: Proceedings of the 38th SIGMOD Conference, Amsterdam, The Netherlands, June 2019. https://doi.org/10.1145/3299869.3324959
21. Gupta, S., Purandare, S., Ramachandra, K.: Aggify: lifting the curse of cursor loops using custom aggregates. In: Proceedings of the SIGMOD, Portland, OR, USA, June 2020. https://doi.org/10.1145/3318464.3389736
22. Hirn, D., Grust, T.: PL/SQL without the PL. In: Proceedings of the SIGMOD (2020). https://doi.org/10.1145/3318464.3384678
23. Hirn, D., Grust, T.: One WITH RECURSIVE is worth many GOTOs. In: Proceedings of the SIGMOD (2021). https://doi.org/10.1145/3448016.3457272
24. Lawson, C.: How functions can wreck performance. Oracle Mag. **IV**(1) (2005). http://www.oraclemagician.com/mag/magic9.pdf
25. Maple, C.: Geometric design and space planning using the marching squares and marching cube algorithms. In: Proceedings of the Geometric Modeling and Processing, London, UK (2003). https://doi.org/10.1109/GMAG.2003.1219671
26. Michie, D.: "Memo" functions and machine learning. Nature **218**(306) (1968). https://doi.org/10.1038/218019a0
27. Microsoft SQL Server 2019 Documentation. http://docs.microsoft.com/en-us/sql
28. MySQL 8.0 Documentation. http://dev.mysql.com/doc/
29. Oracle 19c Documentation. http://docs.oracle.com/
30. Passing, L., et al.: SQL- and operator-centric data analytics in relational main-memory databases. In: Proceedings of the EDBT, Venice, Italy (2017)
31. L PostgreSQL (version 13) Documentation. http://www.postgresql.org/docs/13/
32. Raasveldt, M., Mühleisen, H.: Data management for data science: towards embedded analytics. In: Proceedings of the CIDR (2020)
33. Ramachandra, K., Chavan, M., Guravannavar, R., Sudarshan, S.: Program transformations for asynchronous and batched query submission. IEEE TKDE **27**(2) (2015). https://doi.org/10.1109/TKDE.2014.2334302
34. Ramachandra, K., Park, K., Emani, K., Halverson, A., Galindo-Legaria, C., Cunningham, C.: Froid: optimization of imperative programs in a relational database. Proc. VLDB **11**(4) (2018). https://doi.org/10.1145/3186728.3164140
35. Reynolds, J.: Definitional interpreters for higher-order programming languages. In: Proceedings of the ACM (1972). https://doi.org/10.1145/800194.805852
36. Rowe, L., Stonebraker, M.: The POSTGRES data model. In: Proceedings of the VLDB, Brighton, UK, September 1987
37. SQL:1999 Standard: Database Languages-SQL-Part 2: Foundation, ISO/IEC 9075-2:1999

38. Sussmann, G., Steel, G.: Scheme: an interpreter for extended lambda calculus. AI Memo (349) (1975)
39. Zaniolo, C., Yang, M., Das, A., Shkapksy, A., Condie, T., Interlandi, M.: Fixpoint semantics and optimization of recursive datalog programs with aggregates. Theory Pract. Log. Program. **17**(5–6) (2017). https://doi.org/10.1017/S1471068417000436

CircuitFlow: A Domain Specific Language for Dataflow Programming

Riley Evans, Samantha Frohlich(iD), and Meng Wang(✉)(iD)

University of Bristol, Bristol, UK
meng.wang@bristol.ac.uk

Abstract. Dataflow applications, such as machine learning algorithms, can run for days, making it desirable to have assurances that they will work correctly. Current tools are not good enough: too often the interactions between tasks are not type-safe, leading to undesirable runtime errors. This paper presents a new declarative Haskell Embedded DSL (eDSL) for dataflow programming: CircuitFlow. Defined as a Symmetric Monoidal Preorder (SMP) on data that models dependencies in the workflow, it has a strong mathematical basis, refocusing on how data flows through an application, resulting in a more expressive solution that not only catches errors statically, but also achieves competitive runtime performance. In our preliminary evaluation, CircuitFlow outperforms the industry-leading Luigi library of Spotify by scaling better with the number of inputs. The innovative creation of CircuitFlow is also of note, exemplifying how to create a modular eDSL whose semantics necessitates effects, and where storing complex type information for program correctness is paramount.

Keywords: eDSL · Domain-specific languages · Haskell · Dataflow programming

1 Introduction

CircuitFlow's domain is *dataflow programming* [7], which deals with processing data through transformations with interlinking dependencies. Inputs are transformed into outputs by *tasks*, organised into *workflows* taking the form of Directed Acyclic Graphs (DAGs) encoding dependencies, where the directionality indicates the direction the data is flowing, and the acyclicity ensures that the data doesn't go round in circles. Dataflow programming is highly applicable with numerous uses spanning from scientific data analysis [10,20] to machine learning [1,41]. Examples include *Data Pipelines, CI Systems, Quartz Composer* [17] and *Spreadsheets*. It also has the following benefits:

Declarative. Describing the shape of the DAG instead of just indicating the connections, provides a more user-friendly and declarative experience.

© Springer Nature Switzerland AG 2022
J. Cheney and S. Perri (Eds.): PADL 2022, LNCS 13165, pp. 79–98, 2022.
https://doi.org/10.1007/978-3-030-94479-7_6

Implicit Parallelism. Since each node in a dataflow is a pure function, it is possible to parallelise implicitly. The purity of the nodes means that outside of data dependencies encoded in the dataflow graph, no node can interact with another. Thus eliminating the ability for a deadlock to occur.

Visual. The dataflow paradigm uses graphs. This provides the programs with a visual interpretation, allowing end-user programmer to reason visually about how data passes through the program, much easier than in an imperative approach [15].

Existing dataflow libraries such as Spotify's Luigi [33] or Apache's Airflow [2] have no mechanism to ensure the dependencies are valid. There is no static checking that the connections in the graph match up, which could cause runtime crashes, or even worse, the bug could go unnoticed and cause havoc in later tasks. Consider an example shown in the docs for Luigi [34] that is made up of two tasks: the first, GenerateWords, generates a list of words and saves it to a file; and the second, CountLetters, counts the number of letters in each of those words. An implementation of this in Luigi could have a very subtle bug! GenerateWords could write the words to a file separated by new lines, while CountLetters expects a comma-separated list. This shows a key flaw in this system, as it is up to the programmer to ensure that they write the outputs correctly, and then that they read that same file in the same way. This error, would not even cause a run-time error, instead, it will just produce the incorrect result. For a developer, this is extremely unhelpful: it means more time is used writing tests—something that no one enjoys. With good development practices, the risk is reduced, but as functional programmers, we know a better way: abstraction and static typing.

Why not eliminate all of this with an abstraction of the reading and writing of many different sources and types? The abstraction will help to ensure correctness of passing data via files by eliminating any possible duplicated code. Instead, just having a uniform interface to test. Then the abstract interface can be combined with the type system so that in each program, it is enforced that the types align.

This promotes the need for a new solution with such features that can safely compose tasks and make use of types to perform static analysis to ensure that dependencies are valid.

We present CircuitFlow, which takes a different line of attack from its predecessing plumbers like Luigi: rather than focus on how to compose tasks together, it defines a declarative language that describes how data flows through a workflow. In CircuitFlow, it would not be possible to feed the output of one task, with the type FileStore [String] into a task that expects a CommaSepFile [String]. The same example, written in CircuitFlow, is defined as:

```
generateWords :: Circuit '[Var] '[()] '[FileStore] '[[String]] N1
generateWords = functionTask (const ["apple", "banana", "grapefruit"])

countLetters :: Circuit '[CommaSepFile] '[[String]] '[FileStore] '[[String]] N1
countLetters = functionTask (map f)
  where
    f word = (concat [word, ":", show (length word)])
```

```
circuit :: Circuit '[Var] '[()] '[FileStore] '[[String]] N1
circuit = generateWords <> countLetters
```

In this example, it will fail to compile, giving the error:

```
> Couldn't match type 'CommaSepFile' with 'FileStore'
```

Benefiting the user since the feedback loop of knowing if the program will succeed is reduced. Previously, the whole data pipeline had to be run, whereas now this information is available at compile-time.

Due to the type heft required for such a language, which includes DataKinds [39], Singletons [9], Type Families [32], Heterogeneous lists [19], Phantom Types (a brief introduction of which can be found in Appendix A of an extended version of this manuscript [11]), it will be embedded.

CircuitFlow draws its origins from monoidal resource theory [6], details of which can be found in Appendix C [11]. It is then compiled down to a Kahn Process Network (KPN) that executes the workflow in parallel, to provide the speed benefits of multi-core processors. The KPN used by CircuitFlow is capable of handling an exception in a task, without causing the full network to crash, allowing computation to continue after for successive inputs.

Contributions: A declarative eDSL for creating dataflow programs that:

- employs state of the art DSL design techniques, including indexed data types à la carte and principled recursion to provide interpretations for the AST.
- uses state of the art Haskell methods to produce a type-safe implementation.
- makes use of indexed functors, extended to support multiple indicies, to construct a type-indexed AST in conjunction with an indexed monadic catamorphism to provide a type-safe translation to a KPN.
- has a strong mathematical grounding in monadic resource theories providing confidence that the language can represent all dataflow diagrams.
- has appealing preliminary benchmark performance against another competing library—outperforming Luigi by almost 4x on large numbers of inputs.
- exemplifies how to create such a language in a modular manner.
- uses the first known implementation of a Kahn Process Network in Haskell.

Examples that demonstrate the language's applicability:

- Machine learning: preprocessing of real world song data in comparison to Spotify's Luigi.
- Build systems: the thesis this paper is based on was compiled using CircuitFlow (details in Appendix B [11]).

2   CircuitFlow Language

A use case for CircuitFlow is building data pipelines for machine learning. Consider the example where an audio streaming service would like to create a playlist full of new songs to listen to. This could require a machine learning model that can predict songs based on the top ten artists and songs that the user has listened to over the last three months. However, each of the months' data is stored in different files that need aggregating together before they can be input into the model. This problem can be drawn up as a dataflow diagram like Fig. 1. To achieve this preprocessing, a software developer at said audio streaming service would need to use the following key features of the CircuitFlow language.

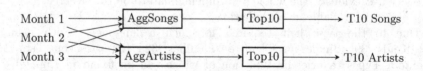

Fig. 1. A dataflow diagram for pre-processing the song data

2.1   DataStores

Dataflow programming revolves around transforming inputs into outputs. Thus the first thing the language needs is a way of getting inputs and writing outputs. For the preprocessing example, this corresponds to a way of interfacing with the different months of song data; a way to pass on the aggregated songs and artists to the top ten calculators; and finally somewhere to store the preprocessed output ready for the machine learning model. In CircuitFlow, DataStores are used to pass values between different tasks, in a closely controlled manner. To abstract over the different ways of storing data, they are defined as a type class:

```
class DataStore f a where
    fetch  :: f a → IO a
    save   :: f a → a → IO ()
    empty :: TaskUUID → JobUUID → IO (f a)
```

The type class provides a way of extracting a value from a DataStore (fetch), a way to write to one (save), and a way of creating an empty one for a specific task. Although the user can define their own, the library comes with predefined DataStores, the simplest is a Var, based on MVars (mutable locations).

```
newtype Var a = Var {unVar :: MVar a} deriving (Eq)
instance DataStore Var a where
    fetch = readMVar · unVar
    save = putMVar · unVar
    empty _ _ = Var <$> newEmptyMVar
```

Var doesn't use its id arguments in empty, however, other predefined stores, such as FileStore and CSVStore, use them to decide where to place the files created.

Combined DataStores. A special case of a DataStore, they allow the interfacing with typed lists, not just a single type. The typed list is a variation on HLists: IHList (defined below). Combined data stores are automatically derived from existing DataStore instances, making it easier for tasks to fetch from multiple inputs by supplying fetch'. (Since tasks can only have one output, there is no need for a save' function.)

data IHList (fs :: [∗ → ∗]) (as :: [∗]) **where**
   HCons' :: f a → IHList fs as → IHList (f ': fs) (a ': as)
   HNil'   :: IHList '[] '[]
class DataStore' (fs :: [∗ → ∗]) (as :: [∗]) **where**
   fetch' :: IHList fs as → IO (HList as)
   empty' :: TaskUUID → JobUUID → IO (IHList fs as)

2.2   Circuit Type

A Circuit represents some computation that has some number of inputs and outputs. In order to statically check dependencies, the Circuit type needs to store a lot of information.

Circuit (insContainerTypes   :: [∗ → ∗]) (insTypes   :: [∗])
   (outsContainerTypes :: [∗ → ∗]) (outsTypes :: [∗]) (nIns :: Nat)

It has five type parameters: insContainerTypes, a type-list of storage types, for example '[VariableStore, CSVStore]; insTypes, a type-list of the types stored in the storage, for example '[Int, [(String, Float)]]; outsContainerTypes and outsTypes mirror that the examples above, but for the outputs instead. The container and value types are separate, due to the need for them to be "unapplied" for the DataStore typeclass. Unfortunately, GHC requires a little more information to perform this match check, such as the seemingly superfluous nIns, a type-level Nat that is the length of the input lists.

2.3   Circuit Constructors

(a) id   (b) replicate   (c) c1 <=> c2   (d) c1 <> c2   (e) task f

Above shows the core constructors of the language along with their diagrammatic representation. Here the relation to resource theories is apparent, the constructors in this library make up a SMP, establishing them as a resource theory able to represent any DAG. More details can be found in appendices C and D [11].

The diagrammatic interpretation also makes translation from dataflow diagrams, such as Fig. 1, to CircuitFlow code easy.

In the language, there are two types of constructors: those that create basic circuits and those that compose them. The behaviour of the constructor is recorded within the types. Here are the types of some basic circuits:

$$\text{id} \quad :: \text{DataStore}'\,'[f]\,'[a] \Rightarrow \text{Circuit}\,'[f]\,'[a]\,'[f]\quad'[a]\quad \text{N1}$$
$$\text{replicate} :: \text{DataStore}'\,'[f]\,'[a] \Rightarrow \text{Circuit}\,'[f]\,'[a]\,'[f,f]\,'[a,a]\,\text{N1}$$

Consider the id constructor, for convenience the nins parameter is shorted with type synonyms, e.g. N1~'Succ 'Zero. It can be seen how the type information for this constructor states that it has 1 input value of type f a and it returns that same value. Each type parameter in id is a phantom type, since there are no values stored in the data type that use the type parameters. The replicate constructor states that a single input value of type f a should be input, and that value should then be duplicated and output. There is also a swap constructor that takes two values as input and swaps their order, and dropL/dropR constructors that will take two inputs and drop the left or the right one respectively.

To use these basic circuits, CircuitFlow provides two constructors named 'beside' and 'then' to compose circuits. The definition of these constructors will require type level calculations. This is where closed type families [8] come in, allowing for type level versions of (+) and (++) [19] (requiring PolyKinds [39]).

The 'Then' Constructor, denoted by <->, is used run one circuit, *then* another, encapsulating the idea of dependencies. Through types, it enforces that the output of the first circuit is the same as the input to the second circuit.

$$(<\!\Leftrightarrow\!>) :: (\text{DataStore}'\,\text{fs as}, \text{DataStore}'\,\text{gs bs}, \text{DataStore}'\,\text{hs cs})$$
$$\Rightarrow \text{Circuit fs as gs bs nfs} \rightarrow \text{Circuit gs bs hs cs ngs} \rightarrow \text{Circuit fs as hs cs nfs}$$

It employs a similar logic to function composition $(\cdot) :: (a \rightarrow b) \rightarrow (b \rightarrow c) \rightarrow (a \rightarrow c)$. The resulting type from this constructor uses the input types from the first argument fs as, and the output types from the second argument hs cs. It then forces the constraint that the output type of the first argument and the input type of the second are the same—gs bs.

The 'Beside' Constructor, denoted by <> is used to run two circuits at the same time. The resulting Circuit has the types of the two circuits appended together.

$$(<\!>) :: (\text{DataStore}'\,\text{fs as}, \text{DataStore}'\,\text{gs bs}, \text{DataStore}'\,\text{hs cs}, \text{DataStore}'\,\text{is ds})$$
$$\Rightarrow \text{Circuit fs as gs bs nfs} \rightarrow \text{Circuit hs cs is ds nhs}$$
$$\rightarrow \text{Circuit (fs :++ hs) (as :++ cs) (gs :++ is) (bs :++ ds) (nfs :+nhs)}$$

This constructor works by making use of the :++ type family to append the input and output type list of the left constructor to those of the right constructor. It also makes use of the :+ type family to sum the number of inputs.

Tasks are made using a smart constructor task, which requires a type level Length. To save boiler-plate, CircuitFlow also provides more handy task smart constructors such as functionTask. This particular smart constructor allows a simple a → b function to be promoted to a task. It comes in useful returning to the music preprocessing example as it simplifies the definition of a task that finds the top ten songs or artists: functionTask (take 10).

2.4   CircuitFlow in Action

$$preProcPipeline = organiseIns <\!\!\!> (\quad (aggSongs <\!\!\!> top10 \; \texttt{"t10s.csv"})$$
$$<\!\!> (aggArtists <\!\!\!> top10 \; \texttt{"t10a.csv"}))$$

The above CircuitFlow circuit solves the music processing example. organiseIns replicates the input values so that they are passed into both aggSongs and aggArtists. Again, it can be seen how this structure of tasks directly correlates with the dataflow diagram previously seen in Fig. 1. This helps to make it easier when designing circuits as it can be constructed visually level by level.

2.5   mapC Operator

Currently a circuit has a static design: once created it cannot change. There are times when this could be a flaw in the language. For example, when there is a dynamic number of inputs. CircuitFlow's mapC allows for dynamic circuits. This constructor maps a circuit on an input containing a list of items. The input is fed one at a time into the inner circuit, accumulated back into a list, and then output.

$$mapC :: (DataStore' \; '[f] \; '[[a]], DataStore \; g \; [b])$$
$$\Rightarrow Circuit \; '[Var] \; '[a] \; '[Var] \; '[b] \; N1 \rightarrow Circuit \; '[f] \; '[[a]] \; '[g] \; '[[b]] \; N1$$

3   CircuitFlow Under the Hood

This section explores the embedding of the CircuitFlow language into Haskell and how it is translated down to be executed.

3.1   Circuit API

The constructors for the language are actually *smart constructors* [35], providing a more elegant way to build the AST that represents the circuit. They bring the benefits of extensibility and modularity usually found in a shallow embedding, while still having a fixed core AST that can be used for interpretation.

IFunctor. The fixed core AST is implemented via a jacked up version of the traditional capturing of an abstract datatype as a fixed Functor story [13]. Instead of Functor, a type class called IFunctor [26] (also known as HFunctor [18]) is used as it is able to maintain the type indices, which in the case of CircuitFlow, are the all important dependency phantom type parameters. IFunctor can be thought of as a Functor transformer: it is able to change the structure of a Functor, whilst preserving the values inside it. IFunctors can also be used to mark recursive points of data types, as long as they are paired with a matching IFix to tie the recursive knot. As Circuit has five type parameters, it needs $IFunctor_5$ and $IFix_5$.

$$\textbf{type}\ (\leadsto)\ f\ g = \forall a.f\ a \rightarrow g\ a$$
$$\textbf{class IFunctor iF where}$$
$$\qquad imap :: (f \leadsto g) \rightarrow iF\ f \leadsto iF\ g$$
$$\textbf{newtype IFix iF a}$$
$$\qquad = IIn\ (iF\ (IFix\ iF)\ a)$$

$$\textbf{class IFunctor}_5\ \textbf{iF where}$$
$$imap_5$$
$$\qquad :: (\forall a \dots e.f\ a \dots e \rightarrow g\ a \dots e)$$
$$\qquad \rightarrow iF\ f\ a \dots e \rightarrow iF\ g\ a \dots e$$
$$\textbf{newtype IFix}_5\ \textbf{iF a} \dots \textbf{e}$$
$$\qquad = IIn_5\ (iF\ (IFix_5\ iF)\ a \dots e)$$

Indexed Data Types à la Carte. When building an eDSL one problem that becomes quickly prevalent is the so called *Expression Problem* [37]. A popular solution is *Data types à la carte* [36]: it combines constructors using the co-product of their signatures. This technique makes use of standard functors, however, an approach using IFunctors is described in *Compositional data types* [3]. This approach is upgraded further to add support for five type indices:

$$\textbf{data}\ (iF :+: iG)\ (f' :: i \rightarrow j \rightarrow k \rightarrow l \rightarrow m \rightarrow *)\ (a :: i) \dots (e :: m)$$
$$= L :: iF\ f'\ a \dots e \rightarrow (iF :+: iG)\ f'\ a \dots e\ |\ R :: iG\ f'\ a \dots e \rightarrow (iF :+: iG)\ f'\ a \dots e$$

Using the :+: operator comes with problem of many L's and R's, when creating the AST. The solution, extended from [36] to also accommodate five type parameters, is to introduce a type class :≺: that injects them automatically.

Data types for each constructor can now be defined individually. The Then (<≻>) constructor is used as an example, however, the process can be applied to all constructors in the language.

$$\textbf{data Then}\ (iF :: [* \rightarrow *] \rightarrow [*] \rightarrow [* \rightarrow *] \rightarrow [*] \rightarrow Nat \rightarrow *)$$
$$\qquad (insS\ :: [* \rightarrow *])\ (insT\ :: [*])$$
$$\qquad (outsS :: [* \rightarrow *])\ (outsT :: [*])\ (nins :: Nat)\ \textbf{where}$$
$$Then :: (DataStore'\ fs\ as, DataStore'\ gs\ bs, DataStore'\ hs\ cs)$$
$$\qquad \Rightarrow iF\ fs\ as\ gs\ bs\ nfs \rightarrow iF\ gs\ bs\ hs\ cs\ ngs \rightarrow Then\ iF\ fs\ as\ hs\ cs\ nfs$$

Each iF denotes the recursive points in the data type, with the subsequent type arguments mirroring those seen in Sect. 2.3. A corresponding $IFunctor_5$ instance formalises the points of recursion, by describing how to transform the structure inside it. The smart constructor, that injects the L's and R's automatically can be defined for Then adding one extra constraint, to the constructor defined in Sect. 2.3 (Then :≺: iF), allowing the smart constructor to produce a node in the AST for any sum of data types, that includes the Then data type.

Representing a Circuit. Once each constructor has been defined, they can be combined together to form the CircuitF type to represent a circuit. IFix$_5$ then ties the recursive knot to define the Circuit type.

type CircuitF = Id :+: Replicate :+: Then :+: ... :+: Task :+: Map
type Circuit = IFix$_5$ CircuitF

Now that it is possible to build a Circuit, which can be considered a specification for how to execute a set of tasks, there needs to be a mechanism in place to execute the specification.

3.2 Network Typeclass

A Network represents a mechanism for executing the computation described by a Circuit. To allow for multiple execution mechanisms, a Network type class defines the key features each network requires:

```
class Network n where
    startNetwork :: Circuit insS insT outsS outsT nIns
                    → IO (n  insS insT outsS outsT)
    stopNetwork  :: n insS insT outsS outsT → IO ()
    write        :: IHList insS insT          → n insS insT outsS outsT → IO ()
    read         :: n insS insT outsS outsT → IO (IHList outsS outsT)
```

This type class requires that a network has 4 different functions: startNetwork is responsible for converting the circuit into the underlying representation for a process network: it will be discussed in more detail in Sect. 3.4; stopNetwork is for cleaning up the network after it is no longer needed. For example, stopping any threads running. This could be particularly important if embedding a circuit into a larger program, where unused threads could be left hanging; write should take some input values and add them into the network, so that they can be processed; read should retrieve some output values from the network. nIns is required for the translation of Circuit to Network, therefore it is not included in the type of a network.

3.3 The Basic Network Representation

A BasicNetwork is an implementation of a Network that uses a Kahn Process Network (KPN). This means that each task in a circuit will run on its own separate thread, with inputs being passed between them on unbounded channels (from Control.Concurrent). A BasicNetwork stores the multiple input and output channels, to do so it leverages a special case of IHList.

```
data PipeList (fs :: [* → *]) (as :: [*]) where
    PipeCons :: Chan (f a) → PipeList fs as → PipeList (f ': fs) (a ': as)
    PipeNil  :: PipeList '[] '[]
```

Using these PipeLists, BasicNetwork is defined using record syntax allowing for named fields, with accessors automatically generated.

```
data BasicNetwork (insS  :: [∗ → ∗]) (insT  :: [∗])
                  (outsS :: [∗ → ∗]) (outsT :: [∗]) where
  BasicNetwork :: {
    threads :: Map TaskUUID ThreadId,    -- allows threads to be managed
    jobs    :: Map JobUUID  JobStatus,   -- avoids duplicate job UUIDs
    ins     :: PipeList inpS  inpT,      -- to feed in inputs
    outs    :: PipeList outsS outsT      -- to retrieve outputs
  } → BasicNetwork inS insT outsS outsT
```

The Network type instance for a BasicNetwork is relatively trivial to implement using Control.Monad's **forM_** if given a function to transform a Circuit to it.

```
instance Network BasicNetwork where
  startNetwork  = buildBasicNetwork   -- Defined soon...
  stopNetwork n = forM_ (threads n) killThread
  write uuid xs n = writePipes xs (ins n)
  read n        = readPipes (outs n)
```

The writePipes function will input a list of values into each of the respective pipes. The readPipes function will make a blocking call to each channel to read an output from it. This function will block till an output is read from every output channel.

3.4 Translation to a BasicNetwork

There is now a representation for a Circuit that the user will build, and a representation used to execute the Circuit. However, there is no mechanism to convert between them. This can be achieved by folding the circuit data type into a network. This fold, however, will need to create threads and channels, both of which are IO actions, and of course it will also need to deal with the numerous type parameters of Circuit. Such requirements lead to an exciting take on the *catamorphism* method for performing generalised folding of an abstract datatype.

Indexed Monadic Catamorphism. The use of a catamorphism removes the recursion from any folding of the datatype. This means that the algebra can focus on one layer at a time. This also ensures that there is no re-computation of recursive calls, as this is all handled by the catamorphism. icata is able to fold an IFix iF a and produce an item of type f a. It uses the algebra argument as a specification of how to transform a single layer of the datatype. Normal catamorphisms can use monadic computations if defined as follows:

```
cataM :: (Traversable f, Monad m) ⇒ (∀a.f a → m a) → Fix f → m a
cataM algM (In x) = algM =≪ mapM (cataM algM) x
```

This monadic catamorphism [12] follows a similar pattern to a standard catamorphism, but instead uses functions such as a monadic map—mapM :: Monad m $\Rightarrow$ $(a \rightarrow m\,b) \rightarrow f\,a \rightarrow m\,(f\,b)$. This allows the monadic catamorphism to be applied recursively on the data type being folded.

A similar technique can also be applied to indexed catamorphisms to gain a monadic version [3], however, to do so an indexed monadic map has to be introduced. imapM is the indexed equivalent of mapM, it performs a natural transformation, but is capable of also using monadic computation. This is included in the IFunctor type class, and facilitates the definition of icataM.

For Circuit, there is one final step that needs to be done: accommodating the five type parameters. To do this, IFunctor's imapM gets gifted the type parameters to complete the IFunctor$_5$ class and allow the definition of icataM$_5$.

BuildNetworkAlg. The final piece of the translation puzzle is an algebra for the fold. However, a standard algebra will not be able to complete this transformation. Consider an example Circuit with two tasks executed in sequence: task1 $\Leftrightarrow$ task2. In a standard algebra, both sides of the Then constructor would be evaluated independently. In this case it would produce two disjoint networks, both with their own input and output channels. The algebra for Then, would then need to join the output channels of task1 with the input channels of task2. However, it is not possible to join channels together. Instead, the output channels from task1 need to be accessible when creating task2. This is referred to as a *context-sensitive* or *accumulating* fold. An accumulating fold forms series of nested functions, that collapse to give a final value once the base case has been applied. A simple example of an accumulating fold could be, implementing foldl in terms of foldr.

To be able to have an accumulating fold inside an indexed catamorphism a carrier data type is required to wrap up this function. This carrier, which shall be named AccuN, contains a function that when given a network that has been accumulated up to that point, then it is able to produce a network including the next layer in a circuit. This can be likened to the lambda function given to foldr, when defining foldl. The type of the layer being folded will be Circuit a b c d e.

```
newtype AccuN n asS asT a b c d e = AccuN
  { unAccuN :: n asS asT a b → IO (n asS asT c d) }
```

This newtype has two additional type parameters at the beginning, namely: asS and asT. They represent the input types to the initial circuit. Since the accumulating fold will work layer by layer from the top downwards, these types will remain constant and never change throughout the fold.

Classy Algebra. To ensure that the approach remains modular, the algebra takes the form of a type class: the interpretation of a new constructor is just a new type class instance.

```
class (Network n, IFunctor₅ iF) ⇒ BuildNetworkAlg n iF where
  buildNetworkAlg :: iF (AccuN n asS asT) bsS bsT csS csT nbs
                    → IO ((AccuN n asS asT) bsS bsT csS csT nbs)
```

This algebra type class takes two parameters: n and iF. The n is constrained to have a Network instance, this allows the same algebra to be used for defining folds for multiple network types. The iF is the IFunctor that this instance is being defined for, an example is Then or Id. This algebra uses the AccuN data type to perform an accumulating fold. The input to the algebra is an IFunctor with the inner elements containing values of type AccuN. The function can be retrieved from inside AccuN to perform steps that are dependent on the previous, for example, in the Then constructor.

The Initial Network. Given the use of an accumulating fold, one important question needs to be answered: what happens on the first layer? The fold needs an initialNetwork that has matching input and output types:

```
initialNetwork
  :: ∀insS insT.(InitialPipes insS insT) ⇒ IO (BasicNetwork insS insT insS insT)
initialNetwork = do
  ps ← initialPipes :: IO (PipeList insS insT)
  return (BasicNetwork empty empty ps ps)
```

The InitialPipes type class constructs an initialPipes based on the type required in the initial network.

The Translation. Now that the algebra type class, and the initial input to the accumulating fold is defined, each instance of the type class can be defined.

Basic Constructors. There are several constructors that just manipulate the output PipeList, these constructors are Id, Replicate, Swap, DropL, and DropR. The Swap constructor takes two inputs and then swaps them over:

```
instance BuildNetworkAlg BasicNetwork Swap where
  buildNetworkAlg Swap = return $ AccuN (λn → do
    let PipeCons c1 (PipeCons c2 PipeNil) = outs n
    return $ BasicNetwork
      (threads n) (jobs n) (ins n)
      (PipeCons c2 (PipeCons c1 PipeNil)))
```

The instance for Swap, defines a function wrapped by AccuN, that takes the current accumulated network, up to this point. It then transforms the outputs by swapping c1 and c2, and building a new BasicNetwork. All other leaf constructors will follow this pattern.

Task. In a BasicNetwork, a task will run as a separate thread, to do this forkIO :: IO () → IO ThreadId will be used. Using this function requires some IO () computation to run, this will be defined by taskExecutor, which will read a value from each of input channels, execute the task with those inputs, and then write the output to the output channels. This computation is then repeated forever. Making use of the taskExecutor, the algebra instance for Task is as:

```
instance BuildNetworkAlg BasicNetwork Task where
  buildNetworkAlg (Task t) = return $ AccuN (λn → do
    out       ← PipeCons <$> newChan <*> return PipeNil
    taskUUID ← genUnusedTaskUUID (threads n)
    threadId  ← forkIO (taskExecuter (Task t) taskUUID (outputs n) output)
    return $ BasicNetwork
      (M.insert taskUUID threadId (threads n)) (jobs n) (inputs n) output
```

This instance first creates a new output channel, this will be given to the task to send its outputs on. It then forks a new thread with the computation generated by taskExecutor. The executor is given the output values of the accumulated network and the output channel, just created. The resulting network has the same inputs, but now adds a new thread id to the list and the outputs set to be the output channels from the task.

Then. The Then constructor is responsible for connecting circuits in sequence. When converting this to a network, this will involve making use of the accumulated network value to generate the next layer. The instance is defined as:

```
instance BuildNetworkAlg BasicNetwork Then where
  buildNetworkAlg (Then (AccuN fx) (AccuN fy))
    = return $ AccuN (fx >==> fy)
```

This instance has an interesting definition: firstly it takes the accumulated network n as input. It then uses the function fx, with the input n to generate a network for the top half of the Then constructor. Finally, it takes the returned network, from the top half of the constructor, and generates a network using the function fy representing the bottom half of the constructor.

Beside. The Beside (<>) constructor places two circuits side by side. This is the most tedious algebra to define as the accumulated network needs to be split in half to pass to the two recursive sides of Beside. Details of its translation can be found in Appendix E [11].

CircuitFlow also uses the ExceptT monad transformer to fail gracefully.

4   Benchmarks

We use the audio streaming example from Sect. 2 to perform the benchmarking. It is also the main application domain of Luigi which we will compare with.

Haskell benchmarks were taken using criterion [29]; Python 3.8.5 benchmarks with pytest − benchmark [23]. Each benchmark is tested on thirteen different numbers of inputs: 1, 10, 100, 200, then at intervals of 200 until 2000, with measurements repeated and summarised as a mean average. Three months of one of the author's own audio history is used, to ensure that the data closely aligns with the real world. This allows for the evaluation of how each implementation scales with more inputs. All benchmarks take place on an Intel(R) Core(TM) i5-4690 CPU at 3.50 GHz (4 cores and no hyper-threading), with 8 GB of RAM booting Ubuntu 20.04.

Multi-core Haskell. By default the Haskell runtime does not enable multi-core processing. Considering the aim of this project partly involves making CircuitFlow run in parallel, multi-core processing is crucial. To enable this the -threaded flag is set when building the binary. Then, using the runtime options, the number of threads can be set by adding +RTS -N flags when running the binary. The -N allows the runtime to select the optimal number of threads for the program.

Parallel vs Serial. The first test will ensure that CircuitFlow's parallelisation has a positive effect on run-times. To ensure that the test is fair, the serial implementation will make use of the same tasks in the pre-processing pipeline. The inputs and outputs will just be manually fed into each task, in a sequential way. The results show that CircuitFlow does indeed provide a performance gain, with a mean speedup of 1.53x.

Profiling the circuit shows that a significant proportion of time is spend reading CSV files. Optimising speed of CSV parsing and how often a CSV is read via caching would improve runtime. Another area for improvement is that there is an expectation on the user to know where is best to split up the workflow into tasks. It would be beneficial if a circuit could automatically fuse tasks together, then it would have a positive effect on the runtime.

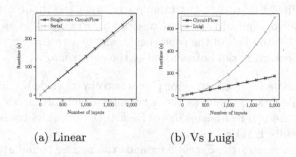

(a) Linear   (b) Vs Luigi

Fig. 2. CircuitFlow benchmarks

1 Core Circuit vs Serial. Another interesting scenario to test is checking if the network structure adds additional overhead, in a situation where there is only 1 core. To test this, the multi-core support of the Haskell runtime will not be enabled: this will then simulate multiple cores with context switching. Figure 2a, shows the results of this benchmark. It shows that both the linear and single core implementation scale together in a linear fashion. Most importantly, CircuitFlow only adds a minor overhead over a linear implementation. This will be particularly helpful for a user which needs to run code on multiple types of devices. There is no need for them to create a different implementation for devices where parallelisation may not be possible.

CircuitFlow vs Luigi. The final benchmark on CircuitFlow is comparing it to widely used library: Luigi by Spotify [33]. Since Luigi uses a Data Process Network (DPN), it can use any number of threads: in this test it is set to 4—the same as CircuitFlow. Figure 2b, shows the results of the benchmark.

This shows that CircuitFlow performs better than Luigi on larger numbers of inputs. CircuitFlow scales linearly with the number of inputs, whereas Luigi's runtime appears to grow at a quicker rate than linear.

Why is CircuitFlow So Good? Luigi and CircuitFlow have their differences, which will likely explain why there is a difference in run times, especially with larger numbers of inputs.

More Lightweight. Luigi is a far more complex library with advanced features, not included in CircuitFlow, that may slow Luigi down—one such feature is back filling. This allows Luigi to avoid running tasks that have already been run. This feature means that before executing a task the Luigi scheduler has to check if a task has already been executed. This adds additional overhead to the scheduler that CircuitFlow does not have. Although this feature does have its benefits, after the first run of Luigi all run times after are very quick as no tasks will need to be executed. If CircuitFlow were to implement this feature any overhead it adds will be partially mitigated by the checks being distributed across multiple threads, instead of in one central scheduler.

Computation Models. The two libraries use variants of the same computation model: CircuitFlow uses a KPN and Luigi uses a DPN [22]. This difference is the main reason why CircuitFlow scales linearly when it needs to process more input values. CircuitFlow makes use of buffered channels to keep a queue of all inputs that need to be processed. However, Luigi does not rely on this design, instead it has a pool of workers with a scheduler controlling what is executed on each worker. It is this scheduler that causes Luigi to scale non-linearly. As the number of inputs grow, the scheduler will have to schedule more and more tasks: this process is not $\mathcal{O}(n)$.

Multi-processing in Python. CircuitFlow makes use of a static number of threads defined by the number of tasks in a circuit. Luigi on the other hand can support any number of workers, however, Luigi suffers from a downfall of Python: threads cannot run in parallel due to the Global Interpreter Lock. To avoid this Luigi uses processes not threads, which adds extra overhead. Luigi also creates a new process for each invocation of a task, which CircuitFlow does not do. This means that Luigi will start 8000 processes vs CircuitFlow's 4 threads for the 2000 inputs benchmark. CircuitFlow's static number of threads could also be considered a downside due to the lack of flexibility depending on run-time values. To combat this more combinators can be introduced that allow for branching or other similar operations, in fact, mapC is a combinator of this type.

5   Discussion and Related Work

In this section, we cover the embedding techniques that we build upon and how our process can be replicated. We also discuss other popular workflow libraries including imperative and functional ones, comparing them to CircuitFlow.

Summary of Embedding Techniques and their General Use. CircuitFlow, which can be more generally be seen as an eDSL whose semantics needs to use effects and has rich types to verify program correctness, has been created in a modular manner that doesn't compromise on performance. The pivotal parts of CircuitFlow's creation can be replicated to produce such other eDSLs. The process is one of three parts. The first is the curation of the type information. In the case of CircuitFlow, this was dependency information, and was achieved using Haskell's approximation of dependant types (DataKinds [39] and Singletons [9] for value promotion/demotion to/from the type level; Type Families [32] for type information manipulation; and Heterogeneous lists [19] for, well, storing more than one type in a list). The second act follows the same beats as the classic embedding story [13]: each construct is created as a separate fixed functor, where all constructs can be composed together with the beloved *Data types à la carte*, and semantics provided through a "classy" algebra. The story just needs to be jacked up to accommodate the type information and effects, with the trick being the switch to indexed functors [18,26] and a monadic catamorphism [12]. Finally, the choice of underlying semantics is key for speed as that is ultimately what will be running. Our choice of KPNs assisted us greatly with CircuitFlow's competitive run-time.

Applicative Functors. An example of capturing parallelism in Haskell is to use applicative functors [27]—a technique employed by the Haxl library [24]. This approach can leverage the applicative combinators to group together computation that can be performed simultaneously. There is even the ApplicativeDo language extension [25], which desugars do notation down to applicative combinators. However, this approach suffers from some forced sequentiality at points. Take the previously mentioned example Fig. 1, both top ten tasks would be grouped together. Leading to neither task being able to begin until both aggregations have been completed.

Arrows. Another method is arrows [16], used by Funflow based on *Composing Effects into Tasks and Workflows* [30]. Arrows similarly are often used through with the notation obtained from the language extension [31], which introduces a do style notation. They also fall victim to the same problems as applicative functors. Due to the constructor arr consuming a function, it is not possible to inspect inside and fully exploit all cases of parallelisation.

The Funflow library that makes use of arrows, does so by noticing that tasks in workflows are similar to effects in the functional community. It draws from existing work on combining and analysing effects, with categories and arrows, and applies this to constructing workflows.

Symmetric Monoidal Categories (SMCs). Linear Haskell is put to excellent use in *Evaluating Linear Functions to Symmetric Monoidal Categories* [4] to address the problem of over sequentialisation found in applicative functors and arrows. It introduces a new SMC type class that allows for all parallelism to be exposed and exploited in a workflow. The type class adds new combinators for linear Haskell functions, that can be composed in a style that aligns with do notation. It uses atomic types to detail the synchronisation points, and where synchronisation can be discovered by a scheduler. However, it comes with the caveat that it can only compose linear functions.

Pipes. [14] focuses on supporting steaming data, which is beneficial as there is no need to wait for jobs to finish before moving on. This is something that CircuitFlow is also designed to support without any modifications: a network can be started and inputs can be streamed in when they are available.

Luigi [33]. Industry-favourite Luigi, used to orchestrate tasks in a data workflow, is a library that, as we have seen, falls into the trap of un-typed task dependencies. It makes use of a central scheduler and workers, allowing work to be distributed across multiple machines. It also comes with built-in support for many different output formats, such as files in a Hadoop file system.

SciPipe [21]. An approach for orchestrating external jobs is taken by SciPipe, a workflow library for agile development of complex and dynamic bioinformatics pipelines. Unlike CircuitFlow and many other libraries, instead of defining tasks as functions within the embedding language, SciPipe uses Bash commands to easily interact with pre-existing binaries. This allows task to be written in the language most suited for its requirements, however, comes with the downside of the additional infrastructure required to create all these binaries for each task. Due to the separation of tasks into bash scripts, type checking interactions between tasks is significantly harder.

Other Typed Dataflow Libraries. DryadLINQ [40] allows for developers to create parallel programs in SQL-like LINQ expressions. Similarly to CircuitFlow, these can be inspected to find any data-parallel sections and then automatically translated into a distributed execution plan that can run on Dryad—although CircuitFlow currently lacks a distributed network implementation. FlumeJava [5], uses lazy evaluation of operations on parallel data structures, to build a dataflow graph of the steps required. When the value is required the graph is optimised to evaluate the operations in an optimal way. Unlike CircuitFlow, Naiad [28] can execute cyclic dataflow programs. It does so on a distributed system, to help with streaming data analysis or iterative machine learning training.

Staged Selective Parser Combinators [38]. Indexed functors [26], are a new technique for building typed eDSL. This paper makes use of this new tool to have a type index representing the type of a parser. This allows it to make optimisations and translations while ensuring that the value parsed never changes.

6   Conclusion

This paper introduced a new eDSL to declaratively construct data workflows, which are type-safe and competitive in run-time performance. The design of CircuitFlow draws its origins from a strong mathematical background, with each constructor directly representing an axiom in a SMP. This demonstrates the language's completeness at being able to represent any DAG, that a data workflow may need. The battle for type-safety without compromising run-time or modular design was a tough one, but one that can be replicated to great avail when creating languages with a similar requirements.

Acknowledgements. The authors would like to thank Jamie Willis for his insights while creating CircuitFlow and the anonymous reviewers for their constructive and helpful comments.

The work is partly supported by EPSRC Grant *EXHIBIT: Expressive High-Level Languages for Bidirectional Transformations* (EP/T008911/1) and Royal Society Grant *Bidirectional Compiler for Software Evolution* (IESR3170104).

References

1. Abadi, M., et al.: TensorFlow: a system for large-scale machine learning. In: 12th USENIX Symposium on Operating Systems Design and Implementation (OSDI 2016), pp. 265–283. USENIX Association, Savannah, November 2016
2. Apache: Airflow. http://airflow.apache.org
3. Bahr, P., Hvitved, T.: Compositional data types. In: Proceedings of the Seventh ACM SIGPLAN Workshop on Generic Programming, WGP 2011, pp. 83–94. Association for Computing Machinery, New York (2011)
4. Bernardy, J.P., Spiwack, A.: Evaluating linear functions to symmetric monoidal categories. In: Proceedings of the 14th ACM SIGPLAN International Symposium on Haskell, Haskell 2021, pp. 14–26. Association for Computing Machinery, New York (2021)

5. Chambers, C., et al.: Easy, efficient data-parallel pipelines. In: ACM SIGPLAN Conference on Programming Language Design and Implementation (PLDI), 2 Penn Plaza, Suite 701 New York, NY 10121–070, pp. 363–3751 (2010)
6. Coecke, B., Fritz, T., Spekkens, R.W.: A mathematical theory of resources. Inf. Comput. **250**, 59–86 (2016)
7. Dennis, J.B., Misunas, D.P.: A preliminary architecture for a basic data-flow processor. In: Proceedings of the 2nd Annual Symposium on Computer Architecture, ISCA 1975, pp. 126–132. Association for Computing Machinery, New York (1974)
8. Eisenberg, R.A., Vytiniotis, D., Peyton Jones, S., Weirich, S.: Closed type families with overlapping equations. In: Proceedings of the 41st ACM SIGPLAN-SIGACT Symposium on Principles of Programming Languages, POPL 2014, pp. 671–683. Association for Computing Machinery, New York (2014)
9. Eisenberg, R.A., Weirich, S.: Dependently typed programming with singletons. In: Proceedings of the 2012 Haskell Symposium, Haskell 2012, pp. 117–130. Association for Computing Machinery, New York (2012)
10. Erdmann, M., Fischer, B., Fischer, R., Rieger, M.: Design and execution of make-like, distributed analyses based on spotify's pipelining package Luigi. J. Phys. Conf. Ser. **898**, 072047 (2017)
11. Evans, R., Frohlich, S., Wang, M.: CircuitFlow: a domain specific language for dataflow programming (with appendices) (2021)
12. Fokkinga, M.: Monadic maps and folds for arbitrary datatypes. Memoranda Informatica (94–28), June 1994. Imported from EWI/DB PMS [db-utwente:tech:0000003538]
13. Gibbons, J., Wu, N.: Folding domain-specific languages: deep and shallow embeddings (functional pearl). In: Proceedings of the ACM SIGPLAN International Conference on Functional Programming, ICFP 49, August 2014
14. Gonzalez, G.: Pipes. https://hackage.haskell.org/package/pipes
15. Hils, D.D.: Visual languages and computing survey: data flow visual programming languages. J. Vis. Lang. Comput. **3**, 69–101 (1992)
16. Hughes, J.: Generalising monads to arrows. Sci. Comput. Program. **37**(1), 67–111 (2000)
17. Inc, A.: Quartz composer user guide, July 2007
18. Johann, P., Ghani, N.: Foundations for structured programming with GADTs. In: Proceedings of the 35th Annual ACM SIGPLAN-SIGACT Symposium on Principles of Programming Languages, POPL 2008, pp. 297–308. Association for Computing Machinery, New York (2008)
19. Kiselyov, O., Lämmel, R., Schupke, K.: Strongly typed heterogeneous collections. In: Proceedings of the 2004 ACM SIGPLAN Workshop on Haskell, Haskell 2004, pp. 96–107. Association for Computing Machinery, New York (2004)
20. Kotliar, M., Kartashov, A.V., Barski, A.: CWL-Airflow: a lightweight pipeline manager supporting Common Workflow Language. GigaScience **8**(7), giz084 (2019)
21. Lampa, S., Dahlö, M., Alvarsson, J., Spjuth, O.: SciPipe: a workflow library for agile development of complex and dynamic bioinformatics pipelines. GigaScience **8**(5), giz044 (2019)
22. Lee, E.A., Parks, T.M.: Dataflow process networks. Proc. IEEE **83**(5), 773–801 (1995)
23. Maries, I.C.: Time. https://pypi.org/project/pytest-benchmark/
24. Marlow, S., Brandy, L., Coens, J., Purdy, J.: There is no fork: an abstraction for efficient, concurrent, and concise data access. In: Proceedings of the 19th ACM SIGPLAN International Conference on Functional Programming, ICFP 2014, pp. 325–337. Association for Computing Machinery, New York (2014)

25. Marlow, S., Peyton Jones, S., Kmett, E., Mokhov, A.: Desugaring Haskell's do-notation into applicative operations. SIGPLAN Not. **51**(12), 92–104 (2016)
26. McBride, C.: Functional pearl: Kleisli arrows of outrageous fortune. J. Funct. Program (2011, accepted for publication)
27. Mcbride, C., Paterson, R.: Applicative programming with effects. J. Funct. Program. **18**(1), 1–13 (2008)
28. Murray, D., McSherry, F., Isaacs, R., Isard, M., Barham, P., Abadi, M.: Naiad: a timely dataflow system. In: Proceedings of the 24th ACM Symposium on Operating Systems Principles (SOSP), pp. 439–455. ACM, November 2013
29. O'Sullivan, B.: Criterion. http://www.serpentine.com/criterion/
30. Parès, Y., Bernardy, J.P., Eisenberg, R.A.: Composing effects into tasks and workflows. In: Proceedings of the 13th ACM SIGPLAN International Symposium on Haskell, Haskell 2020, pp. 80–94. Association for Computing Machinery, New York (2020)
31. Paterson, R.: A new notation for arrows. In: International Conference on Functional Programming, pp. 229–240. ACM Press, September 2001
32. Schrijvers, T., Peyton Jones, S., Chakravarty, M., Sulzmann, M.: Type checking with open type functions. In: Proceedings of the 13th ACM SIGPLAN International Conference on Functional Programming, ICFP 2008, pp. 51–62. Association for Computing Machinery, New York (2008)
33. Spotify: Spotify: Luigi. https://github.com/spotify/luigi
34. Spotify: Tasks, April 2020. https://luigi.readthedocs.io/en/stable/tasks.html
35. Svenningsson, J., Axelsson, E.: Combining deep and shallow embedding of domain-specific languages. Comput. Lang. Syst. Struct. **44**, 143–165 (2015). sI: TFP 2011/12
36. Swierstra, W.: Data types á la carte. J. Funct. Program. **18**(4), 423–436 (2008)
37. Wadler, P.: The expression problem, November 1998
38. Willis, J., Wu, N., Pickering, M.: Staged selective parser combinators. Proc. ACM Program. Lang. **4**(ICFP), 1–30 (2020)
39. Yorgey, B.A., Weirich, S., Cretin, J., Peyton Jones, S., Vytiniotis, D., Magalhães, J.P.: Giving haskell a promotion. In: Proceedings of the 8th ACM SIGPLAN Workshop on Types in Language Design and Implementation, TLDI 2012, pp. 53–66. Association for Computing Machinery, New York (2012)
40. Yu, Y., et al.: DryadLINQ: a system for general-purpose distributed data-parallel computing using a high-level language. In: Proceedings of the 8th USENIX Conference on Operating Systems Design and Implementation, OSDI 2008, pp. 1–14. USENIX Association, USA (2008)
41. Zaharia, M., Chowdhury, M., Franklin, M.J., Shenker, S., Stoica, I.: Spark: cluster computing with working sets. In: Proceedings of the 2nd USENIX Conference on Hot Topics in Cloud Computing, HotCloud 2010, p. 10. USENIX Association, USA (2010)

Languages, Methods and Tools

Timed Concurrent Language for Argumentation: An Interleaving Approach

Stefano Bistarelli[1], Maria Chiara Meo[2], and Carlo Taticchi[1(✉)]

[1] University of Perugia, Perugia, Italy
{stefano.bistarelli,carlo.taticchi}@unipg.it
[2] University "G. d'Annunzio" of Chieti-Pescara, Chieti, Italy
mariachiara.meo@unich.it

Abstract. Time is a crucial factor in modelling dynamic behaviours of intelligent agents: in a real-world environment, activities have a determined temporal duration and the behaviour of agents is influenced by the actions previously taken. In this paper, we propose a language for modelling concurrent interaction between agents that also allows the specification of temporal intervals in which particular actions occur. Such a language exploits a timed version of Abstract Argumentation Frameworks to realise a shared memory used by the agents both to communicate and to reason on the acceptability of their beliefs with respect to a given time interval. An interleaving model on a single processor is used for basic computation steps (with maximal parallelism for time elapsing). Following this approach, at each moment only one of the enabled agents is executed.

Keywords: Argumentation theory · Concurrency · Interleaving

1 Introduction

Agents in distributed environments can perform operations that affect the behaviour of other components. To describe the interactions that ma take place between intelligent agents, many formalisms have been proposed for modelling concurrent systems. Concurrent Constraint Programming (CC) [24], for example, relies on a constraint store of shared variables in which agents can read and write in accordance with some properties posed on the variables. The basic operations that can be executed by agents in the CC framework are a blocking *Ask* and an atomic *Tell*. These operations realise the interaction with the store and also allow one to deal with partial information.

When dealing with concurrent interactions, the notion of time plays a fundamental role: in many "real-life" applications, the activities have a temporal duration (that can be even interrupted) and the coordination of such activities has to take into consideration this timeliness property. The interacting actors are mutually influenced by their actions, meaning that *A* reacts accordingly to the timing and quantitative aspects related to *B*'s behaviour, and vice versa. Moreover, the information brought forward by debating agents that interact in a dynamic environment can be affected by time constraints limiting, for instance, the influence of some arguments in the system to a

© Springer Nature Switzerland AG 2022
J. Cheney and S. Perri (Eds.): PADL 2022, LNCS 13165, pp. 101–116, 2022.
https://doi.org/10.1007/978-3-030-94479-7_7

certain time lapse. A mechanism for handling time is therefore required to better model the behaviour of intelligent agents involved in argumentation processes.

In [5], we introduced *tcla*, a timed extension of the Concurrent Language for Argumentation [3,6], which models dynamic interactions between agents (using basic actions like *add*, *rmv*, *check* and *test*) and exploits notions from Argumentation Theory to reason about shared knowledge. The time extension is based on the hypothesis of *bounded asynchrony*: the computation takes a bounded period of time and is measured by a discrete global clock. Parallel operations are expressed in [5] in terms of maximal parallelism. According to the maximal parallelism policy (applied, for example, in the original works as [22] and [23]), at each moment every enabled agent of the system is activated. However, this setting implies the existence of an unbounded number of processors ready to handle the execution of a program.

With this paper we revise *tcla* semantics by considering a paradigm where the parallel operator is interpreted in terms of interleaving. The interleaving approach limits the number of enabled agents executed at a time, mimicking the limited number of available processors as in the real world. We still assume maximal parallelism for actions depending on time. In other words, time passes for all the parallel processes involved in a computation. This is accomplished by allowing all the time-only dependent actions (that we identify through τ-transitions) to concurrently run with at most one action manipulating the store (a ω-transition). This approach, analogous to that one adopted in [13], is different from that one of [4, 12] (where maximal parallelism was assumed for any kind of action), and it is also different from the one considered in [8], where time does not elapse for timeout constructs.

The rest of the paper is organised as follows: in Sect. 2 we summarise the background notions that will be used to present our proposal; Sect. 3 presents the interleaving version of *tcla*, providing both the syntax and the operational semantics; Sect. 4 exemplifies the use of timed paradigms in *tcla*; in Sect. 5 we describe a working implementation of *tcla*; Sect. 6 features related works relevant to our study; Sect. 7, finally, concludes the paper by also indicating possible future research lines.

2   Background

Argumentation Theory aims to understand and model the human natural fashion of reasoning, allowing one to deal with uncertainty in non-monotonic (defeasible) reasoning. In his seminal paper [14], Dung defines the building blocks of abstract argumentation.

Definition 1 (AFs). *Let U be the set of all possible arguments[1], which we refer to as the "universe". An Abstract Argumentation Framework is a pair $\langle Arg, R \rangle$ where $Arg \subseteq U$ is a set of adopted arguments and R is a binary relation on Arg (representing attacks among adopted arguments).*

AFs can be represented through directed graphs, that we depict using the standard conventions. For two arguments $a, b \in Arg$, the notation $(a, b) \in R$ (or, equivalently, $a \rightarrow b$) represents an attack directed from a against b.

---

[1] The set U is not present in the original definition by Dung and we introduce it for our convenience to distinguish all possible arguments from the adopted ones.

Definition 2 (Acceptable Argument). *Given an AF $F = \langle A, R \rangle$, an argument $a \in A$ is acceptable with respect to $D \subseteq A$ if and only if $\forall b \in A$ such that $(b, a) \in R$, $\exists c \in D$ such that $(c, b) \in R$, and we say that a is* **defended** *from D.*

Given an argument framework F we use A_F to refer to the arguments of F and R_F to refer to the attack relation of F. We identify the sets of attacking arguments as follows.

Definition 3 (Attacks). *Let $F = \langle A, R \rangle$ be an AF, $a \in A$ and $S \subseteq A$. We define the sets $a_F^+ = \{b \in A \mid (a, b) \in R\}$ and $S_F^+ = \bigcup_{a \in S} a_F^+$ (we will omit the subscript F when it is clear from the context).*

The notion of defence can be used for identifying subsets of "good" arguments. The goal is to establish which are the acceptable arguments according to a certain semantics, namely a selection criterion. Non-accepted arguments are rejected. Different kinds of semantics have been introduced [1,14] that reflect desirable qualities for sets of arguments. We first give the definition for the extension-based semantics, namely admissible, complete, stable, semi-stable, preferred, and grounded semantics (denoted with *adm, com, stb, sst, prf* and *gde*, respectively, and generically with σ).

Definition 4 (Extension-based semantics). *Let $F = \langle Arg, R \rangle$ be an AF. A set $E \subseteq Arg$ is conflict-free in F, denoted $E \in S_{cf}(F)$, if and only if there are no $a, b \in E$ such that $(a, b) \in R$. For $E \in S_{cf}(F)$ we have that:*

- $E \in S_{adm}(F)$ *if each $a \in E$ is defended by E;*
- $E \in S_{com}(F)$ *if $E \in S_{adm}(F)$ and $\forall a \in Arg$ defended by E, $a \in E$;*
- $E \in S_{stb}(F)$ *if $\forall a \in Arg \setminus E$, $\exists b \in E$ such that $(b, a) \in R$;*
- $E \in S_{sst}(F)$ *if $E \in S_{com}(F)$ and $E \cup E^+$ is maximal[2];*
- $E \in S_{prf}(F)$ *if $E \in S_{adm}(F)$ and E is maximal;*
- $E \in S_{gde}(F)$ *if $E \in S_{com}(F)$ and E is minimal.*

Moreover, if E satisfies one of the above properties for a certain semantics, we say that E is an extension for that semantics (for example, if $E \in S_{adm/com/stb/sst/prf/gde}(F)$ we say that E is an admissible/complete/stable/semi-stable/preferred/grounded extension).

Besides enumerating the extensions for a certain semantics σ, one of the most common tasks performed on AFs is to decide whether an argument a is accepted in some extension of $S_\sigma(F)$ or in all extensions of $S_\sigma(F)$. In the former case, we say that a is *credulously* accepted with respect to σ; in the latter, a is instead *sceptically* accepted with respect to σ.

Example 1. In Fig. 1 we provide an example of AF where sets of extensions are given for all the mentioned semantics: $S_{cf}(F) = \{\{\}, \{a\}, \{b\}, \{c\}, \{d\}, \{a,c\}, \{a,d\}, \{b,d\}\}$, $S_{adm}(F) = \{\{\}, \{a\}, \{c\}, \{d\}, \{a,c\}, \{a,d\}\}$, $S_{com}(F) = \{\{a\}, \{a,c\}, \{a,d\}\}$, $S_{prf}(F) = \{\{a,c\}, \{a,d\}\}$, $S_{stb}(F) = \{\{a,d\}\}$, and $S_{gde}(F) = \{\{a\}\}$. The singleton $\{e\}$ is not conflict-free because e attacks itself. The argument b is not contained in any

---

[2] The set $E \cup E^+$ is also called range of E [10].

admissible extension because it is not defended from the attack of a. The empty set $\{\}$, and the singletons $\{c\}$ and $\{d\}$ are not complete extensions because a, which is not attacked by any other argument, has to be contained in all complete extensions. The maximal admissible extensions $\{a,c\}$ and $\{a,d\}$ are preferred, while the minimal complete $\{a\}$ is the (unique) grounded extension. Then, the arguments in the subset $\{a,d\}$, that conduct attacks against all the other arguments (namely b, d and e), represent a stable extension. To conclude the example, we want to point out that argument a is sceptically accepted with respect to the complete semantics, since it appears in all three subsets of $S_{com}(F)$. On the other hand, arguments c and d, each of which is in one complete extension only, are credulously accepted with respect to the complete semantics.

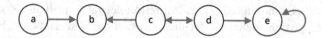

Fig. 1. Example of abstract argumentation framework.

Many of the above-mentioned semantics (such as the admissible and the complete ones) exploit the notion of defence to decide whether an argument is part of an extension or not. The phenomenon for which an argument is accepted in some extension because it is defended by another argument belonging to that extension is known as *reinstatement* [9]. In the same paper, Caminada also give a definition for a reinstatement labelling.

Definition 5 (Reinstatement labelling). *Let* $F = \langle Arg, R \rangle$ *and* $\mathbb{L} = \{$in, out, undec$\}$. *A labelling of* F *is a total function* $L : Arg \to \mathbb{L}$. *We define* $in(L) = \{a \in Arg \mid L(a) = $ in$\}$, $out(L) = \{a \in Arg \mid L(a) = $ out$\}$ *and* $undec(L) = \{a \in Arg \mid L(a) = $ undec$\}$. *We say that* L *is a reinstatement labelling if and only if it satisfies the following:*

- $\forall a,b \in Arg$, *if* $a \in in(L)$ *and* $(b,a) \in R$ *then* $b \in out(L)$;
- $\forall a \in Arg$, *if* $a \in out(L)$ *then* $\exists b \in Arg$ *such that* $b \in in(L)$ *and* $(b,a) \in R$.

In other words, an argument is labelled in if all its attackers are labelled out, and it is labelled out if at least one in node attacks it. In all other cases, the argument is labelled undec. A labelling-based semantics [1] associates with an AF a subset of all the possible labellings. In Fig. 2 we show an example of reinstatement labelling on an AF in which arguments a and c highlighted in green are in, red ones (b and d) are out, and the yellow argument e (that attacks itself) is undec.

Given a labelling L, it is also possible to identify a correspondence with the extension-based semantics [1]. In particular, the set of in arguments coincides with a complete extension, while other semantics can be obtained through restrictions on the labelling as shown in Table 1.

Table 1. Reinstatement labelling vs semantics.

Labelling restrictions	Semantics
No restrictions	Complete
Empty undec	Stable
Minimal undec	Semi-stable
Maximal in	Preferred
Maximal out	Preferred
Maximal undec	Grounded
Minimal in	Grounded
Minimal out	Grounded

3 Syntax and Semantics

The syntax of our timed concurrent language for argumentation, *tcla*, is presented in Table 2, where P, C, A and E denote a generic process, a sequence of procedure declarations (or clauses), a generic agent and a generic guarded agent, respectively. Moreover $t \in \mathbb{N} \cup \{+\infty\}$.

Table 2. *tcla* syntax.

$$P ::= C.A$$
$$C ::= p(x) :: A \mid C.C$$
$$A ::= success \mid failure \mid add(Arg,R) \rightarrow A \mid rmv(Arg,R) \rightarrow A \mid E \mid A\|A \mid \exists_x A \mid p(x)$$
$$E ::= c\text{-}test_t(a,l,\sigma) \rightarrow A \mid s\text{-}test_t(a,l,\sigma) \rightarrow A \mid check_t(Arg,R) \rightarrow A \mid E+E \mid E+_P E \mid E\|_G E$$

Communication between *tcla* agents is implemented via shared memory, similarly to *cla* [3,6] and CC [24], and opposed to other languages (e.g., CSP [16] and CCS [19]) based on message passing. In the following, we denote by $\mathcal{E}$ the class of guarded agents and by $\mathcal{E}_0$ the class of guarded agents such that all outermost guards have $t = 0$ (note that a Boolean syntactic category could be introduced in replacement of $\mathcal{E}_0$ to handle guards and allow for finer distinctions). In a *tcla process* $P = C.A$, A is the initial agent to be executed in the context of the set of declarations C.

Fig. 2. Example of reinstatement labelling. (Color figure online)

The operational model of *tcla* processes can be formally described by a labeled transition system $T = (Conf, Label, \rightarrow)$, where we assume that each transition step exactly takes one time-unit. Configurations (in) *Conf* are pairs consisting of a process and an AF $F = \langle Arg, R \rangle$ representing the common knowledge base. $\mathscr{L} = \{\tau, \omega\}$ is the set of labels that we use to distinguish "real" computational steps performed by processes which have the control (label ω) from the transitions which model only the passing of time (label τ). So ω-actions are those performed by processes that modify the store (*add*, *rmv*), check the store (*check_t*, *c-test_t*, *s-test_t*), call a procedure, and correspond to exceeding a timeout (*check_0*, *c-test_0*, *s-test_0*). On the other hand, τ-actions are those performed by timeout processes (*check_t*, *c-test_t*, *s-test_t*) in case they do not have control of the processor.

The transition relation $\xrightarrow{\omega} \subseteq Conf \times Conf$ is the least relation satisfying the rules in Tables 3 and 4, and it characterizes the (temporal) evolution of the system. So, $\langle A, F \rangle \xrightarrow{\omega} \langle A', F' \rangle$ means that, if at time t we have the process A and the AF F, then at time $t + 1$ we have the process A' and the AF F'.

In Tables 3 and 4 we give the definitions for the transition rules. The agents *success* and *failure* represent a successful and a failed termination, respectively, so they may not make any further transition. Action prefixing is denoted by $\rightarrow$, non-determinism is introduced via the guarded choice construct $E + E$, if-then-else statements can be realised through $+_P$, parallel and guarded parallel compositions are denoted by $\|$ and $\|_G$, and a notion of locality is introduced by the agent $\exists_x A$, which behaves like A with argument x considered local to A, thus hiding the information on x provided by the external environment. Moreover, we have the c-test_t$(a, l, \sigma) \rightarrow A$, s-test_t$(a, l, \sigma) \rightarrow A$ and check_t$(Arg, R) \rightarrow A$ constructs, which are explicit timing primitives introduced in order to allow for the specification of timeouts. In Tables 3 and 4 we have omitted the symmetric rules for the choice operator $+$ and for the two parallel composition operators $\|$ and $\|_G$. Indeed, $+$ is commutative, so $E_1 + E_2$ produces the same result as (that is, is congruent to) $E_2 + E_1$. The same is also true for $\|$ and $\|_G$. Note that $+$, $\|$ and $\|_G$ are also associative. Moreover *success* and *failure* are the identity and the absorbing elements under the parallel composition $\|$, respectively (namely for each agent A, we have that $A \| success$ and $A \| failure$ are the agents A and *failure*, respectively).

In the following we give an operational semantics of *tcla*, where the parallel operator is modelled in terms of *interleaving*. While in the *maximal parallelism* paradigm, at each moment, every enabled agent of the system is activated, in the interleaving paradigm, agents may have to wait for the processor to be "free". Clearly, since we have dynamic process creation, a maximal parallelism approach has the disadvantage that, in general, it implies the existence of an unbound number of processes. On the other hand a naive interleaving semantic could be problematic from the time viewpoint, as in principle the time does not pass for enabled agent which are not scheduled.

For the operational semantics of *tcla* we follow a solution analogous to that one adopted in [4]: we assume that the parallel operator is interpreted in terms of interleaving, as usual, however we must assume maximal parallelism for actions depending on time. In other words, time passes for all the parallel processes involved in a computation. Practically, we use τ-actions to make the time pass for agents who do not require the processor.

We will usually write a *tcla* process $P = C.A$ as the corresponding agent A, omitting C when not required by the context. Suppose we have an agent A whose knowledge base

Table 3. *tcla* operational semantics (part I).

$\langle add(Arg',R') \to A, \langle Arg,R\rangle\rangle \xrightarrow{\omega} \langle A, \langle Arg \cup Arg', R \cup R''\rangle\rangle$	Addition
where $R'' = \{(a,b) \in R' \mid a,b \in Arg \cup Arg'\}$	
$\langle rmv(Arg',R') \to A, \langle Arg,R\rangle\rangle \xrightarrow{\omega} \langle A, \langle Arg \setminus Arg', R \setminus \{R' \cup R''\}\rangle\rangle$	Removal
where $R'' = \{(a,b) \in R \mid a \in Arg' \lor b \in Arg'\}$	
$\dfrac{Arg' \subseteq Arg \land R' \subseteq R \quad t > 0}{\langle check_t(Arg',R') \to A, \langle Arg,R\rangle\rangle \xrightarrow{\omega} \langle A, \langle Arg,R\rangle\rangle}$	Check (1)
$\dfrac{Arg' \not\subseteq Arg \lor R' \not\subseteq R \quad t > 0}{\langle check_t(Arg',R') \to A, \langle Arg,R\rangle\rangle \xrightarrow{\omega} \langle check_{t-1}(Arg',R') \to A, \langle Arg,R\rangle\rangle}$	Check (2)
$\langle check_t(Arg',R') \to A,F\rangle \xrightarrow{\tau} \langle check_{t-1}(Arg',R') \to A,F\rangle \quad t > 0$	Check (3)
$\langle check_0(Arg',R') \to A,F\rangle \xrightarrow{\omega} \langle failure,F\rangle$	Check (4)
$\dfrac{\exists L \in S_\sigma(F) \mid l \in L(a) \quad t > 0}{\langle c\text{-}test_t(a,l,\sigma) \to A,F\rangle \xrightarrow{\omega} \langle A,F\rangle}$	Credulous Test (1)
$\dfrac{\forall L \in S_\sigma(F) \mid l \notin L(a) \quad t > 0}{\langle c\text{-}test_t(a,l,\sigma) \to A,F\rangle \xrightarrow{\omega} \langle c\text{-}test_{t-1}(a,l,\sigma) \to A,F\rangle}$	Credulous Test (2)
$\langle c\text{-}test_t(a,l,\sigma) \to A,F\rangle \xrightarrow{\tau} \langle c\text{-}test_{t-1}(a,l,\sigma) \to A,F\rangle \quad t > 0$	Credulous Test (3)
$\langle c\text{-}test_0(a,l,\sigma) \to A,F\rangle \xrightarrow{\omega} \langle failure,F\rangle$	Credulous Test (4)
$\dfrac{\forall L \in S_\sigma(F).l \in L(a) \quad t > 0}{\langle s\text{-}test_t(a,l,\sigma) \to A,F\rangle \xrightarrow{\omega} \langle A,F\rangle}$	Sceptical Test (1)
$\dfrac{\exists L \in S_\sigma(F).l \notin L(a) \quad t > 0}{\langle s\text{-}test_t(a,l,\sigma) \to A,F\rangle \xrightarrow{\omega} \langle s\text{-}test_{t-1}(a,l,\sigma) \to A,F\rangle}$	Sceptical Test (2)
$\langle s\text{-}test_t(a,l,\sigma) \to A,F\rangle \xrightarrow{\tau} \langle s\text{-}test_{t-1}(a,l,\sigma) \to A,F\rangle \quad t > 0$	Sceptical Test (3)
$\langle s\text{-}test_0(a,l,\sigma) \to A,F\rangle \xrightarrow{\omega} \langle failure,F\rangle$	Sceptical Test (4)
$\dfrac{\langle E_1,F\rangle \xrightarrow{\omega} \langle A,F\rangle, \quad E_1 \notin \mathscr{E}_0, \quad A_1 \notin \mathscr{E}}{\langle E_1 +_P E_2,F\rangle \xrightarrow{\omega} \langle A_1,F\rangle}$	If Then Else (1)
$\dfrac{\langle E_1,F\rangle \xrightarrow{\xi} \langle E_1',F\rangle, \quad E_1 \notin \mathscr{E}_0, \quad E_1' \in \mathscr{E}}{\langle E_1 +_P E_2,F\rangle \xrightarrow{\xi} \langle E_1' +_P E_2,F\rangle} \qquad \dfrac{E_1 \in \mathscr{E}_0, \langle E_2,F\rangle \xrightarrow{\xi} \langle A_2,F\rangle}{\langle E_1 +_P E_2,F\rangle \xrightarrow{\xi} \langle A_2,F\rangle} \quad \xi \in \{\tau,\omega\}$	If Then Else (2)

Table 4. *tcla* operational semantics (part II).

$\dfrac{\langle E_1,F\rangle \xrightarrow{\omega} \langle A_1,F\rangle, \langle E_2,F\rangle \xrightarrow{\tau} \langle A_2,F\rangle \quad E_1,E_2 \notin \mathscr{E}_0, \quad A_1 \notin \mathscr{E}}{\langle E_1 \|_G E_2,F\rangle \xrightarrow{\omega} \langle A_1\|A_2,F\rangle}$	Guarded Parallelism (1)
$\dfrac{\langle E_1,F\rangle \xrightarrow{\xi} \langle E_1',F\rangle, \langle E_2,F\rangle \xrightarrow{\tau} \langle E_2',F\rangle, \quad E_1,E_2 \notin \mathscr{E}_0, \quad E_1',E_2' \in \mathscr{E}}{\langle E_1\|_G E_2,F\rangle \xrightarrow{\xi} \langle E_1'\|_G E_2',F\rangle} \quad \xi \in \{\tau,\omega\}$	Guarded Parallelism (2)
$\dfrac{E_1 \in \mathscr{E}_0, \langle E_2,F\rangle \xrightarrow{\xi} \langle A_2,F\rangle}{\langle E_1\|_G E_2,F\rangle \xrightarrow{\xi} \langle A_2,F\rangle} \quad \xi \in \{\tau,\omega\}$	Guarded Parallelism (3)
$\dfrac{\langle E_1,F\rangle \xrightarrow{\omega} \langle A_1,F\rangle, \quad E_1 \notin \mathscr{E}_0 \quad A_1 \notin \mathscr{E}}{\langle E_1 + E_2,F\rangle \xrightarrow{\omega} \langle A_1,F\rangle}$	Non Determinism (1)
$\dfrac{\langle E_1,F\rangle \xrightarrow{\xi} \langle E_1',F\rangle, \langle E_2,F\rangle \xrightarrow{\tau} \langle E_2',F\rangle}{\langle E_1 + E_2,F\rangle \xrightarrow{\xi} \langle E_1' + E_2',F\rangle} \qquad \dfrac{E_1 \in \mathscr{E}_0, \langle E_2,F\rangle \xrightarrow{\xi} \langle A_2,F\rangle}{\langle E_1 + E_2,F\rangle \xrightarrow{\xi} \langle A_2,F\rangle} \quad \xi \in \{\tau,\omega\}$	Non Determinism (2)
$\dfrac{\langle A_1,F\rangle \xrightarrow{\xi} \langle A_1',F'\rangle, \langle A_2,F\rangle \xrightarrow{\tau} \langle A_2',F'\rangle}{\langle A_1\|A_2,F\rangle \xrightarrow{\xi} \langle A_1'\|A_2',F'\rangle} \quad \xi \in \{\tau,\omega\}$	Parallelism (1)
$\dfrac{\langle A_1,F\rangle \xrightarrow{\xi} \langle A_1',F'\rangle, \langle A_2,F\rangle \not\xrightarrow{\tau}}{\langle A_1\|A_2,F\rangle \xrightarrow{\xi} \langle A_1'\|A_2,F'\rangle} \quad \xi \in \{\tau,\omega\}$	Parallelism (2)
$\dfrac{\langle A[y/x],F\rangle \xrightarrow{\xi} \langle A',F'\rangle \quad \xi \in \{\tau,\omega\}}{\langle \exists_x A,F\rangle \xrightarrow{\xi} \langle A',F'\rangle}$ with y fresh	Hidden Variables
$\langle p(y),F\rangle \xrightarrow{\omega} \langle A[y/x],F\rangle$ with $p(x) :: A$ and $x \in \{a,l,\sigma,t\}$	Procedure Call

is represented by an AF $F = \langle Arg, R \rangle$. An $add(Arg', R')$ action performed by the agent results in the addition of a set of arguments $Arg' \subseteq U$ (where U is the universe) and a set of relations R' to the AF F. When performing an Addition, (possibly) new arguments are taken from $U \setminus Arg$. We want to make clear that the tuple (Arg', R') is not an AF, indeed it is possible to have $Arg' = \emptyset$ and $R' \neq \emptyset$, which allows to perform an addition of only attack relations to the considered AF. It is as well possible to add only arguments to F, or both arguments and attacks. Intuitively, $rmv(Arg, R)$ allows to specify arguments and/or attacks to remove from the knowledge base. Removing an argument from an AF requires to also remove the attack relations involving that argument and trying to remove an argument (or an attack) which does not exist in F will have no consequences.

The operator $check_t(Arg', R')$ realises a timed construct and is used to verify whether, in a given time interval, the specified arguments and attack relations are contained in the set of arguments and attacks of the knowledge base, without introducing any further change. If $t > 0$ and the check is positive, the operation succeeds and the agent $check_t(Arg', R') \rightarrow A$ can perform a ω-action in the agent A (Rule Check (1)). If $t > 0$ but the check is not satisfied, then the control is repeated at the next time instant and the value of the counter t is decreased; note that in this case we use the label ω, since a check on the store has been performed (Rule Check (2)). As shown by axiom Check (3), the counter can be decreased also by performing a τ-action: intuitively, this rule is used to model the situation in which, even though the evaluation of the timeout started already, another (parallel) process has the control. In this case, analogously to the approach in [13] and differently from the approach in [8], time continues to elapse (via τ-actions) also for the timeout process. Axiom Check (4) shows that, if the timeout is exceeded, i.e., the counter t has reached the value of 0, then the process $check_t(Arg', R') \rightarrow A$ fails.

The rules Credulous Test (1)–(4) and Sceptical Test (1)–(4) in Table 3 are similar to rules Check (1)–(4) described before. Observe that we have two distinct test operations, both requiring the specification of an argument $a \in A$, a label $l \in \{in, out, undec\}$ and a semantics $\sigma \in \{adm, com, stb, prf, gde\}$. The credulous c-$test_t(a, l, \sigma)$, with $t > 0$, succeeds if there exists at least one extension of $S_\sigma(F)$ whose corresponding labelling L is such that $L(a) = l$. Similarly, the sceptical s-$test_t(a, l, \sigma)$, with $t > 0$, succeeds if a is labelled l in all possible labellings $L \in S_\sigma(F)$. The operator $+_P$ is left-associative and realises an if-then-else construct: if we have $E_1 +_P E_2$ and E_1 is successful, than E_1 will be always chosen over E_2, even if E_2 is also successful, so in order for E_2 to be selected, it has to be the only one that succeeds. The guarded parallelism $\|_G$ is designed to allow all the operations for which the guard in the inner expression is satisfied. In more detail, $E_1\|_G E_2$ is successful when either E_1, E_2 or both are successful and all the operations that can be executed are executed. This behaviour is different both from classical parallelism (for which all the agents have to succeed in order for the procedure to succeed) and from nondeterminism (that only selects one branch).

The remaining operators are classical concurrency compositions. Rules Parallelism (1)–(2) in Table 4 model the parallel composition operator in terms of *interleaving*, since only one basic ω-action is allowed for each transition (i.e., for each unit of time). This means that the access to the shared AF F is granted to one process at a time. However, time passes for all the processes appearing in the $\|$ context at the external level, as shown by rule Parallelism (1), since τ-actions are allowed together with a ω-action. On the other hand, as shown by rule Parallelism (2), a parallel component is allowed to proceed in isolation if (and only if) the other parallel component cannot perform a τ-action. To summarise, we adopt maximal parallelism for time elapsing (i.e., τ-actions) and an interleaving model for basic computation steps (i.e., ω-actions). By transition rules, an agent in a parallel composition obtained through $\parallel$ succeeds only if all the agents succeed. The parallel composition operator enables the specification of complex concurrent argumentation processes: for example, a debate involving many agents that asynchronously provide arguments can be modelled as a parallel composition of add operations performed on the knowledge base. Any agent composed through $+$ is chosen if its guards succeed; the existential quantifier $\exists_x A$ behaves like agent A where variables in x are local to A. Finally, the procedure call (rule PC) has a single parameter which can be an argument, a label among in, out and undec, a semantics σ, or a instant of time. If necessary, the procedure call can be clearly extended for allowing more than one parameter.

In the following we provide the definition for the observables of the language, which are clearly based only on ω-actions.

Definition 6 (Observables for *tcla*). *Let* $P = C.A$ *be a tcla process. We define*

$$\mathscr{O}_{io}(P) = \lambda F. \ \{F_1 \cdots F_n \cdot ss \mid F = F_1 \text{ and } \langle A, F_1 \rangle \xrightarrow{\omega}{}^* \langle success, F_n \rangle\} \cup$$
$$\{F_1 \cdots F_n \cdot ff \mid F = F_1 \text{ and } \langle A, F_1 \rangle \xrightarrow{\omega}{}^* \langle failure, F_n \rangle\}.$$

4   Modelling a Dialogue

In this section, we provide an example of how *tcla* programs can be used to model debates involving several agents taking "turns" to assert their beliefs. A possible use case for *tcla* can be identified in modelling information sharing for common resource management. This problem can be instantiated as done in [15,20] as a debate in a multi-agent environment where argumentation techniques are exploited for arriving to desirable outcomes. We start from the scenario proposed in [20], where three counterparts debate on the use of fertilisers for oyster production.

Example 2. We have three agents: Alice (a farmer), Bob (an oyster farmer) and Carol (a state representative). They are debating on the impact of the fertilisers on the oysters as reported in the following:

- **Alice:** *using a lot of fertiliser helps to have a big yield* (argument a);
- **Bob:** *using a lot of fertiliser pollutes the lake and harms the oyster* (argument b);
- **Carol:** *using a lot of fertiliser increases the risk of control* (argument c);
- **Carol:** *using more fertiliser than the norm implies a fine* (argument d);
- **Alice:** *there is no risk of being controlled because of lack of means* (argument e);
- **Carol:** *an important polluting event can lead to harden the norms* (argument f);
- **Alice:** *lake pollution is not linked to pesticides* (argument g).

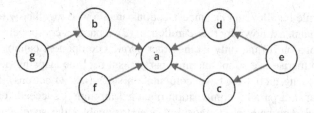

Fig. 3. AF obtained starting from the arguments of Alice, Bob and Carol.

A total of seven arguments are presented, upon which the AF of Fig. 3 is built. We can write a *tcla* program emulating such an exchange of arguments, using three agents in parallel to model the behaviour of Alice, Bob and Carol, respectively. Each agent inserts the arguments at its disposal into the knowledge base through add operations. The first argument to appear in the debate is a, and since it does not attack any other argument, it can be directly added to the AF. The arguments that come after and attack a, namely b, c, d and f, are not brought forward before a itself has been added. Indeed, although *tcla* allows to add arguments and attacks to the knowledge base at separate times, in this particular example we want arguments that come after a, namely b, c, d and f, to be added together with their attacks toward a. Also the order in which the arguments are added must be respectful of the timing with which the debate between the three contenders takes place. To ensure that those arguments will always be added after a, agents acting in place of Bob and Carol have to perform, beforehand, a check operation to verify whether a belongs to the shared memory. Only once the check succeeds, the agents can go on with the execution. Analogously, Alice will check the arguments c and d before adding e (which attacks them), and the argument b before adding g. The resulting program is shown in Table 5. Since parallel executions are handled via interleaving, only one agent will operate on the knowledge base at a time, simulating the alternation of the three counterparts in exchanging arguments during the debate. Check operations, in particular, allow agents to wait for their turn to "speak". In this example, we specify a timeout of 9 instants of time, meaning that the check will be repeated up to 9 times, until it is either satisfied or expired. In our case, checks will always succeed before their timeouts. Note that a shorter timeout cannot guarantee the successful termination of all check operations[3]. Different solutions can also be implemented. For instance, arguments c and d could be added with two distinct operations, or also, together with f.

---

[3] Using a maximal parallelism approach for the parallel composition, a timeout of 4 time units would have been sufficient.

Table 5. *tcla* program realising the AF of Fig. 3.

$add(\{a\},\{\}) \rightarrow$
$\quad check_9(\{c,d\},\{\}) \rightarrow Add(\{e\},\{(e,c),(e,d)\}) \rightarrow success \parallel_G$
$\quad check_9(\{b\},\{\}) \rightarrow add(\{g\},\{(g,b)\}) \rightarrow success$
$\parallel$
$check_9(\{a\},\{\}) \rightarrow add(\{b\},\{(b,a)\}) \rightarrow Success$
$\parallel$
$check_9(\{a\},\{\}) \rightarrow add(\{c,d\},\{(c,a),(d,a)\}) \rightarrow success \parallel_G$
$check_9(\{a\},\{\}) \rightarrow add(\{f\},\{(f,a)\}) \rightarrow success$

5   *tcla* Simulator

We developed a working implementation for the interleaving version of *tcla*. Some of the operations had their syntax translated (see Table 6) to enable users for manually specifying *tcla* programs. The core of our implementation consists of a Python script that covers three fundamental tasks: it serves as interpreter for the *tcla* syntax, it executes programs taken in input, and it communicates with the web interface. The interpreter is built using ANTLR[4], a parser generator for reading, processing, executing, and translating structured text. We start from a grammar file defining the constructs given in Table 2. Any source program, then, is parsed according to the grammar and a parse tree is generated. Each node of this tree corresponds to one operation to perform, whose behaviour is defined in a dedicated Python class. Visiting the parse tree is equivalent to executing the corresponding program.

Table 6. Implementation of *tcla* operations

tcla syntax	Implementation
$add(Arg,R)$	add(Arg,R)
$rmv(Arg,R)$	rmv(Arg,R)
$check_t(Arg,R)$	check(t,Arg,R)
$c\text{-}test_t(a,l,\sigma)$	ctest(t,{a},l,σ)
$s\text{-}test_t(a,l,\sigma)$	stest(t,{a},l,σ)
$E+\cdots+E$	sum(E,...,E)
$E\parallel_G\cdots\parallel_G E$	gpar(E,...,E)
$E+_P E$	(E)+P(E)

The parallel execution of ω-actions is handled through interleaving: only one ω-action can be executed at each step. Such a behaviour is accomplished by means of a Python lock object which acts as a synchronisation primitive, entrusting the control of

---

[4] ANTLR website: https://www.antlr.org.

the shared memory to one action at a time. In detail, when an ω-action is ready to be executed, it tries to acquire the lock object. If the object is unlocked, it immediately changes its status to locked, and the action continues its execution. Before proceeding to the subsequent step, the action releases the lock, that becomes unlocked again. If, on the other hand, the object is locked, the action cannot be executed (because another ω-action has already been granted such privilege upon the acquisition of the lock) and thus it will be postponed to the next step. Practically, we rewrite the parse tree of the program so that to each node representing an ω-action A that cannot be executed at a given step s is assigned a child node which is a clone of A itself, except for possible timeouts, that are decreased by one. Failed attempts of execution also consume a unit of time: when the condition of a guarded ω-action is not satisfied, its timeout is decreased and the execution is postponed by one step.

Differently form ω-actions, τ-actions do not directly interact with the underlying knowledge base, as they are used to make time pass for timeout operations. Several τ-actions can be executed in parallel with an ω-action at each step. To obtain maximal parallelism for τ-actions, we synchronise the threads that implement the agents by keeping track of time elapsing in each parallel branch of the execution.

The input program is provided to the Python script through a web interface (see Fig. 4), developed in HTML and JavaScript. After the program has been executed, its output is also shown within the interface. We have two main areas, one for the input and the other one for the output. The user enters a program in the dedicated text box (either manually or by selecting one of the provided examples), after which there are two ways to proceed: by clicking on the "Run All" button the whole program is executed at once and the final result is displayed in the output area; alternatively, by clicking on the "Run 1 Step" button, it is possible to monitor the execution step by step. The interface communicates with the underlying Python engine through an Ajax call which passes the program as parameter and asynchronously retrieves the output. After the execution of

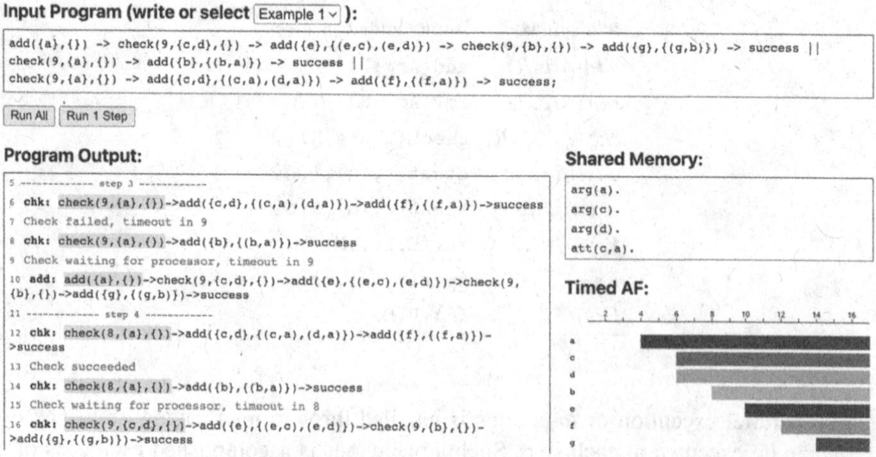

Fig. 4. Example of a *tcla* program executed form the web interface.

(a step of) the program, three different components are simultaneously visualised in the output area, namely the program output, the state of the shared memory and a timeline representing the behaviour of arguments during time. The program output box shows the results of the execution, divided by steps. The beginning of each step is marked by a separating line explicitly showing the step number. The shared memory box is updated after each step of the execution and shows the AF used as knowledge base. Finally, the bottom-left box contains the visual representation of arguments during time and shows the temporal evolution of the AF used by the *tcla* program. Time is reported on the x axis and each bar of the timeline shows the intervals of time during which an argument is contained in the shared memory.

6   Related Work

A formalism for expressing dynamics in AFs is defined in [21] as a *Dynamic Argumentation Framework* (DAF). This kind of frameworks allows for instantiating Dung-style AFs by considering "evidence" (a set of arguments to adopt) from a universe of arguments. DAF generalises AFs by adding the possibility of modelling changes, but, contrary to our study, it does not consider how such modifications affect the semantics and does not allow to model the behaviour of concurrent agents.

In our model, AFs are equipped with a universe of arguments that agents use to insert new information into the knowledge base. The problem of combining AFs (i.e., merging arguments and attacks of two different AFs) is addressed in [2], that studies the computational complexity of verifying if a subset of arguments is an extension for a certain semantics in incomplete argumentation frameworks. The incompleteness is considered both for arguments and attack relations. Similarly to our approach, arguments (and attacks) can be brought forward by agents and used to build new acceptable extensions. On the other hand, the scope of [2] is focused on a complexity analysis and does not provide implementations for the merging.

Given the very nature of argumentation, it is reasonable to assume that the interaction between entities is regulated by the passing of time [17, 18]. Timed Abstract Argumentation Frameworks (TAFs) [7, 11] have been proposed to meet the need for including the notion of time into argumentation processes. The existence of arguments in a TAF is regulated by a function that determines the exact intervals of time in which every argument is available within the framework. In [5] we used *tcla* construct to dynamically instantiate a TAF. The interleaving approach we propose with the current work, however, is not suitable for that task: since only one agent can interact with the store at once, it is not possible to model a TAF in which, for instance, two different arguments are added and removed in the same instant of time.

A collection of process calculi is presented in [8] as a solution for the lack of formal definitions of languages like Linda, JavaSpaes and TSpaes. To this regard, an operational semantics is introduced for enabling formal reasoning and also allowing the systematic comparison of primitives with respect to their expressiveness. Although the authors consider the passing of time (which is represented as divided into discrete intervals), time does not elapse for timeout constructs. In our work, instead, also timeout processes can make time pass.

Related to our work, [4,12] extend CC with timed constructs, also based on the hypothesis of bounded asynchrony. In both approaches, time elapsing is measured by means of a global clock and each time instant is marked through action prefixing. The resulting timed languages are able to describe the behaviour of intelligent agents interacting within a dynamic environment. Apart from the different field of application (as constraint systems in [4]), the main difference with our work lies in the fact that the authors of [4,12] assume maximal parallelism, instead of interleaving, for concurrent actions.

Interleaving is used in [13] to model parallel composition of actions in the context of a temporal logic based on CC. The main purpose of the paper is to devise a logic for reasoning about the correctness of timed concurrent constraint programs. Indeed, the authors focus on providing soundness and completeness of a related proof system, rather than modelling complex reasoning processes in multi-agent systems. Consequently, a major difference with our work is that information in [13] is monotonically accumulated in the shared memory (as per classical CC tell operation) and cannot be retracted by the agents.

7   Conclusion

We presented a formalisation of *tcla* based on two kinds of actions, τ-actions and ω-actions, which realise time elapsing and computation steps, respectively. Parallel composition of τ-actions is handled through maximal parallelism, while for ω-actions we adopt an interleaving approach. Indeed, it seems more adequate to the nature of timeout operators not to interrupt the elapsing of time, once the evaluation of a timeout has started. Clearly one could start the elapsing of time when the time out process is scheduled, rather than when it appears in the top-level current parallel context. This modification could easily be obtained by adding a syntactic construct to differentiate active timeouts from inactive ones, and by accordingly changing the transition system. One could also easily modify the semantics (both operational and denotational) to consider a more liberal assumption which allows multiple ask actions in parallel. As future work, we first plan to use existential quantifiers to extend our language by allowing the agents to have local stores. Then, we would like to compare the interleaving approach introduced in this paper with the implementation based on maximal parallelism given in [5]. In this regard, we could devise a set of benchmark programs to highlight any differences between the two proposals.

References

1. Baroni, P., Caminada, M., Giacomin, M.: An introduction to argumentation semantics. Knowl. Eng. Rev. **26**(4), 365–410 (2011)
2. Baumeister, D., Neugebauer, D., Rothe, J., Schadrack, H.: Verification in incomplete argumentation frameworks. Artif. Intell. **264**, 1–26 (2018)
3. Bistarelli, S., Taticchi, C.: Introducing a tool for concurrent argumentation. In: Faber, W., Friedrich, G., Gebser, M., Morak, M. (eds.) JELIA 2021. LNCS (LNAI), vol. 12678, pp. 18–24. Springer, Cham (2021). https://doi.org/10.1007/978-3-030-75775-5_2

4. Bistarelli, S., Gabbrielli, M., Meo, M.C., Santini, F.: Timed soft concurrent constraint programs. In: Lea, D., Zavattaro, G. (eds.) COORDINATION 2008. LNCS, vol. 5052, pp. 50–66. Springer, Heidelberg (2008). https://doi.org/10.1007/978-3-540-68265-3_4

5. Bistarelli, S., Meo, M.C., Taticchi, C.: Timed concurrent language for argumentation. In: Proceedings of CILC 2021–36th Italian Conference on Computational Logic, volume 3002 of CEUR Workshop Proceedings, pp. 1–15. CEUR-WS.org (2021)

6. Bistarelli, S., Taticchi, C.: A concurrent language for argumentation. In: Proceedings of AI^3 2020–4th Workshop on Advances in Argumentation in Artificial Intelligence, co-located with AIxIA 2020–19th International Conference of the Italian Association for Artificial Intelligence, volume 2777 of CEUR Workshop Proceedings, pp. 75–89. CEUR-WS.org (2020)

7. Budán, M.C., Gómez Lucero, M.J., Chesñevar, C.I., Simari, G.R.: Modeling time and valuation in structured argumentation frameworks. Inf. Sci. **290**, 22–44 (2015)

8. Busi, N., Gorrieri, R., Zavattaro, G.: Process calculi for coordination: from Linda to JavaSpaces. In: Rus, T. (ed.) AMAST 2000. LNCS, vol. 1816, pp. 198–212. Springer, Heidelberg (2000). https://doi.org/10.1007/3-540-45499-3_16

9. Caminada, M.: On the issue of reinstatement in argumentation. In: Fisher, M., van der Hoek, W., Konev, B., Lisitsa, A. (eds.) JELIA 2006. LNCS (LNAI), vol. 4160, pp. 111–123. Springer, Heidelberg (2006). https://doi.org/10.1007/11853886_11

10. Caminada, M.: Semi-stable semantics. In: Proceedings of COMMA 2006 - 1st International Conference on Computational Models of Argument, volume 144 of Frontiers in Artificial Intelligence and Applications, pp. 121–130. IOS Press (2006)

11. Cobo, M.L., Martínez, D.C., Simari, G.R.: On admissibility in timed abstract argumentation frameworks. In: Proceedings of ECAI 2010 - 19th European Conference on Artificial Intelligence, volume 215 of Frontiers in Artificial Intelligence and Applications, pp. 1007–1008. IOS Press (2010)

12. de Boer, F.S., Gabbrielli, M., Meo, M.C.: A timed concurrent constraint language. Inf. Comput. **161**(1), 45–83 (2000)

13. de Boer, F.S., Gabbrielli, M., Meo, M.C.: A timed Linda language and its denotational semantics. Fundam. Informaticae **63**(4), 309–330 (2004)

14. Dung, P.M.: On the acceptability of arguments and its fundamental role in nonmonotonic reasoning, logic programming and n-person games. Artif. Intell. **77**(2), 321–358 (1995)

15. Emele, C.D., Norman, T.J., Parsons, S.: Argumentation strategies for plan resourcing. In: Proceedings of AAMAS 2011 - 10th International Conference on Autonomous Agents and Multiagent Systems, pp. 913–920. IFAAMAS (2011)

16. Hoare, C.A.R.: Communicating sequential processes. Commun. ACM **21**(8), 666–677 (1978)

17. Mann, N., Hunter, A.: Argumentation using temporal knowledge. In: Proceedings of COMMA 2008 - 2nd International Conference on Computational Models of Argument, volume 172 of Frontiers in Artificial Intelligence and Applications, pp. 204–215. IOS Press (2008)

18. Marcos, M.J., Falappa, M.A., Simari, G.R.: Dynamic argumentation in abstract dialogue frameworks. In: McBurney, P., Rahwan, I., Parsons, S. (eds.) ArgMAS 2010. LNCS (LNAI), vol. 6614, pp. 228–247. Springer, Heidelberg (2011). https://doi.org/10.1007/978-3-642-21940-5_14

19. Milner, R.: A Calculus of Communicating Systems. LNCS, vol. 92. Springer, Heidelberg (1980). https://doi.org/10.1007/3-540-10235-3

20. Paget, N., Pigozzi, G., Barreteau, O.: Information sharing for natural resources management. Presented at EUMAS 2013 - 11th European Workshop on Multi-Agent Systems (2013)

21. Rotstein, N.D., Moguillansky, M.O., Garcia, A.J., Simari, G.R.: An abstract argumentation framework for handling dynamics. In: Proceedings of the Argument, Dialogue and Decision Workshop in NMR 2008, pp. 131–139 (2008)

22. Saraswat, V.A., Jagadeesan, R., Gupta, V.: Foundations of timed concurrent constraint programming. In: Proceedings of LICS 1994 - 9th Annual Symposium on Logic in Computer Science, pp. 71–80. IEEE Computer Society (1994)

23. Saraswat, V.A., Jagadeesan, R., Gupta, V.: Timed default concurrent constraint programming. J. Symb. Comput. **22**(5/6), 475–520 (1996)

24. Saraswat, V.A., Rinard, M.: Concurrent constraint programming. In: Proceedings of POPL 1990 - 17th ACM SIGPLAN-SIGACT Symposium on Principles of Programming Languages, pp. 232–245. ACM Press (1990)

Towards Dynamic Consistency Checking in Goal-Directed Predicate Answer Set Programming

Joaquín Arias[1]([✉]) [iD], Manuel Carro[2,3] [iD], and Gopal Gupta[4] [iD]

[1] CETINIA, Universidad Rey Juan Carlos, Madrid, Spain
joaquin.arias@urjc.es
[2] Universidad Politécnica de Madrid, Madrid, Spain
manuel.carro@upm.es,manuel.carro@imdea.org
[3] IMDEA Software Institute, Madrid, Spain
[4] University of Texas at Dallas, Richardson, USA
gupta@utdallas.edu

Abstract. Goal-directed evaluation of Answer Set Programs is gaining traction thanks to its amenability to create AI systems that can, due to the evaluation mechanism used, generate explanations and justifications. s(CASP) is one of these systems and has been already used to write reasoning systems in several fields. It provides enhanced expressiveness w.r.t. other ASP systems due to its ability to use constraints, data structures, and unbound variables natively. However, the performance of existing s(CASP) implementations is not on par with other ASP systems: model consistency is checked once models have been generated, in keeping with the generate-and-test paradigm. In this work, we present a variation of the top-down evaluation strategy, termed *Dynamic Consistency Checking*, which interleaves model generation and consistency checking. This makes it possible to determine when a literal is not compatible with the *denials* associated to the global constraints in the program, prune the current execution branch, and choose a different alternative. This strategy is specially (but not exclusively) relevant in problems with a high combinatorial component. We have experimentally observed speedups of up to 90× w.r.t. the standard versions of s(CASP).

Keywords: Dynamic consistency checking · Goal-directed evaluation · Constraints · Answer set programming

Work partially supported by EIT Digital, MICINN projects RTI2018-095390-B-C33 InEDGEMobility (MCIU/AEI/FEDER, UE), PID2019-108528RB-C21 ProCode, Comunidad de Madrid project S2018/TCS-4339 BLOQUES-CM co-funded by EIE Funds of the European Union, US NSF Grants IIS 1718945, IIS 1910131, IIP 1916206.

© Springer Nature Switzerland AG 2022
J. Cheney and S. Perri (Eds.): PADL 2022, LNCS 13165, pp. 117–134, 2022.
https://doi.org/10.1007/978-3-030-94479-7_8

1   Introduction

s(CASP) [3] is a novel non-monotonic reasoner that evaluates Constraint Answer Set Programs without a grounding phase, either before or during execution. s(CASP) supports predicates and thus retains logical variables (and constraints) both during the execution and in the answer sets. The operational semantics of s(CASP) relies on backward chaining, which is intuitive to follow and lends itself to generating explanations that can be translated into natural language [1]. The execution of an s(CASP) program returns partial stable models: the subsets of the stable models [13] which include only the (negated) literals necessary to support the initial query. To the best of our knowledge, s(CASP) is the only system that exhibits the property of relevance [22]. s(CASP) has been already applied in relevant fields related to the representation of commonsense reasoning:

- An automated reasoner that uses Event Calculus (EC) [2,4] (http://bit.ly/ EventCalculus). s(CASP) can make deductive reasoning tasks in domains featuring constraints involving dense time and continuous properties. It is being used to model real-world avionics systems, to verify (timed) properties, and to identify gaps with respect to system requirements [14].
- The s(CASP) justification framework has been used to bring Explainable Artificial Intelligence (XAI) principles to rule-based systems capturing expert knowledge [1,10].
- It is at the core of two natural language understanding systems [8]: SQuARE, a Semantic-based Question Answering and Reasoning Engine, and StaCACK, Stateful Conversational Agent using Commonsense Knowledge. They use the s(CASP) engine to "truly understand" and perform reasoning while generating natural language explanations for their responses. Building on these systems, s(CASP) was used to develop one of the nine systems selected to participate in the Amazon Alexa Socialbot Grand Challenge 4 [9][1], and is being used to develop a conversational AI chatbot.
- It has been used in ILP systems that generate ASP programs [23] and concurrent imperative programs from behavioral, observable specifications [25].
- A legal expert system [21], developed at the SMU Centre for Computational Law at Singapore, coded rule 34 of Singapore's Legal Profession[2]. Its frontend is a web interface that collects user information, runs queries on s(CASP), and displays the results with explanations in natural language.
- s(LAW), an administrative and judicial discretion reasoner [5], which allows modeling legal rules involving ambiguity and infers conclusions, providing (natural language) justifications based on them.

However, in the standard implementation of s(CASP), the global constraints in a program are checked when a tentative but complete model is computed. This strategy takes a large toll on the performance of programs that generate

---

[1] https://cs.utdallas.edu/computer-scientists-enhance-alexas-small-talk-skills/.
[2] https://github.com/smucclaw/r34_sCASP.

many tentative models and use global constraints to discard those that do not satisfy the specifications of the problem.

In this work, we propose a technique termed *Dynamic Consistency Checking* (DCC) that anticipates the evaluation of global constraints to discard inconsistent models as early as possible. Before adding a literal to the tentative model, DCC checks if any global constraint is violated. If so, this literal is discarded and the evaluation backtracks to look for other alternatives. We show, through several examples, that using this preliminary implementation, s(CASP) with DCC is up to 90× faster. Section 2 contains an overview of the syntax, operational semantics, and implementation of s(CASP). Section 3 explains the motivation behind DCC with examples, and describes its design and implementation Sect. 4 presents the evaluating results of several benchmarks using s(CASP) with DCC enabled or not. Finally, in Sect. 5 we draw conclusions and propose future work. All the program and files used or mentioned in this paper are available at http:// platon.etsii.urjc.es/~jarias/papers/dcc-padl21/.

2   Background: S(CASP)

An s(CASP) program is a set of clauses of the following form:

$$a :\text{-} c_a, b_1, \ldots, b_m, \text{not } b_{m+1}, \ldots, \text{not } b_n.$$

where a and $b_1, \ldots, b_n$ are atoms. An atom is either a propositional variable or the expression $p(t_1, \ldots, t_n)$ if p is an n-ary predicate symbol and $t_1, \ldots, t_n$ are terms. A term is either a variable x_i or a function symbol f of arity n, denoted as f/n, applied to n terms, e.g., $f(t_1, t_2, \ldots, t_n)$, where each t_i is in turn a term. A function symbol of arity 0 is called a constant. Therefore, s(CASP) accepts terms with the same conventions as Prolog: f(a, b) is a term, and so are f(g(X),Y) and [f(a)|Rest] (to denote a list with head f(a) and tail Rest). Program variables are usually written starting with an uppercase letter[3], while function and predicate symbols start with a lowercase letter. Numerical constants are written solely with digits.

The term c_a is a simple constraint or a conjunction of constraints: an expression establishing relations among variables in some constraint system [18]. Similar to CLP, s(CASP) is parametrized w.r.t. the constraint system, from which it inherits its semantics. Since the execution of an s(CASP) program needs negating constraints, soundness requires that this can be done in the chosen constraint system by means of a finite disjunction of basic constraints [11,24].

At least one of a, b_i, or not b_i must be present. When the head a is not present, it is supposed to be substituted by the head *false*. Headless rules have then the form

$$:\text{-} c_a, b_1, \ldots, b_m, \text{not } b_{m+1}, \ldots, \text{not } b_n.$$

and their interpretation is that the conjunction of the constraints and goals has to be false, so at least one constraint or goal has to be false. For example, the

---

[3] There are additional syntactical conventions to distinguish variables and non-variables that are of no interest here.

rule :-p, q, expresses that the conjunction of atoms p ∧ q cannot be true: either p, q, or both, have to be false in any stable model. ASP literature often uses the term *constraint* to denote these constructions. To avoid the ambiguity that may arise from using the same name for constraints appearing among (free) variables during program execution and in the final models and for rules without heads, we will refer to headless rules as *denials* [19].

The execution of an s(CASP) program starts with a *query* of the form

$$?- c_a, b_1, \ldots, b_m, \text{not } b_{m+1}, \ldots, \text{not } b_n.$$

The s(CASP) answers to a query are *partial* stable models where each one is a subset of a stable model that satisfies the constraints, makes non-negated atoms true, makes the negated atoms non-provable, and, in addition, includes only atoms that are relevant to support the query. Additionally, for each partial stable model s(CASP) returns on backtracking *partial answer sets* with the justification tree and the bindings for the free variables of the query that correspond to the most general unifier (*mgu*) of a successful top-down derivation.

While mainstream ASP systems such as clingo [12] require a preliminary grounding phase, s(CASP) executes predicate ASP programs and retains logical variables both during the execution and in the answer sets. As a consequence of the grounding phase, ASP systems featuring constraints may suffer a loss of communication from elimination of variables, and face difficulties when having to deal with large domains [7], which still have to be discrete. On the other hand, the execution methods for CASP systems are notably complex. For example, EZSMT [6] needs explicit hooks to communicate the ASP solver and the constraint solver used.

2.1 Execution Procedure of s(CASP)

Let us present an abridged description of the top-down strategy of s(CASP):

1. Rules expressing the constructive negation of the predicates in the original ASP program are synthesized. We call this the *dual program*. Its mission is to provide a means to constructively determine the conditions and constraints under which calls to non-propositional predicates featuring variables would have failed: if we want to know when a rule such as p(X,Y):-q(X), not r(Y) succeeds, the dual program computes the constraints on Y under which the call r(Y) would fail. This is an extension of the usual ASP semantics that is compatible with the case of programs that can be finitely grounded[4]. A description of the construction of the dual program can be found in [2,3,17].
2. The original program is checked for loops of the form r:-q, not r. and introduces additional denials to ensure that the models satisfy ¬q ∨ r, even if the atoms r or q are not needed to solve the query. This is done by building a dependency graph of the program and detecting the paths where this may happen, including call paths across calls. Therefore, for the program:

---

[4] Note that, in the presence of function symbols and constraints on dense domains, this is in general not the case for s(CASP) programs.

```
1  p :- not q.          2  q :- not p.          3  r :- not r.
```

s(CASP) will determine that there are no stable models, regardless of the initial query. For the propositional case, such an analysis can be precise. For the non-propositional case, an over-approximation is calculated. In both cases, denials that are not used during program evaluation can be generated. These may impose a penalty in execution time, but are safe.

3. The denials generated in point 2, together with any denials present in the original program, are collected in predicates synthesized by the compiler that are evaluated by adding an auxiliary goal, nmr_check/0, at the end of the top-level query.

4. The union of the original program, the dual program, and the denials is handled by a top-down algorithm that implements the stable model semantics.

Point number 4 is specially relevant. The dual program (point 1) is synthesized by means of program transformations drawing from classical logic. However, its intended meaning differs from that of first-order logic. That is so because it is to be executed by a metainterpreter that does not implement the inference mechanisms of first-order logic, as it is designed to ensure that the semantics of answer set programs is respected (see Sect. 2.4). In particular, it treats specifically cyclic dependencies involving negation.

2.2 Unsafe Variables and Uninterpreted Function Symbols

The following code, from [2, Pag. 9] has variables that would be termed as *unsafe* in regular ASP systems: variables that appear in negated atoms in the body of a clause, but that do not appear in any positive literal in the same body.

```
1  p(X):- q(X, Z), not r(X).        3  q(X, a):- X #> 5.
2  p(Z):- not q(X, Z), r(X).        4  r(X):- X #< 1.
```

Since s(CASP) synthesizes explicit constructive goals for these negated goals, the aforementioned code can be run as-is in s(CASP). The query ?-p(A). generates three different answer sets, one for each binding:

```
{ p(A| {A #> 5}), q(A| {A #> 5}, a), not r(A| {A #> 5}) }
   A #> 5
{ p(A| {A \= a}), not q(B| {B #< 1}, A| {A \= a}), r(B| {B #< 1}) }
   A \= a
{ p(a), not q(B| {B #< 1}, a), r(B| {B #< 1}) }
   A = a
```

where the notation V|{C} for a variable V is intended to mean that V is subject to the constraints in {C}. The constraints A = 5, A $\neq$ a, and A = a correspond to the bindings of variable A that make the atom from the query ?-p(A) belong to the stable model.

Another very relevant point where s(CASP) differs from ASP is in the possibility of using arbitrary uninterpreted function symbols to build, for example, data structures. While in mainstream ASP implementations these could give rise to an infinite grounded program (i.e., if the program does not have the *bound-term-depth* property), the s(CASP) execution model can deal with them similarly to Prolog, with the added power of the use of constructive negation in the execution and in the returned models.

Example 1. The predicate member/2 below, from [2, Pag. 11], models the membership to a list as it is usual in (classical) logic programming. The query is intended to derive the conditions for one argument not to belong to a given list.

```
1  member(X, [X|Xs]).                    3  list([1,2,3,4,5]).
2  member(X, [_|Xs]):- member(X, Xs).    4  ?- list(A), not member(B, A).
```

This program and query return in s(CASP) the following model and bindings:
```
{ list([1,2,3,4,5]),
    not member(B| {B \= 1,B \= 2,B \= 3,B \= 4,B \= 5}, [1,2,3,4,5]),
    not member(B| {B \= 1,B \= 2,B \= 3,B \= 4,B \= 5}, [2,3,4,5]),
    not member(B| {B \= 1,B \= 2,B \= 3,B \= 4,B \= 5}, [3,4,5]),
    not member(B| {B \= 1,B \= 2,B \= 3,B \= 4,B \= 5}, [4,5]),
    not member(B| {B \= 1,B \= 2,B \= 3,B \= 4,B \= 5}, [5]),
    not member(B| {B \= 1,B \= 2,B \= 3,B \= 4,B \= 5}, []) }
    A = [1,2,3,4,5], B \= 1, B \= 2, B \= 3, B \= 4, B \= 5
```

I.e., for variable B not to be a member of the list [1,2,3,4,5] it has to be different from each of its elements.

2.3   s(CASP) as a Conservative Extension of ASP

The behavior of s(CASP) and ASP is the same for propositional programs. They differ in programs with unsafe variables (not legal in mainstream ASP systems), programs that could create unbound data structures, or whose variable ranges are defined in infinite domains (either unbound or bound but dense). Such programs are outside the standard domain of ASP systems as they cannot be finitely grounded, For them, s(CASP) extends ASP consistently.

In addition, the domain of the variables is implicitly expanded to include a domain which can be potentially infinite. Let us use the following example, from [2, Pag. 12], where we are interested in knowing whether p(X) (for some X) is or not part of a stable model:

```
1  d(1).                                 2  p(X) :- not d(X).
```

The only constant in the program is 1, which is the only possible domain for X in the second clause. That clause is not legal for ASP, as X is an unsafe variable (Sect. 2.2). Adding a domain predicate call for it (i.e., adding d(X) to the body of the second clause), makes its model be {d(1)} (not p(1) is implicit).

That second clause is however legal in s(CASP). Making the query ?-p(X) returns the *partial* model {p(X| {X \= 1}), not d(X|{X \= 1})} stating that p(X) and not d(X) are true when X \= 1, which is consistent with, but more general than, the model given by ASP. As the model is partial, only the atoms (perhaps negated) involved in the proof for ?-p(X) appear in that model.

```
1   scasp(Query) :-
2       solve(Query,[],Mid),
3       solve_goal(nmr_check,Mid,Model),
4       print_just_model(Model).
5
6   solve([],In,['$success'|In]).
7   solve([Goal|Gs],In,Out) :-
8       solve_goal(Goal,In,Mid),
9       solve(Gs,Mid,Out).
10
11  solve_goal(Goal,In,Out) :-
12      user_defined(Goal), !,
13      check_loops(Goal,In,Out).
14  solve_goal(Goal,In,Out) :-
15      Goal=forall(Var,G), !,
16      c_forall(V,G,In,Out).

17  solve_goal(Goal,In,Out) :-
18      call(Goal),
19      Out=['$success',Goal|In].
20
21  check_loops(Goal,In Out) :-
22      loop_type(Goal,In,Loop),
23      s_loop(Loop,Goal,In,Out).
24
25  s_loop(odd,_,_,_) :- fail.
26  s_loop(even,G,In,[chs(G)|In]).
27  s_loop(no_loop,G,In,Out) :-
28      pr_rule(G, Body),
29      solve(Body,[G|In],Out).
30  s_loop(proved,G,In,[proved(G)|In]).
31  s_loop(positive,_,_,_) :- fail.
```

Fig. 1. Outline of the s(CASP) interpreter's code implemented in Ciao Prolog.

2.4 The s(CASP) Interpreter

Queries to the original program extended with the dual rules are evaluated by a runtime environment. This is currently a metainterpreter (see Fig. 1) in Prolog that executes an algorithm [15] that has similarities with SLD resolution. But it takes into account specific characteristics of ASP and the dual programs, such as the denials, the different kinds of loops, and the introduction of universal quantifiers in the body of the clauses:

1. The query Query is evaluated invoking solve/3 in line 2 starting with an empty model represented as the empty list [].
2. After the query evaluation, and to ensure that the returned model, Mid, is consistent with the denials, nmr_check (item 3 in page 7) is evaluated in line 3.
3. In line 4, the models that are consistent (and their justifications), Model, are output by print_just_model/1.
4. The predicate solve/3 receives a list with the literals in the query (or in the body of some rule) and evaluates them, one by one, invoking solve_goal/3.

5. When the literal is a user defined predicate (line 12), the interpreter checks if there is a loop invoking `check_loops/3`. Three main cases are distinguished by `type_loop/3`:

   Odd loop. When a call eventually invokes itself and there is an odd number of intervening negations (as in, e.g., p:- q. q:- not r. r:- p.), the evaluation fails in line 25, to avoid contradictions of the form $p \wedge \neg p$, and backtracking takes place.

   Even loop. When there is an even number of intervening negations (as in p:- not q. q:- r. r:- not p.), the metainterpreter succeeds in line 26 to generate several stable models, such as {p, not q, not r} and {q, r, not p}.

   No loop. If no loops are detected, in line 27 the interpreter invokes `pr_rule/2` to retrieve the rule that unifies with the goal G and continues the evaluation by invoking `solve/3` with the literals of the rule.

6. The construction `forall(Var, G)` in line 15 is the dual of the existential quantifications in the body of the clauses. To evaluate them the runtime environment invokes the predicate `c_forall/4` in line 16, which determines if G holds for all the values of Var—see [3] for implementation details.

7. Finally, operations involving constraints and/or builtins are natively handled by invoking `call/1` in line 18.

3   Dynamic Consistency Checking in s(CASP)

The Dynamic Consistency Checking proposal of [16] is designed for propositional programs, while our proposal can also take care of predicate ASP programs. It is based on anticipating the evaluation of denials to fail as early as possible

3.1   Motivation

As we mentioned before, a denial such as :-p, q, expresses that the conjunction of atoms p $\wedge$ q cannot be true: either p, q, or both, have to be false in any stable model. In predicate ASP the atoms have variables and a denial such as :-p(X), q(X,Y) means that:

$$false \;\; \leftarrow \;\; \exists x, y \; (\; p(x) \wedge q(x,y) \;)$$

i.e., p(X) and q(X,Y) can not be simultaneously true for any possible values of X and Y in any stable model. To ensure that the tentative partial model is consistent with this denial, the compiler generates a rule of the form

$$\forall x, y \; (chk_i \;\; \leftrightarrow \;\; \neg (\; p(x) \wedge q(x,y) \;) \;)$$

and to ensure that each sub-check (chk_i) is satisfied, they are included in the rule $nmr\_check \leftarrow chk_1 \wedge \cdots \wedge chk_k \wedge \ldots$, which is transparently called after the program query by the s(CASP) interpreter (see Fig. 1, line 3).

However, this generate-and-test strategy has a high impact on the performance of programs that create many tentative models and use denials to discard those that do not satisfy the constraints of the problem.

```
1  reachable(V) :- chosen(a, V).
2  reachable(V) :- chosen(U, V), reachable(U).
3  chosen(U, V) :- edge(U, V), not other(U, V).    % Choose or not an
4  other(U, V) :- edge(U, V), not chosen(U, V).     % edge of the graph.
5
6  :- vertex(U), not reachable(U).        % Every vertex must be reachable.
7  :- chosen(U, W), U \= V, chosen(V, W).      % Do not choose edges to or
8  :- chosen(W, U), U \= V, chosen(W, V).      % from the same vertex.
9  #show chosen/2.
10
11  ?- reachable(a).                       % Is there a path from a to a?
```

Fig. 2. Code of the Hamilonian problem á la ASP, available at hamiltonian.pl.

```
1  % Graph        6  edge(b, a).    11  edge(c, d).
2  vertex(a).     7  edge(b, d).    12  edge(d, a).
3  vertex(b).     8  edge(a, c).    13  edge(c, a).
4  vertex(c).     9  edge(a, b).    14  edge(a, d).
5  vertex(d).    10  edge(b, c).    15  edge(d, b).
```

Fig. 3. Graph with 4 nodes available at graph_4.pl.

Example 2 (Hamiltonian path problem). Consider the Hamiltonian path problem, in which for a given graph we search for a cyclic path that visits each node of the graph only once. The standard ASP code for this problem, available at hamiltonian.pl, is in Fig. 2. The conditions of the problem are captured (i) in line 6 to discard tentative paths that do not visit all the nodes, and (ii) in lines 7–8 to discard paths that have edges violating the properties of the Hamiltonian path. For the query in line 11, using the graph in Fig. 3 there are three stable models, one for each Hamiltonian cycle:

```
{ chosen(a,c),   chosen(c,d),   chosen(d,b),   chosen(b,a),... }
{ chosen(a,b),   chosen(b,c),   chosen(c,d),   chosen(d,a),... }
{ chosen(a,d),   chosen(d,b),   chosen(b,c),   chosen(c,a),... }
```

As mentioned before, the standard s(CASP) execution follows a generate-and-test scheme, choosing a cycle that reaches node a from node a and then discards any cycle in which:

– Not all vertices are reached (line 6), e.g., {chosen(a,b),chosen(b,a)}.
– Two chosen edges reach / leave the same vertex (line 7), e.g., {chosen(a, b), chosen(d,b), chosen(b,a)}   or   {chosen(a,b), chosen(b,d), chosen(b,a)}.

As a consequence, if the evaluation chooses an edge that breaks any of these conditions, trying combinations with the rest of the edges would be misused effort.

3.2 Outline of the DCC Approach

The main idea behind our proposal is to anticipate the evaluation of the denials to fail and backtrack as early as possible. When an atom involved in a denial is a candidate to be added to a tentative model, the denial is checked to ensure that it is not already violated. By contrast, the classical implementation of s(CASP) checked the tentative model as a whole once it had been completely built. The latter is akin to the generate-and-test approach to combinatorial problems, while the former tries to cut the search early.

In the most general case, DCC can take the form of a constraint-and-test instance. While detecting some denial violations can be performed by just checking the current state of the (partial) candidate model, better, more powerful algorithms can impose additional constraints on the rest of the atoms belonging to the partial model and also on the parts of the denials that remain to be checked.

These constraints can propagate additional conditions through the candidate model to ensure that it is consistent with the denials. These conditions will also remain active for the rest of the construction of the model, so that they can be carried forward, further reducing the search space. Note that since s(CASP) includes constraints á la CLP, the effect is very similar to the constraint propagation mechanisms that take place in constraint satisfaction systems, therefore making a full s(CASP) + DCC system an instance of a constraint-and-generate evaluation engine.

The current implementation, which we describe in this paper, is a *proof of concept* that only checks grounds literals and does not anticipate the consistency check of constrained literals. As we will see later, this does not have a negative impact on the soundness of the system.

3.3 Implementation of DCC in s(CASP)

The implementation of s(CASP) + DCC is available as part of the source code of s(CASP) at https://gitlab.software.imdea.org/ciao-lang/scasp.

Compilation of the Denials. As we mentioned before, the denials are compiled in such a way that the interpreter checks consistency by proving that forall possible values, the negation of the denial is satisfied. For example, for the denial :-p(X), q(X,Y), the compiler generates the rule:

```
1  chk1 :- forall(X, forall(Y, not chk_body(X,Y))).
2  not chk_body(X,Y) :- not p(X).
3  not chk_body(X,Y) :- p(X), not q(X,Y).
```

The last clause includes a call to p(X) to avoid duplicated solutions provided by the two clauses. If the interpreter is able to prove that for all the possible values of X and Y the tentative partial model is consistent with the predicate not chk_body(X,Y), then it means that the tentative partial model is a stable partial model.

The approach followed by the DCC proposal is to detect when a rule like the above determines that a model candidate is inconsistent. If that is the case, s(CASP) fails and provokes backtracking to explore the generation of a different model. In the example above, if a model being generated is consistent with p(X) ∧ q(X,Y), then it should be discarded.

Since it is only necessary to check for violation of denials when adding a goal involved in one of the denials, the compiler creates a series of rules that state what has to be checked for in case a goal involved in the denial is generated. For the case above, if p(X) is added, then q(X,Y) has to be checked to ensure it does not hold, and the other way around. This is represented as:

```
1  dcc(p(X), [q(X,Y)]).
2  dcc(q(X,Y), [p(X)]).
```

which can be understood as "if p(X) is present, check that q(X,Y) is not present".

In general, given a user defined denial[5] of the form :-c_a, b_1, ..., b_n for each (negated) literal b_k, of a user defined predicate, the compiler generates a DCC rule dcc(b_k, [c_a, ..., b_{k-1}, b_{k+1}, ...]) for each $k, 1 \leq k \leq n$.

```
1   % The only clauses that changes        13  holds_dcc([],_).
2   s_loop(even,G,In,[chs(G)|In]) :-        14  holds_dcc([F_A|F_As],In) :-
3        eval_dcc(G,In).   % New call       15      holds_dcc_(F_A,In),
4   s_loop(no_loop,G,In,Out) :-             16      holds_dcc(F_As,In).
5        pr_rule(G, Body),                  17
6        solve(Body,[G|In],Out),            18
7        eval_dcc(G,In).   % New call       19  holds_dcc_(F_A,In) :-
8                                           20      user_defined(F_A), !,
9   eval_dcc(G,In):-                        21      member(F_A,In).
10       \+ ( ground(G),                    22  holds_dcc_(F_A,In) :-
11           pr_dcc_rule(G,F_Atoms),        23      call(F_A).
12           holds_dcc(F_Atoms,In) ).
```

Fig. 4. Outline of the changes to the s(CASP) interpreter extended with DCC.

Extending the s(CASP) Interpreter with DCC. Figure 4 shows the relevant fragment of the s(CASP) interpreter extended with Dynamic Consistency Checking. The basic intuition is that as soon as an atom that is involved in a denial is a candidate to be added to a model, DCC checks whether the candidate

---

[5] The current implementation does not check denials introduced due to olon loops.

model is consistent with the rest of the atoms (including builtins) in that denial. Depending on the result of this check, the candidate atom is added or not. The modified interpreter performs the following steps:

1. The DCC check starts when the interpreter proves that a goal G holds, by invoking the predicate `eval_dcc/2`. If it succeeds, G is added to the model and the evaluation continues. Otherwise, an inconsistency has been detected and backtracking takes place.
2. The current implementation of `eval_dcc/2` only evaluates fully instantiated goals. Therefore, if the G is not ground (line 10), `eval_dcc/2` succeeds and the evaluation continues. This is not a source of unsoundness, as in any case the whole set of denials are checked before finally returning a model.
3. Otherwise, `dcc_rule(G,F_Atoms)` (line 11) retrieves the DCC rules that involve goal G. If there are no DCC rules, `eval_dcc/2` succeeds.
4. Since one atom in the rule (G) is to be added to the model, we need to ensure that not all the rest of the atoms in the rule (F_Atoms) appear in the candidate model In. In order not to instantiate the model, this is done by checking with `holds_dcc(F_Atoms,In)` whether *all* the atoms appear in In[6] and then negating (by failure) the calling predicate.

Let us consider a program including the denial `:-p(X), q(X,Y)`. When the evaluation of `p(1)` succeeds, and before it is added to the tentative model, the interpreter calls `eval_dcc(p(1),[...])`, where `[...]` is the current tentative model. Since `p(1)` is ground, `pr_dcc_rule(p(1),F_Atoms)` retrieves in F_Atoms a list of the atoms that cannot be true in the model—in this case, `[q(1,Y)]`. Then, the interpreter checks if the literals in `[q(1,Y)]` are true in the current (tentative) model In. If that is the case, `holds_dcc([q(1,Y)],[...])` succeeds, `eval_dcc/2` fails, and the interpreter backtracks because the denial has been violated. Otherwise, the evaluation continues.

It is easy to see that this implementation of dynamic consistency checking is *complete*, i.e., we do not lose answers: since only ground goals are checked, there is no risk of instantiating free variables which could restrict degrees of freedom of the tentative model and therefore potentially removing solutions. Furthermore, to ensure *correctness*, we keep the non-monotonic rule checking that is performed once the tentative model is found. Note that non-ground goals are at the moment not subject to DCC rules, but they may be involved in denials, and denials of atoms not needed to support the query must be checked.

DCC is also used during the execution of the `nmr_check` predicate. As we mentioned before (item 3 in page 5), denials are compiled into a synthesized goal, `nmr_check`, that is executed after a model has been generated. During its execution, DCC rules are actively used to look for atoms that are introduced and when an inconsistency is flagged, execution fails and backtracks.

Example 3 (Cont. Example 2). Let us consider the Hamiltonian program in Fig. 2. As explained above, the compiler generates the DCC rules below. For this example each denial is translated into two specialized rules.

---

[6] For builtins: checking that they succeed if evaluated in the environment of the model.

```
1  dcc(vertex(U), [not reachable(U)]).
2  dcc(not reachable(U), [vertex(U)]).
3  dcc(chosen(U,W), [U \= V, chosen(V,W)]).
4  dcc(chosen(V,W), [chosen(U,W), U \= V]).
5  dcc(chosen(W,U), [U \= V, chosen(W,V)]).
6  dcc(chosen(W,V), [chosen(W,U), U \= V]).
```

By invoking scasp --dcc[7] hamiltonian.pl graph_4.pl, s(CASP) evaluates the query ?-reachable(a) following a goal-directed strategy. Let us refer to the code in Fig. 2 and the graph in Fig. 3 to explain how the evaluation with DCC takes place:

1. The query unifies with the clause in line 1 but the goal chosen(a,a) fails because edge(a,a) does not exist.
2. From the clause in line 2, chosen(b,a) is added to the tentative model, because no DCC rule succeeds. The goal reachable(b) is then called.
3. The goal reachable(b) unifies with the clause in line 1 and chosen(a,b) is added, because it is consistent with chosen(b,a).
4. As the query succeeds for the model {chosen(b,a), chosen(a,b), reachable(a), reachable(b), ...}, s(CASP) invokes nmr_check.
5. nmr_check executes checks for all the denials. The code corresponding to line 6 is:

```
1  chk1 :- forall(U, not chk1_1(U))).
2  not chk1_1(U) :- not vertex(U).
3  not chk1_1(U) :- vertex(U), reachable(U).
```

   i.e., all vertices (vertex(U)) must be reachable (reachable(U)). For vertices U = a and U = b, reachable(a) and reachable(b) are already in the model, so there is nothing to check. But for vertex U = c, reachable(c) is not in the model and therefore reachable(c) has to be invoked while checking the denials.
6. From the clause in line 1, chosen(a,c) is selected to be added to the model, but it is discarded by DCC, because of the DCC rule dcc(chosen(V,W), [chosen(U,W), U \=V]), corresponding to the denial in line 7. Note that this DCC rule is instantiated to dcc(chosen(a,c), [c \= b, chosen(a,b)]) and the literal chosen(a,b) is already in the model.
7. The evaluation backtracks and continues the search using another edge.

The denial in line 6 makes the interpreter to select edges to reach all vertices. The interleaving of the dynamic consistency checking prunes the search, which, as shown in Sect. 4, improves performance.

---

[7] The --dcc flag imply the use of --prev_forall, valid for non-constrained programs.

4   Evaluation

In this section we compare the performance of s(CASP) with and without DCC using a macOS 11.5.2 Intel Core i7 at 2.6 GHz. We use s(CASP) version 0.21.10.09 available at https://gitlab.software.imdea.org/ciao-lang/scasp and, as mentioned before, all the benchmarks used or mentioned in this paper are available at http://platon.etsii.urjc.es/~jarias/papers/dcc-padl21.

Table 1. Performance comparison: s(CASP) and s(CASP)+DCC.

	Speedup	s(CASP)	s(CASP)+DCC
Hamiltonian (4 vertices)	10.0	11.985	**1.196**
Hamiltonian (7 vertices)	41.1	134.460	**3.191**
n_queens (n=4)	4.3	8.147	**1.910**
n_queens (n=5)	4.9	92.756	**18.786**
n_queens (n=6)	90.8	1362.840	**15.001**
n_queens_attack (n=6)	1.0	77.039	76.827

Table 1 shows the results of the performance comparison (in seconds), and the speedup of s(CASP) with DCC w.r.t. s(CASP) – note that DCC activates the use of the *forall* predicate optimized for non-constrained programs, therefore, for a fair comparison, s(CASP) w.o. DCC should be executed including the --prev_forall flag.

First, we evaluate the Hamiltonian path problem (Example 2) using the encoding in Fig. 2 (available at hamiltonian.pl) and the graph with 4 vertices in Fig. 3 (available at graph_4.pl). We see that s(CASP) with DCC obtains a speedup of **10.0×**. When the size of the graph is increased by adding three vertices[8] we obtain a speedup of **41.1×**.

We also evaluated the performance of s(CASP) with DCC with the well-known n-queens problem, using two different versions. These examples are especially interesting, as they have no finite grounding and thus cannot be run by other implementations of the stable model semantics. In particular, the size of the board is not fixed by the programs and therefore the same code can be used to find solutions to several board sizes.

The first version, n_queens (available at n_queens.pl), uses denials to discard solutions where two queens attack each other. The speedup obtained by s(CASP) with DCC ranges from **4.3×** (for $n = 4$) to **90.8×** (for $n = 6$).

The second version is the one presented in [15, Pag. 37] (available at n_queens_attack.pl). In this case, the predicate attack/3 is used to check whether a candidate queen attacks any previously selected queen. This version does not have denials, as the check is done as part of the computation, and therefore DCC checks are not useful.

---

[8] The graph with seven vertices is available at graph_7.pl.

Two interesting conclusions can be drawn from the numbers in the table:

- The execution time of n_queens_attack does not significantly change using or not DCC, which supports our assumption that the overhead of using DCC checks when they are not needed is negligible.
- On the other hand, the DCC-enabled execution for the version with denials (n_queens, column "s(CASP)+DCC") is faster than the version without denials (n_queens_attack, column "s(CASP)") for a factor of **4.1×**. This can be attributed to the runtime being sophisticated enough to perform checks earlier and more efficiently than the hand-crafted code, even with the current, preliminary implementation.

Table 2. Models generated and/or discarded: s(CASP) vs. s(CASP)+DCC.

	#models returned	#models discarded		#DCC detected
		s(CASP)	s(CASP)+DCC	
Hamiltonian (4 vertices)	3	7	7	52
Hamiltonian (7 vertices)	1	13	13	34
n_queens (n=4)	2	253	0	44
n_queens (n=5)	10	3116	0	167
n_queens (n=6)	4	46652	0	742

Table 2 sheds some additional light on the effectiveness of DCC. It contains, for the same benchmarks as Table 1, how many models were returned, how many candidate models were discarded by nmr_check after they were generated (column "#models discarded – s(CASP)"), how many (partial) candidate models were discarded using DCCs (column "#models discarded – s(CASP) + DCC") and how many times the dynamic consistency checking detects an inconsistency and backtracks (column "#DCC detected").

Let us first focus on the n_queens benchmark[9]. As the size of the board grows, the number of models that are completely generated and discarded by s(CASP) without using DCCs grows exponentially; this is of course the reason why its execution time also increases very quickly. If we look at the column "#models discarded – s(CASP) + DCC" we see that, when DCC is active, none of final models is discarded by nmr_check. That means that all models not consistent with the denials have been removed early, while they were being built. We also see that the number of times that DCC rules were activated is much smaller than the number of times that nmr_check was executed—early pruning made it possible to avoid attempting to generate many other candidate models. On top of that, executing DCC rules is done directly in Prolog, while nmr_check is executed using the s(CASP) metainterpreter, and the former is considerably faster than the latter. This adds to the advantage of early pruning.

---

[9] n_queens_attack does not have denials, hence we do not include it in this table.

The Hamiltonian path benchmark is different and very interesting. The number of models discarded by `nmr_check` is the same regardless of whether DCC is activated or not. That means that the DCC could not detect inconsistencies in candidate models. In this case the advantage of using DCC comes from applying it when `nmr_check` is invoked to ensure that the final model is consistent with the denials. `nmr_check` is executed as a piece of (synthesized) code by the metainterpreter. The denials in the Hamiltonian path not only check, but also generate new atoms which are checked by the DCC. This accelerates the execution of `nmr_check`, making it fail earlier, and it is the cause of the speedup of the Hamiltonian path benchmark.

5   Conclusions

In this paper, we have reported on a preliminary design and implementation of Dynamic Consistency Checking (DCC), a technique that anticipates the consistency evaluation of tentative models in s(CASP), a goal-directed (predicate) Constraint Answer Set Programming. This technique translates the denials to check them as early as possible rather than when a full model is found for a given query. Its ability to detect inconsistencies before a literal is added to the tentative model greatly increases the performance. With respect with executions without DCC. Early denial checking can also beat programs that use auxiliary predicates explicitly called from the user code to check for inconsistencies.

The current DCC implementation can still be improved, in particular to properly handle constraints by reducing the domain of constrained variables: checking denials using literals with constrained variables has to keep track of the domains of the variables, while avoiding introducing non-determinism when conflicting values are removed from the domain of the variables.

References

1. Arias, J., Carro, M., Chen, Z., Gupta, G.: Justifications for goal-directed constraint answer set programming. In: Proceedings 36th International Conference on Logic Programming (Technical Communications). EPTCS, vol. 325, pp. 59–72. Open Publishing Association (2020). https://doi.org/10.4204/EPTCS.325.12
2. Arias, J., Carro, M., Chen, Z., Gupta, G.: Modeling and Reasoning in Event Calculus using Goal-Directed Constraint Answer Set Programming. Theory and Practice of Logic Programming, pp. 1–30 (2021). https://doi.org/10.1017/S1471068421000156
3. Arias, J., Carro, M., Salazar, E., Marple, K., Gupta, G.: Constraint answer set programming without grounding. Theor. Pract. Logic Program. 18(3–4), 337–354 (2018). https://doi.org/10.1017/S1471068418000285
4. Arias, J., Chen, Z., Carro, M., Gupta, G.: Modeling and reasoning in event calculus using goal-directed constraint answer set programming. In: Gabbrielli, M. (ed.) LOPSTR 2019. LNCS, vol. 12042, pp. 139–155. Springer, Cham (2020). https://doi.org/10.1007/978-3-030-45260-5_9

5. Arias, J., Moreno-Rebato, M., Rodriguez-García, J.A., Ossowski, S.: Modeling administrative discretion using goal-directed answer set programming. In: Alba, E., et al. (eds.) CAEPIA 2021. LNCS (LNAI), vol. 12882, pp. 258–267. Springer, Cham (2021). https://doi.org/10.1007/978-3-030-85713-4_25

6. Balduccini, M., Lierler, Y.: Constraint answer set solver EZCSP and why integration schemas matter. Theor. Pract. Logic Program. **17**(4), 462–515 (2017). https://doi.org/10.1017/S1471068417000102

7. Banbara, M., Kaufmann, B., Ostrowski, M., Schaub, T.: Clingcon: the next generation. Theor. Pract. Log. Program. **17**(4), 408–461 (2017). https://doi.org/10.1017/S1471068417000138

8. Basu, K., Varanasi, S., Shakerin, F., Arias, J., Gupta, G.: Knowledge-driven natural language understanding of english text and its applications. In: Proceedings of the AAAI Conference on Artificial Intelligence, vol. 35, pp. 12554–12563 (2021)

9. Basu, K., et al.: CASPR: a commonsense reasoning-based conversational Socialbot. In: 4th Proceedings of Alexa Prize (Alexa Prize 2021) (2021)

10. Chen, Z., Marple, K., Salazar, E., Gupta, G., Tamil, L.: A physician advisory system for chronic heart failure management based on knowledge patterns. Theor. Pract. Logic Program. **16**(5–6), 604–618 (2016). https://doi.org/10.1017/S1471068416000429

11. Dovier, A., Pontelli, E., Rossi, G.: A necessary condition for constructive negation in constraint logic programming. Inf. Process. Lett. **74**(3–4), 147–156 (2000)

12. Gebser, M., Kaminski, R., Kaufmann, B., Schaub, T.: Multi-shot ASP solving with clingo. Theor. Pract. Logic Program. **19**(1), 27–82 (2019). https://doi.org/10.1017/S1471068418000054

13. Gelfond, M., Lifschitz, V.: The stable model semantics for logic programming. In: 5th International Conference on Logic Programming, pp. 1070–1080 (1988). http://www.cse.unsw.edu.au/~cs4415/2010/resources/stable.pdf

14. Hall, B., et al.: Knowledge-Assisted reasoning of model-augmented system requirements with event calculus and goal-directed answer set programming. In: Proceedings 8th Workshop on Horn Clause Verification and Synthesis (2021)

15. Marple, K., Bansal, A., Min, R., Gupta, G.: Goal-Directed execution of answer set programs. In: Schreye, D.D., Janssens, G., King, A. (eds.) Principles and Practice of Declarative Programming, PPDP 2012, Leuven, Belgium - 19–21 September 2012, pp. 35–44. ACM (2012). https://doi.org/10.1145/2370776.2370782

16. Marple, K., Gupta, G.: Dynamic consistency checking in goal-directed answer set programming. Theor. Pract. Loging Program. **14**(4–5), 415–427 (2014). https://doi.org/10.1017/S1471068414000118

17. Marple, K., Salazar, E., Gupta, G.: Computing Stable Models of Normal Logic Programs Without Grounding. arXiv:1709.00501 (2017). http://arxiv.org/abs/1709.00501

18. Marriott, K., Stuckey, P.J.: Programming with Constraints: An Introduction. MIT Press, Cambridge (1998)

19. Mellarkod, V.S., Gelfond, M., Zhang, Y.: Integrating Answer Set Programming and Constraint Logic Programming. Technical Report, Texas Tech University, October 2008, this is a long version of [20]. https://www.depts.ttu.edu/cs/research/documents/46.pdf

20. Mellarkod, V.S., Gelfond, M., Zhang, Y.: Integrating answer set programming and constraint logic programming. Ann. Math. Artif. Intell. **53**(1–4), 251–287 (2008)

21. Morris, J.: Constraint answer set programming as a tool to improve legislative drafting: a rules as code experiment. In: ICAIL, pp. 262–263. ACM (2021)

22. Pereira, L.M., Aparício, J.N.: Relevant counterfactuals. In: EPIA 89, 4th Portuguese Conference on Artificial Intelligence, Lisbon, Portugal, 26–29 September 1989, Proceedings, pp. 107–118 (1989). https://doi.org/10.1007/3-540-51665-4_78
23. Shakerin, F., Gupta, G.: Induction of non-monotonic logic programs to explain boosted tree models using LIME. In: AAAI 2019, pp. 3052–3059, January–February 2019. https://doi.org/10.1609/aaai.v33i01.33013052
24. Stuckey, P.: Constructive negation for constraint logic programming. In: Proceedings LICS 1991, pp. 328–339 (1991)
25. Varanasi, S.C., Salazar, E., Mittal, N., Gupta, G.: Synthesizing imperative code from answer set programming specifications. In: Gabbrielli, M. (ed.) LOPSTR 2019. LNCS, vol. 12042, pp. 75–89. Springer, Cham (2020). https://doi.org/10.1007/978-3-030-45260-5_5

Implementing Stable-Unstable Semantics with ASPTOOLS and Clingo

Tomi Janhunen[✉]

Tampere University, Tampere, Finland
Tomi.Janhunen@tuni.fi

Abstract. Normal logic programs subject to stable model semantics cover reasoning problems from the first level of polynomial time hierarchy (PH) in a natural way. Disjunctive programs reach one level beyond this, but the access to the underlying NP oracle(s) is somewhat implicit and available for the programmer using the so-called saturation technique. To address this shortcoming, stable-unstable semantics was proposed, making oracles explicit as subprograms having no stable models. If this idea is applied recursively, any level of PH can be reached with normal programs only, in analogy to quantified Boolean formulas (QBFs). However, for the moment, no native implementations of stable-unstable semantics have emerged except via translations toward QBFs. In this work, we alleviate this situation with a translation of (effectively) normal programs that combines a main program with any fixed number of oracles subject to stable-unstable semantics. The result is a disjunctive program that can be fed as input for answer set solvers supporting disjunctive programs. The idea is to hide saturation from the programmer altogether, although it is exploited by the translation internally. The translation of oracles is performed using translators and linkers from the ASPTOOLS collection while Clingo is used as the back-end solver.

1 Introduction

The semantics of answer set programming paradigm (see, e.g., [6,22] for an overview) rests on the notion of *stable models* first proposed for *normal* logic programs (NLPs) [15] and later generalized for *disjunctive* logic programs (DLPs) [16]. The known complexity results [9,30] indicate that NLPs subject to stable model semantics cover reasoning problems from the first level of polynomial time hierarchy (PH) in a natural way while DLPs reach one level beyond. In the latter case, however, the access to underlying NP oracle(s) is somewhat implicit and best understood via the so-called *saturation* technique from the original complexity result [9]. When using saturation, the programmer is confronted with the fact that an oracle must be essentially expressed as a Boolean satisfiability problem, which differs from NLPs with respect to both syntax and semantics (cf. Sect. 5). In spite of this mismatch, saturation has been successfully applied when expressing properties pertaining to the second-level of PH [10,13], e.g., when using meta-programming techniques together with saturation.

© Springer Nature Switzerland AG 2022
J. Cheney and S. Perri (Eds.): PADL 2022, LNCS 13165, pp. 135–153, 2022.
https://doi.org/10.1007/978-3-030-94479-7_9

The *stable-unstable semantics* [3] was proposed as a remedy to the problems identified above. The main ideas are (i) to use NLPs when encoding problems, (ii) to make a subprogram acting as an oracle explicit, and (iii) to change the mode of reasoning from stability to instability for the oracle.[1] If this idea is applied in a nested fashion by merging NLPs recursively as *combined programs*, any level of PH can be reached with NLPs only, in analogy to *quantified Boolean formulas* (QBFs). In a nutshell, according to the stable-unstable semantics, we seek a stable model M for the main NLP P such that the NLP Q acting as the oracle has no stable model N that agrees with M about the truth values of atoms shared by P and Q. In contrast with QBFs, this leaves the quantification of atoms implicit, i.e., the atoms of P are existentially quantified while the local atoms of Q are effectively universal. There are follow-up approaches [1,11] that make the quantification of atoms explicit. Regardless of this objective, the semantics of quantified programs is still aligned with the stable-unstable semantics, see [1, Theorem 7] and [11, Appendix B] for details. For the purposes of this work, however, implicit quantification is very natural, since the quantification of atoms can be controlled in terms of #show-statements directly supported by Clingo.

For the moment, no native implementations of stable-unstable semantics have emerged except via translations toward QBFs [3,11]. The goal of this work is to alleviate this situation with a translation of (effectively) normal programs that combines a main program P with any fixed number of oracle programs $P_1, \ldots, P_n$ subject to stable-unstable semantics. In this way, we facilitate the incorporation of several oracles although, in principle, they could be merged into a single oracle first. The result of the translation is a DLP that can be fed as input for answer set solvers supporting DLPs. Thus we are mainly concentrating on search problems that reside on the second level of polynomial hierarchy.

One central idea behind our approach is to hide saturation from the programmer altogether, even though it is exploited by the translation internally. The reason behind this is that encoding saturation is error-prone when using non-ground rules with first-order variables. To this end, consider positive rules

$$\mathtt{u} \mid \mathtt{p}_1(\boldsymbol{X}_1) \mid \ldots \mid \mathtt{p}_k(\boldsymbol{X}_k) \leftarrow \mathtt{p}_{k+1}(\boldsymbol{X}_{k+1}), \ldots, \mathtt{p}_{k+m}(\boldsymbol{X}_{k+m}), \\ \mathtt{d}_1(\boldsymbol{Y}_1), \ldots, \mathtt{d}_n(\boldsymbol{Y}_n). \tag{1}$$

used to encode an oracle where the special atom $\mathtt{u}$ denotes *unsatisfiability*, $\mathtt{p}_i$:s are application predicates subject to saturation, and $\mathtt{d}_j$:s are domain predicates. In general, their argument lists $\boldsymbol{X}_i$:s and $\boldsymbol{Y}_j$:s consist of first-order terms and the domain predicates in the rule body restrict the possible values of variables occurring in the rule. Modern grounders are also able to infer part of this domain information based on the occurrences of predicates elsewhere in a program. Now, the saturating rules $\mathtt{p}_i(\boldsymbol{t}) \leftarrow \mathtt{u}$ should be generated for every *ground* (non-input) atom $\mathtt{p}_i(\boldsymbol{t})$ appearing in the ground rules of the oracle (see Definition 8 for details). Overseeing this objective presumes an understanding of which ground rules are actually produced for the oracle and, therefore, it becomes inherently difficult to find non-ground counterparts for the saturating rules for individual

---

[1] In terms of QBFs, this amounts to treating a QBF $\exists X \forall Y \phi$ as $\exists X \neg \exists Y \neg \phi$.

predicates $p_i(X)$. In the worst case, the only option is to accompany each rule (1) of the oracle with saturating rules of the forms $p_i(X_i) \leftarrow u, d_1(Y_1), \ldots, d_n(Y_n)$ for every $1 \leq i \leq k + m$. The number of such rules may get high and it is an extra burden for the programmer to keep these rules in synchrony with (1) when the rules encoding the oracle are further elaborated.

Our implementation is based on translators and linkers available under the ASPTOOLS[2] collection. Moreover, we expect that the grounding component of Clingo, namely Gringo, is used for instantiation. Thus we can use any Clingo program as the main program, exploiting extended rule types, proper disjunctive rules, and optimization as needed. As regards oracles, the translation-based approach of [21] sets the limits for their support in contrast with main programs. Due to existing normalization tools [4,5], aggregates can be used. However, the use of disjunction in rule heads is restricted, i.e., only head-cycle-free disjunctions can be tolerated, as they can be translated away. Finally, optimization does not make sense in the context of oracles—supposed to have no stable models.

The rest of this article is organized as follows. In Sect. 2, we recall the syntax and the semantics of logic programs, including stable-unstable semantics. An account of the modularity properties of stable models is given in Sect. 3. Then, we concentrate on translations required in the subsequent treatment of oracles, i.e., the translation of NLPs into propositional clauses in Sect. 4 and the saturation technique in Sect. 5. Then we are ready to present our saturation-based technique for linking a main program with oracle programs in Sect. 6. The details of the implementation, including a saturating translator UNSAT2LP, are presented in Sect. 7. Moreover, we illustrate practical modeling with stable-unstable semantics in terms of the *point of no return* problem [2] involving a non-trivial oracle which is challenging to encode in ASP directly. The paper is concluded by Sect. 8 including a plan for future work.

2   Preliminaries

In this section, we review the syntax and semantics of logic programs and, in particular, the fragments of normal and disjunctive programs in the propositional case. Thus, as regards syntax, a *logic program* is a set of *rules* of form[3]

$$a_1 \mid \ldots \mid a_k \leftarrow b_1, \ldots, b_n, \text{not } c_1, \ldots, \text{not } c_m. \tag{2}$$

where $a_1, \ldots, a_k, b_1, \ldots, b_n$, and $c_1, \ldots, c_m$, are (propositional) atoms and "not" denotes negation by default. *Literals* are either atoms "a" or their negations "not a", also called *positive* and *negative* literals, respectively. Using shorthands A, B, and C for the sets of atoms involved in (2), the rule can be abbreviated as $A \leftarrow B, \text{not } C$ where "not C" stands for the set of negative conditions $\{\text{not } c \mid c \in C\}$. The intuition behind a rule is that some atom from the *head* A of the

---

[2] https://github.com/asptools.

[3] The syntax of logic programs has been generalized, e.g., with choice, cardinality, and weight rules in [32], but such extensions can be translated back to normal rules [4].

rule can be inferred true whenever the *body* of the rule is satisfied, i.e., when all atoms of B are true and no atom of C is true by any other rules in the program.

A rule (2) is *proper disjunctive*, if $k > 1$, *normal*, if $k = 1$, and a *constraint* if $k = 0$. A rule (2) is a *fact*, if $k > 0$, $n = 0$, and $m = 0$ and then $\leftarrow$ is typically omitted. A *normal (logic) program* (NLP) consists of normal rules only whereas a *disjunctive (logic) program* (DLP) allows for any number of head atoms in its rules. Additionally, a program is called *positive* if $m = 0$ for all of its rules (2).

2.1   Minimal and Stable Models

Turning our attention to semantics, let $\mathrm{At}(P)$ denote the *signature* of a program P, i.e., $A \cup B \cup C \subseteq \mathrm{At}(P)$ for every rule $A \leftarrow B, \mathrm{not}\ C$ of P.[4] The semantics of a *positive* DLP P is determined as follows. An *interpretation* I of P is simply any subset of $\mathrm{At}(P)$ considered to be true under I. A (positive) rule $A \leftarrow B$ of P is satisfied in an interpretation $I \subseteq \mathrm{At}(P)$ of P, if $B \subseteq I$ implies $A \cap I \neq \emptyset$. A *model* of P is an interpretation $M \subseteq \mathrm{At}(P)$ satisfying all rules of P. A model M of P is a (subset) minimal model of P if there is no other model M' of P such that $M' \subset M$. The set of minimal models of P is denoted by $\mathrm{MM}(P)$.

By the definitions above, a positive DLP may have no minimal models ($P_1 = \{a. \leftarrow a.\}$), a unique minimal model ($P_2 = \{a \leftarrow a.\}$), or several minimal models ($P_3 = \{a \mid b.\}$). A widely agreed semantics of NLPs and DLPs is given by their stable models [15,16] based on the Gelfond-Lifschitz reduct of a logic program P with respect to a model candidate M. The reduced program is

$$P^M = \{(A \leftarrow B) \mid (A \leftarrow B, \mathrm{not}\ C) \in P,\ A \neq \emptyset,\ B \subseteq M,\ \text{and}\ C \cap M = \emptyset\}. \quad (3)$$

Definition 1 (Gelfond and Lifschitz [15,16]). *A model M of a program P is stable if and only if $M \in \mathrm{MM}(P^M)$.*

We let $\mathrm{SM}(P)$ denote the set of stable models of P. It should be noted that Definition 1 covers constraints (2) with $k = 0$ by the requirement that M is a *model* of P, i.e., for every rule $A \leftarrow B, \mathrm{not}\ C$ of P, $B \subseteq M$ and $C \cap M = \emptyset$ imply $A \cap M \neq \emptyset$, thus treating default negation in rule bodies classically.

2.2   Stable-Unstable Semantics

The original definition of stable-unstable semantics adds one subprogram as an oracle to the main program. To cater for more flexible use cases, we formulate a generalized definition with any fixed number $n \geq 0$ of oracles. While there is no real reason to restrict the main program P, it is assumed that oracles P_i are effectively NLPs containing no rule $a \leftarrow B, \mathrm{not}\ C$ such that $a \in \mathrm{At}(P)$. Thus oracles may not *define* any concepts for the main program, they simply receive some facts as input, relating to the stable models of the main program.

---

[4] Typically, $\mathrm{At}(P)$ is selected to be minimal in this respect, i.e., it only contains atoms that actually appear in P. But larger sets might be used, e.g., if P resulted from rewriting and certain atoms were removed, but the semantics of P is unaffected.

Definition 2. *A model M of a program P is stable-unstable with respect to oracle programs $P_1, \ldots, P_n$ if and only if $M \in \mathrm{SM}(P)$ and for every oracle P_i with $1 \leq i \leq n$, $\mathrm{SM}(P_i \cup \{a. \mid a \in M \cap \mathrm{At}(P_i)\}) = \emptyset$.* –

Note that if there is an (input) atom $a \in \mathrm{At}(P) \cap \mathrm{At}(P_i)$ such that $a \notin M$, then a will remain false by default in the context of the oracle P_i whose rules may not have a as the head. Moreover, when $n = 0$, we obtain the standard stable semantics (cf. Definition 1) as a special case of Definition 2.

3 Modularity

In this section, we adopt the Gaifman-Shapiro-style module architecture of DLPs from [24]. The respective modularity properties of stable models enable the modular (de)composition of DLPs. Programs are encapsulated as follows.

Definition 3. *A program module Π is a quadruple $\langle P, I, O, H \rangle$ where*

1. *P is a logic program,*
2. *I, O, and H are pairwise disjoint sets of input, output, and hidden atoms;*
3. *$\mathrm{At}(P) \subseteq \mathrm{At}(\Pi) = I \cup O \cup H$; and*
4. *if $A \neq \emptyset$ for some rule $A \leftarrow B$, not C of P, then $A \cap (O \cup H) \neq \emptyset$.*

The program interface of a module Π splits the signature $\mathrm{At}(\Pi)$ in three disjoint parts that serve the following purposes. The *visible* part $\mathrm{At}_v(\Pi) = I \cup O$ of $\mathrm{At}(\Pi)$ can be accessed by other modules to supply input for Π or to utilize its output. The *input signature* I and the *output signature* O of Π are also denoted by $\mathrm{At}_i(\Pi)$ and $\mathrm{At}_o(\Pi)$, respectively. The *hidden* atoms in the difference $\mathrm{At}_h(\Pi) = \mathrm{At}(\Pi) \backslash \mathrm{At}_v(\Pi) = H$ can be used to formalize some internal (auxiliary) concepts of Π. The fourth requirement of Definition 3 ensures that every rule with a non-empty head must mention at least one non-input atom from $O \cup H$. This is a particular relaxation for disjunctive rules—note that the head of a normal rule cannot be an input atom by this requirement, but the heads of disjunctive rules may refer to input atoms as well. Thus, every rule in a module Π must contribute to the *definition* of at least one atom in $O \cup H$.

Example 1. Consider a module Π having only one rule $a \mid b \leftarrow \mathrm{not}\ c$ such that $I = \{b, c\}$, $O = \{a\}$, and $H = \emptyset$. Therefore, the overall signature $\mathrm{At}(\Pi) = \{a, b, c\}$. The requirements of Definition 3 are met. The fourth one is satisfied because the head $a \mid b$ mentions the output atom a besides the input atom b. ∎

A module Π corresponds to a conventional logic program when $\mathrm{At}_i(\Pi) = \emptyset = \mathrm{At}_h(\Pi)$ and then the semantics of the module $\Pi = \langle P, \emptyset, O, \emptyset \rangle$ is given by $\mathrm{SM}(P) \subseteq 2^{\mathrm{At}_o(\Pi)} = 2^O$ directly. Hidden atoms become only relevant, when we compare programs or modules with each other, e.g., using the notion of *visible equivalence* [17]. Then, the idea is that each stable model M is reduced to $M \backslash H = M \cap (I \cup O)$, i.e., hidden atoms are neglected in comparisons but they do not affect stability by any means. However, to cover input atoms, the definition of stable models must be generalized, e.g., according to [24].

Definition 4. *Given a program module $\Pi = \langle P, I, O, H \rangle$, the reduct of P with respect to a set $M \subseteq \text{At}(\Pi)$ and the input signature I, denoted by $P^{M,I}$, contains a positive disjunctive rule $(A \backslash I) \leftarrow (B \backslash I)$ if and only if there is a rule $A \leftarrow B,$ not C of P such that $A \neq \emptyset$, $A \cap I \cap M = \emptyset$, $B \cap I \subseteq M$, and $M \cap C = \emptyset$.*

In analogy to (3), the reduct $P^{M,I}$ evaluates all negative literals in rule bodies of P and, in addition, all input atoms appearing elsewhere in P. Intuitively, if the satisfaction of a rule $A \leftarrow B,$ not C under M depends on the remaining atoms in the rule, the respective reduced rule $(A \backslash I) \leftarrow (B \backslash I)$ is included in $P^{M,I}$. The head $A \backslash I$ of any such rule is necessarily non-empty when $A \neq \emptyset$ by Item 4 in Definition 3 and $P^{M,I}$ is guaranteed to possess (minimal) classical models. Potential constraints of P with $A = \emptyset$ are covered in analogy to Definition 1.

Definition 5. *A model $M \subseteq \text{At}(\Pi)$ of a program module $\Pi = \langle P, I, O, H \rangle$, is stable if and only if $M \backslash I \in \text{MM}(P^{M,I})$.*

As for programs, we let $\text{SM}(\Pi)$ denote the set of stable models of Π.

Example 2. The module Π from Example 1 has four stable models in total, i.e., $\text{SM}(\Pi)$ equals to $\{\{a\}, \{b\}, \{c\}, \{b, c\}\}$. To verify that $M = \{a\}$ is indeed stable, we note that $P^{M,I} = \{a.\}$ with a minimal model $\{a\}$ and $\{a\} \backslash \{b, c\} = \{a\}$. ∎

Inputs to modules can also be taken into account by other means: an input $M \cap I$ defined by an interpretation $M \subseteq \text{At}(\Pi)$ could be added to Π as a set of facts [25]. The other option is to amend modules with *input generators* [31] that can be used to capture stable models of modules using Definition 1 and the standard reduct (3). Unfortunately, stable models of program modules do not provide a fully *compositional* semantics for logic programs: taking simple unions of modules does not guarantee that the stable models of the union could be obtained as straightforward combinations of the stable models for the modules involved. Towards this goal, two modules Π_1 and Π_2 are eligible for composition only if their output signatures are disjoint and they *respect each other's hidden atoms*, i.e., $\text{At}_h(\Pi_1) \cap \text{At}(\Pi_2) = \emptyset$ and $\text{At}_h(\Pi_2) \cap \text{At}(\Pi_1) = \emptyset$.

Definition 6 (Composition [24]). *The composition of logic program modules $\Pi_1 = \langle P_1, I_1, O_1, H_1 \rangle$ and $\Pi_2 = \langle P_2, I_2, O_2, H_2 \rangle$, denoted by $\Pi_1 \oplus \Pi_2$, is*

$$\langle P_1 \cup P_2, (I_1 \backslash O_2) \cup (I_2 \backslash O_1), O_1 \cup O_2, H_1 \cup H_2 \rangle \tag{4}$$

if $O_1 \cap O_2 = \emptyset$ and Π_1 and Π_2 respect each other's hidden atoms.

As demonstrated in [24], the conditions of Definition 6 do not yet imply the desired relationship of stable models in general. The conditions can be suitably tightened using the *positive dependency graph* of the composition $\Pi_1 \oplus \Pi_2$. Generally speaking, the *positive dependency graph* $\text{DG}^+(\Pi)$ associated with a program module $\Pi = \langle P, I, O, H \rangle$ is the pair $\langle O \cup H, \leq \rangle$ where $b \leq a$ holds for any atoms a and b of $O \cup H$ if there is a rule $A \leftarrow B,$ not C of P such that $a \in A$ and $b \in B$. A *strongly connected component* (SCC) S of $\text{DG}^+(P)$ is a maximal set

$S \subseteq \mathrm{At}(P)$ such that $b \leq^* a$ holds for every $a, b \in S$, i.e., all atoms of S depend positively on each other. If the composition $\Pi_1 \oplus \Pi_2$ is defined, the members of the composition are *mutually dependent* if and only if $\mathrm{DG}^+(\Pi_1 \oplus \Pi_2)$ has an SCC S such that $S \cap \mathrm{At}_o(\Pi_1) \neq \emptyset$ and $S \cap \mathrm{At}_o(\Pi_2) \neq \emptyset$, i.e., the SCC in question is effectively *shared* by Π_1 and Π_2. Then, following [24], the *join* $\Pi_1 \sqcup \Pi_2$ of Π_1 and Π_2 is defined as $\Pi_1 \oplus \Pi_2$, provided $\Pi_1 \oplus \Pi_2$ is defined and Π_1 and Π_2 are mutually *independent*. The key observation from the viewpoint of compositional semantics is that stable models do not tolerate positive recursion across module boundaries. Thus, independence leads to a natural relationship[5] between the sets of stable models $\mathrm{SM}(\Pi_1 \sqcup \Pi_2)$, $\mathrm{SM}(\Pi_1)$, and $\mathrm{SM}(\Pi_2)$ as detailed below.

Theorem 1 (Module Theorem [24]). *If Π_1 and Π_2 are program modules such that $\Pi_1 \sqcup \Pi_2$ is defined, then $\mathrm{SM}(\Pi_1 \sqcup \Pi_2) = \mathrm{SM}(\Pi_1) \bowtie \mathrm{SM}(\Pi_2)$.*

In Theorem 1, the operation $\bowtie$ denotes a *natural join* of *compatible* stable models, i.e., $M_1 \cup M_2$ belongs to $\mathrm{SM}(\Pi_1) \bowtie \mathrm{SM}(\Pi_2)$ if and only if $M_1 \in \mathrm{SM}(\Pi_1)$, $M_2 \in \mathrm{SM}(\Pi_1)$, and $M_1 \cap \mathrm{At}_v(\Pi_2) = M_2 \cap \mathrm{At}_v(\Pi_1)$. Theorem 1 is easily generalized for finite joins of modules: if $\Pi_1 \sqcup \cdots \sqcup \Pi_n = \bigsqcup_{i=1}^{n} \Pi_i$ is defined, then

$$\mathrm{SM}(\textstyle\bigsqcup_{i=1}^{n} \Pi_i) = \bowtie_{i=1}^{n} \mathrm{SM}(\Pi_i). \tag{5}$$

Example 3. Let us consider modules $\Pi_1 = \langle \{a \leftarrow \mathrm{not}\ b.\}, \{b\}, \{a\}, \emptyset \rangle$, $\Pi_2 = \langle \{b \leftarrow \mathrm{not}\ c.\}, \{c\}, \{b\}, \emptyset \rangle$, and $\Pi_3 = \langle \{c \leftarrow \mathrm{not}\ a.\}, \{a\}, \{c\}, \emptyset \rangle$. The respective sets of stable models are $\mathrm{SM}(\Pi_1) = \{\{a\}, \{b\}\}$, $\mathrm{SM}(\Pi_2) = \{\{b\}, \{c\}\}$, and $\mathrm{SM}(\Pi_3) = \{\{c\}, \{a\}\}$. The joins between the three modules are well-defined, since the output signatures are disjoint, no atoms are hidden, and no positive recursion is involved. Thus, we obtain by Theorem 1 that

$$\mathrm{SM}(\Pi_1 \sqcup \Pi_2) = \mathrm{SM}(\Pi_1) \bowtie \mathrm{SM}(\Pi_2) = \{\{a\}, \{b\}\} \bowtie \{\{b\}, \{c\}\} = \{\{a, c\}, \{b\}\}$$

where the compatibility of stable models depends on $\mathrm{At}_i(\Pi_1) = \{b\} = \mathrm{At}_o(\Pi_2)$. When incorporating $\mathrm{SM}(\Pi_3) = \{\{a\}, \{c\}\}$, we observe no models compatible with the ones listed above, i.e., $\mathrm{SM}(\bigsqcup_{i=1}^{3} \Pi_i) = \bowtie_{i=1}^{3} \mathrm{SM}(\Pi_i) = \emptyset$. ∎

Finally, it is worth noting that oracles P_i, as detailed in Definition 2, can be viewed as modules $\Pi_i = \langle P_i, I_i, \emptyset, H_i \rangle$ that can be composed/joined with the main module $\Pi = \langle P, \emptyset, O, \emptyset \rangle$. By hiding all non-input atoms in the oracle modules, they cannot interfere with the atoms of Π in any well-defined compositions. However, since the visible parts $M \cap I_i$ of stable models $M \in \mathrm{SM}(\Pi_i)$ are essentially witnesses for rejecting particular stable models of the main module, the relationship behind stable-unstable semantics cannot be expressed with $\bowtie$ directly. This goes back to insisting on instability (cf. Theorem 4 in Sect. 6).

---

[5] The respective property of propositional formulas ϕ_1 and ϕ_2 is formalized by $\mathrm{CM}(\phi_1 \wedge \phi_2) = \mathrm{CM}(\phi_1) \bowtie \mathrm{CM}(\phi_2)$ where $\mathrm{CM}(\phi) \subseteq 2^{\mathrm{At}(\phi)}$ gives the classical models of ϕ.

4 Translating NLPs into SAT

In the forthcoming translations, we need to express *normal* logic programs as sets of propositional clauses as an intermediary step. The goal of this section is to recollect some results in this respect. A *clause* is an expression of the form

$$a_1 \vee \ldots \vee a_m \vee \neg b_1 \vee \ldots \vee \neg b_n \qquad (6)$$

where $a_1, \ldots, a_m$ and $b_1, \ldots, b_n$ are (propositional) atoms. Given a set of clauses S, we write $\mathrm{At}(S)$ for the signature of S in analogy to the signature of a logic program (cf. Sect. 2). In the same way, an *interpretation* I for S is any subset of $\mathrm{At}(S)$ so that an atom $a \in \mathrm{At}(S)$ is considered *true* if $a \in I$ and *false*, otherwise. A clause C of form (6) is satisfied by I, denoted by $I \models C$, if and only if some $a_i \in I$ or some $b_j \notin I$. An interpretation $M \subseteq \mathrm{At}(S)$ is a *(classical) model* of S, denoted by $M \models S$, if and only if $M \models C$ for every clause C of S. Then, let $\mathrm{CM}(S) = \{M \subseteq \mathrm{At}(S) \mid M \models S\}$. The signature $\mathrm{At}(S)$ can be partitioned into $\mathrm{At_i}(S)$, $\mathrm{At_o}(S)$, and $\mathrm{At_h}(S)$, if we wish to treat S as a module $\langle S, I, O, H \rangle$ [19] in analogy to Sect. 3, keeping the semantics $\mathrm{CM}(S)$ intact.

Due to the greater expressive power of NLPs—relating to both default negation and recursive definitions—the translations from NLPs to SAT incur at least some blow-up. If no auxiliary atoms are introduced, the translation based on *loop formulas* [28,29] is deemed worst-case exponential [26]. However, if new atoms are allowed, polynomial transformations become feasible, e.g., quadratic [27] and even sub-quadratic [17]. We adopt loop formulas for a brief illustration but exploit the most compact translation in the actual implementation. But, in contrast with [29], we use bd as a *new name* for a rule body B, not C. This amounts to a Tseitin transformation [33] of rule bodies. These new atoms enable a linear translation for the first part of the translation (Items 1 and 2 below) that captures Clark's *completion* [7] for the program. The last item is based on loops $L \subseteq \mathrm{At}(P)$ which strongly connected in the same way as SCCs but not necessarily maximal as sets. Thus, an SCC S may induce several loops.

Definition 7 ([29]). *Given an NLP P, the translation* $\mathrm{Tr}_{SAT}(P)$· *contains for every* $a \in \mathrm{At}(P)$ *and the defining rules* $a \leftarrow B_i, \mathrm{not}\ C_i$ *of a in P with* $1 \leq i \leq k$,

1. *clauses* $a \vee \neg bd_1, \ldots, a \vee \neg bd_k$ *and a clause* $\neg a \vee bd_1 \vee \ldots \vee bd_k$,
2. *for each body indexed by* $1 \leq i \leq k$, *a clause* $bd_i \vee \neg B \vee C$,[6]
   clauses $\{\neg bd_i \vee b \mid b \in B_i\}$, *and clauses* $\{\neg bd_i \vee \neg c \mid c \in C_i\}$;

and for every loop $\emptyset \subset L \subseteq \mathrm{At}(P)$ *and the related externally supporting rules* $a \leftarrow B_i, \mathrm{not}\ C_i$ *of P with a head* $a \in L$, *positive body* $B_i \cap L = \emptyset$, *and* $1 \leq i \leq k$,

3. *clauses* $\{bd_1 \vee \ldots \vee bd_k \vee \neg a \mid a \in L\}$.

Intuitively, the clauses of the first item express $a \leftrightarrow bd_1 \vee \ldots \vee bd_k$ for each atom a while the second item establishes equivalences $bd_i \leftrightarrow B_i \wedge \neg C_i$ for each

---

[6] A set of literals is understood disjunctively as part of a disjunction.

rule body indexed by $1 \leq i \leq k$. If $k = 1$ for an atom a, then we can forget about bd_1 and encode $a \leftrightarrow B_i \wedge \neg C_i$ directly with the respective clauses. Last, the clauses in the third item essentially express a loop formula $\neg bd_1 \wedge \ldots \wedge \neg bd_k \rightarrow \neg L$ falsifying all atoms of the loop L in case they lack *external support* altogether.

Theorem 2 ([29]). *Let P be an NLP and $\text{Tr}_{SAT}(P)$ its translation into SAT.*

1. *If $M \in \text{SM}(P)$, then $N \models \text{Tr}_{SAT}(P)$ for a unique truth assignment $N = M \cup \{bd \mid (a \leftarrow B, \text{not } C) \in P, B \subseteq M, C \cap M = \emptyset, \text{ and } bd \text{ names } (B, \text{not } C)\}$.*
2. *If $N \models \text{Tr}_{SAT}(P)$, then $M = N \cap \text{At}(P) \in \text{SM}(P)$.*

The translation is also applicable to modules $\Pi = \langle P, I, O, H \rangle$ by neglecting input atoms having no defining rules in program P. The resulting SAT-module $\langle \text{Tr}_{SAT}(P), I, O, H' \rangle$ extends H to H' with new names bd introduced by $\text{Tr}_{SAT}(\cdot)$.

Example 4 Consider a program module $\Pi = \langle P, \{c\}, \{a, b\}, \emptyset \rangle$ based on:

$$a \leftarrow b, \text{not } c. \qquad b \leftarrow a. \qquad a \leftarrow c.$$

The module has two stable models $\{\}$ and $\{a, b, c\}$. The translation into SAT is:

$$
\begin{array}{llll}
a \vee \neg bd_1, & a \vee \neg bd_2, & \neg a \vee bd_1 \vee bd_2, & [a \leftrightarrow bd_1 \vee bd_2] \\
bd_1 \vee \neg b \vee c, & \neg bd_1 \vee b, & \neg bd_1 \vee \neg c, & [bd_1 \leftrightarrow b \wedge \neg c] \\
bd_2 \vee \neg c, & \neg bd_2 \vee c, & & [bd_2 \leftrightarrow c] \\
b \vee \neg a, & \neg b \vee a, & & [b \leftrightarrow a] \\
bd_2 \vee \neg a, & bd_2 \vee \neg b. & & [\neg bd_2 \rightarrow \neg a \wedge \neg b]
\end{array}
$$

Since c is an input atom, it is only treated as a condition in rule bodies. The only non-trivial loop of Π is $\{a, b\}$ that gives rise to the last two clauses of the translation. The resulting SAT-module $\langle \text{Tr}_{SAT}(P), \{c\}, \{a, b\}, \{bd_1, bd_2\} \rangle$ has two satisfying assignments $\{\}$ and $\{a, b, c, bd_2\}$ that capture the stable models of Π. It is important to note that the last two clauses exclude the truth assignment $\{a, b, bd_1\}$ which would suggest an extra (incorrect) stable model $\{a, b\}$ for Π. ∎

5   Saturation

Saturation was introduced in [9] when showing that the main decision problems related to DLPs are complete on the second level of PH. It offers a central primitive for changing the mode of reasoning from *unsatisfiability* to the existence of a stable model. Typically, saturation is used as an integral part of the main program, but the goal of this section is to extract respective subprograms as independent program modules with input interfaces. Therefore, it is assumed below that a SAT-module $\langle S, I, O, H \rangle$ is provided as input. Given an interpretation $N \subseteq \text{At}_i(S)$, we write $S|_N$ for a *partial evaluation* of S obtained by (i) removing $C \in S$ if $N \models l$ for some literal $l \in C$ and (ii) removing from $C \in S$ any literal $l \in C$ such that $N \not\models l$. The translation aims to capture truth assignments N over the set of input atoms I that render $S|_N$ inconsistent.

Definition 8. *Given a SAT-module* $\langle S, I, O, H \rangle$ *encapsulating a set of clauses* S, *the saturation translation* $\mathrm{Tr}_{UNSAT}(S)$ *contains*

1. *for every clause (6), a positive disjunctive rule* $u \mid a_1 \mid \ldots \mid a_m \leftarrow b_1, \ldots, b_n$;
2. *for every atom* $a \in \mathrm{At_h}(S) \cup \mathrm{At_o}(S)$, *the saturating rule* $a \leftarrow u$; *and*
3. *the rule* $u \leftarrow \mathrm{not}\ u$

where $u \notin \mathrm{At}(S)$ *is a new atom. Moreover, we set* $\mathrm{At_i}(\mathrm{Tr}_{UNSAT}(S)) = \mathrm{At_i}(S)$, $\mathrm{At_o}(\mathrm{Tr}_{UNSAT}(S)) = \emptyset$, $\mathrm{At_h}(\mathrm{Tr}_{UNSAT}(S)) = \mathrm{At_o}(S) \cup \mathrm{At_h}(S)$.

All atoms except input atoms are hidden in $\mathrm{Tr}_{\mathrm{UNSAT}}(S)$ because their values are uninteresting (all true) under any stable model of the translation. The intuitive idea of $\mathrm{Tr}_{\mathrm{UNSAT}}(S)$ is that if $S|_N$ is satisfiable for an input interpretation $N \subseteq \mathrm{At_i}(S)$, then the positive rules in $\mathrm{Tr}_{\mathrm{UNSAT}}(S)$ have a $\subseteq$-minimal (classical) model M extending N with $u \notin M$. Then, the rule $u \leftarrow \mathrm{not}\ u$ prevents stability.

Example 5. Consider the following set S of clauses:

$$a \vee b, \qquad \neg a \vee b, \qquad \neg a \vee \neg b.$$

Assuming that b is the only input atom of S, we observe that $S|_\emptyset = \{a, \neg a\}$ is unsatisfiable while $S|_{\{b\}} = \{\neg a\}$ is satisfiable. The translation $\mathrm{Tr}_{\mathrm{UNSAT}}(S)$:

$$u \mid a \mid b. \qquad u \mid b \leftarrow a. \qquad u \leftarrow a, b.$$
$$a \leftarrow u. \qquad u \leftarrow \mathrm{not}\ u.$$

where b is treated as an input atom. The translation has a stable model $\{a, u\}$ indicating that $S|_\emptyset$ is unsatisfiable. Note how this stable model would be excluded if $b \leftarrow u$ were added in the translation. However, if b is added as a fact, there is no way to derive a nor u being false by default. Then, the translation augmented by the fact b has no stable models, indicating that $S|_{\{b\}}$ is satisfiable. ∎

Theorem 3. *Given a SAT-module* $\langle S, I, O, H \rangle$ *and its translation as a program module* $\Pi = \langle P, I, \emptyset, O \cup H \rangle$ *with* $P = \mathrm{Tr}_{UNSAT}(S)$:

1. *If* $S|_N$ *is unsatisfiable for an input interpretation* $N \subseteq I$, *then* $N \cup O \cup H \cup \{u\} \in \mathrm{SM}(\Pi)$.
2. *If* $M \in \mathrm{SM}(\Pi)$ *and* $N = M \cap I$, *then* $M = N \cup O \cup H \cup \{u\}$ *and* $S|_N$ *is unsatisfiable.*

Proof. (1) Let $S|_N$ be unsatisfiable for some $N \subseteq I$ and let $M = N \cup O \cup H \cup \{u\}$. To show $M \in \mathrm{SM}(\mathrm{Tr}_{\mathrm{UNSAT}}(S))$, we should establish that $M \backslash I \in \mathrm{MM}(P^{M,I})$.

(i) Since $u \in M$, the rule $u \leftarrow \mathrm{not}\ u$ does not contribute to the reduct, but $a \leftarrow u$ is included for every $a \in O \cup H$. The rule is satisfied by $M \backslash I = O \cup H \cup \{u\}$. Moreover, the reduct contains $u \mid (A \backslash I) \leftarrow (B \backslash I)$ for every clause $A \vee \neg B \in S$ such that $A \cap N = \emptyset$ and $B \cap I \subseteq N$, i.e., $A \vee \neg B \in S|_N$. This rule is trivially satisfied by $M \backslash I$ containing u. Thus $M \backslash I \models P^{M,I}$. (ii) Suppose that $M' \models P^{M,I}$ for some $M' \subset M \backslash I$. If $u \notin M'$, then $M' \models S|_N$, a contradiction.

Thus $u \in M'$ and since $a \leftarrow u$ is in $P^{M,I}$ for every $a \in O \cup H$ and $M' \models a \leftarrow u$, it follows that $M' = M \backslash I$, a contradiction. Thus, $M \backslash I \in \mathrm{MM}(P^{M,I})$.

(2) Let $M \in \mathrm{SM}(\Pi)$ and $N = M \cap I$. Due to $u \leftarrow \mathrm{not}\ u$ in P, $u \in M$ is necessarily the case. Since $a \leftarrow u$ is contained in $P^{M,I}$ for every $a \in O \cup H$ and $M \models P^{M,I}$ it follows that $O \cup H \subseteq M$ and $M = N \cup O \cup H \cup \{u\}$. Calculating as above, the reduct contains $u \mid (A \backslash I) \leftarrow (B \backslash I)$ for every $A \vee \neg B \in S|_N$. Assuming that $S|_N$ is satisfiable, gives us $M' \models S|_N$ such that $u \notin M'$. It follows that $M' \subset M$ and $M' \models P^{M,I}$, a contradiction. Thus $S|_N$ is unsatisfiable. $\square$

6   Capturing Stable-Unstable Semantics

The goal of this section is to define a translation $\mathrm{Tr}_{\text{ST-UNST}}(\Pi, \Pi_1, \ldots, \Pi_n)$ that captures the stable-unstable semantics of a *main program module* Π combined with *oracle modules* $\Pi_1, \ldots, \Pi_n$. The translation exploits the preceding translations devised in Sects. 4 and 5 as well as modularity properties from Sect. 3. Therefore, we formulate the result for modules with proper interface definitions.

Definition 9. *Given a main program module* $\Pi = \langle P, I, O, H \rangle$ *and oracle modules* $\Pi_1, \ldots, \Pi_n$ *encapsulating NLPs* $P_1, \ldots, P_n$*, the stable-unstable translation*

$$\mathrm{Tr}_{ST\text{-}UNST}(\Pi, \Pi_1, \ldots, \Pi_n) = \Pi \sqcup \bigsqcup_{i=1}^{n} \mathrm{Tr}_{UNSAT}(\mathrm{Tr}_{SAT}(\Pi_i)). \qquad (7)$$

Due to pairwise input-output relationships there are no mutual positive dependencies between the translation $\mathrm{Tr}_{\text{UNSAT}}(\mathrm{Tr}_{\text{SAT}}(\Pi_i))$ of each oracle module Π_i and the main module Π. The same can be stated about the translations of any pair of oracles Π_i and Π_j with $i < j$, because only input atoms are made visible and we may assume without loss of generality that $\mathrm{At_h}(\Pi_i) \cap \mathrm{At_h}(\Pi_j) = \emptyset$, since hidden atoms can always be renamed apart. Moreover, the new atoms (u) introduced by the translation $\mathrm{Tr}_{\text{UNSAT}}(\cdot)$ can be assumed distinct for the oracles $\Pi_1, \ldots, \Pi_n$, say atoms $u_1, \ldots, u_n$. Thus the joins in (7) are well-formed and the resulting signatures of the translation $\Pi' = \mathrm{Tr}_{\text{ST-UNST}}(\Pi, \Pi_1, \ldots, \Pi_n)$ are

1. $\mathrm{At_i}(\Pi') = \mathrm{At_i}(\Pi)$,
2. $\mathrm{At_o}(\Pi') = \mathrm{At_o}(\Pi)$, and
3. $\mathrm{At_h}(\Pi') = \mathrm{At_h}(\Pi) \cup (\bigcup_{i=0}^{n} \mathrm{At}(\mathrm{Tr}_{\text{UNSAT}}(\mathrm{Tr}_{\text{SAT}}(\Pi_i)))) \backslash \mathrm{At_i}(\Pi_i)$.

Theorem 4. *For a main program module* Π*, the NLP oracle program modules* $\Pi_1, \ldots, \Pi_n$ *of* Π*, and their stable-unstable translation:*

1. *If* $\mathrm{Tr}_{ST\text{-}UNST}(\Pi, \Pi_1, \ldots, \Pi_n)$ *has a stable model* N*, then* $M = N \cap \mathrm{At}(\Pi)$ *is stable-unstable model of* Π *with respect to oracles* $\Pi_1, \ldots, \Pi_n$*.*
2. *If* Π *has a stable-unstable model* M *with respect to oracles* $\Pi_1, \ldots, \Pi_n$*, then* $\mathrm{Tr}_{ST\text{-}UNST}(\Pi, \Pi_1, \ldots, \Pi_n)$ *has a stable model* N *such that* $M = N \cap \mathrm{At}(\Pi)$*.*

Proof. Since the joins in Definition 9 are well-formed, we may apply Theorem 1:

$$\mathrm{SM}(\mathrm{Tr}_{\mathrm{ST\text{-}UNST}}(\Pi, \Pi_1, \ldots, \Pi_n)) =$$
$$\mathrm{SM}(\Pi) \bowtie (\bowtie_{i=1}^{n} \mathrm{SM}(\mathrm{Tr}_{\mathrm{UNSAT}}(\mathrm{Tr}_{\mathrm{SAT}}(\Pi_i)))).(8)$$

For brevity, let Π' stand for the entire translation $\mathrm{Tr}_{\mathrm{ST\text{-}UNST}}(\Pi, \Pi_1, \ldots, \Pi_n)$ and Π_i' for the translation $\mathrm{Tr}_{\mathrm{UNSAT}}(\mathrm{Tr}_{\mathrm{SAT}}(\Pi_i))$ of each oracle Π_i with $1 \leq i \leq n$.

By the model correspondence (8) established above, N is a stable model of Π' if and only if $M = N \cap \mathrm{At}(\Pi) \in \mathrm{SM}(\Pi)$ and $N_i = N \cap \mathrm{At}(\Pi_i') \in \mathrm{SM}(\Pi_i')$ for each $1 \leq i \leq n$. By Theorem 3, this holds if and only if $M \in \mathrm{SM}(\Pi)$ and $\mathrm{Tr}_{\mathrm{SAT}}(\Pi_i)|_{M_i}$ is unsatisfiable for each $1 \leq i \leq n$ and the respective input $M_i = N_i \cap \mathrm{At}_{\mathrm{i}}(\Pi_i)$. By Theorem 2, this is equivalent to $M \in \mathrm{SM}(\Pi)$ and each oracle Π_i with $1 \leq i \leq n$ having no stable models given the input M_i, i.e., M is a stable-unstable model of Π with respect to $\Pi_1, \ldots, \Pi_n$. □

Definition 9 and Theorem 4 characterize our method for computing stable-unstable models in the propositional case. Therefore, let us discuss how non-ground programs fit into this scenario. Given a set of non-ground rules P, we write $\mathrm{Gnd}(P)$ for the resulting ground program produced by a grounder such as Gringo in the Clingo system. Since $\mathrm{Gnd}(P)$ depends on the grounder, we leave its exact definition open and assume that the semantics of a non-ground program P is determined by $\mathrm{SM}(\mathrm{Gnd}(P))$ where $\mathrm{Gnd}(P)$ is understood as a propositional program. The signature of $\mathrm{Gnd}(P)$ is also determined during the grounding phase, based on directives supplied by the programmer. Thus, for a non-ground main program P and each non-ground oracle P_i with $1 \leq i \leq n$, we effectively obtain the ground module $\Pi = \langle \mathrm{Gnd}(P), I, O, H \rangle$ and the ground oracle modules $\Pi_i = \langle \mathrm{Gnd}(P_i), I_i, \emptyset, H_i \rangle$ where $1 \leq i \leq n$. Then, stable-unstable models can be computed using the translation $\mathrm{Tr}_{\mathrm{ST\text{-}UNST}}(\Pi, \Pi_1, \ldots, \Pi_n)$ in (7).

7   Implementation and Practical Modeling

In what follows, we describe how our method for computing stable-unstable semantics can be realized in practice using tools available in the ASPTOOLS collection and Clasp as the the back-end solver. Finally, we illustrate practical modeling in terms of an application problem that is challenging to formalize if the goal is to represent the entire problem as a single DLP in Sect. 7.1. The performance of Clingo on the resulting stable-unstable encoding of the problem is screened in Sect. 7.2. Reflecting Definition 9, our implementation involves the following three steps for the *ground* modules Π and $\Pi_1, \ldots, \Pi_n$:

1. translating each oracle module Π_i into SAT, i.e., the SAT module $\mathrm{Tr}_{\mathrm{SAT}}(\Pi_i)$,
2. translating each $\mathrm{Tr}_{\mathrm{SAT}}(\Pi_i)$ into a DLP module $\mathrm{Tr}_{\mathrm{UNSAT}}(\mathrm{Tr}_{\mathrm{SAT}}(\Pi_i))$, and
3. linking the parts of the translation (7) together.

Translating Oracles into SAT. The translation of oracles is based on translators in the LP2SAT family. These translators implement the more compact transformation described in [17], the one described in Sect. 4 is compatible up to forming the completion of the program. In addition, we deploy other tools in order to extend the applicability of our approach somewhat beyond the class of NLPs. In general, it is recommended to use a tool pipeline similar to those used in the latest ASP competitions. Brief descriptions of the tools follow. (i) Remove invisible facts produced by the grounder using LPSTRIP. (ii) Make the symbol table of the program contiguous with LPCAT as described below. (iii) Unwind *head-cycle-free* (HCF) disjunctions by *shifting* [8] as implemented by LPSHIFT. (iv) Translate away aggregates [32] using LP2NORMAL2 [5]. (v) Instrument SCCs with additional rules that guarantee the acyclicity of support within components [12] by calling LP2ACYC. (vi) Produce the respective CNF using LP2SAT and its command-line option -b for a translation in line with [17].

Saturation Transformation. The compiler for the saturation transformation, called UNSAT2LP, is available in the ASPTOOLS collection [21]. The input of the compiler consists of a DIMACS file extended by the definitions of symbols in comments. The translators described in the preceding step produce these definitions automatically and they are crucial information for the linking phase. The compiler UNSAT2LP is directly based on Definition 8. The output is a DLP in the SMODELS format [18], supported by Clingo for backward compatibility.

Linking. Definition 6 provides the specification for a link editor called LPCAT [20]. Given ground program modules $\Pi_1, \ldots, \Pi_n$ as input, assuming that the join $\Pi_1 \sqcup \ldots \sqcup \Pi_n$ is defined, the tool can be used to safely compute their composition. In the output, every atom will have a unique number (i.e., index in the atom table) and atoms are numbered from 1 to n where n gives the number of atoms in the program. The stable models of the resulting ground program are then governed by (5) and they can be computed by invoking Clasp. Other disjunctive solvers can be potentially used, if the final ground program is translated back into symbolic form (e.g., using the program listing tool LPLIST from the ASPTOOLS collection) and parsed again.

7.1 Practical Modeling

Having described the steps of translation involved in our implementation, let us introduce one concrete encoding to demonstrate the use of tools in practice. In the sequel, we use the problem *point of no return* [2] for illustration. The problem was specifically designed to reside on the second level of PH and it requires the representation of an oracle which is non-trivial to encode via saturation directly, due to interlinked reachability and satisfiability conditions. Below we recall the problem, but by using clauses rather than formulas as labels for a digraph.

Definition 10 (Point of No Return). *Given a digraph $G = \langle N, A \rangle$ where $A \subseteq N^2$, a start node $s \in N$, and a labeling function $cl(\cdot)$ that maps each arc $\langle n_1, n_2 \rangle \in A$ to a clause $cl(n_1, n_2)$, a point of no return is a node $n \in N$ so that*

Listing 1. Point of no return: a minimal instance

```
% Assign clauses to arcs        % Arcs
lit(1,2,a).      lit(1,2,b).    % 1 ==   a|b   ==> 2
lit(2,3,n(a)).   lit(2,3,n(b)). % 2 ==  -a|-b  ==> 3
lit(3,4,a).      lit(3,4,n(b)). % 3 ==   a|-b  ==> 4
lit(3,1,n(a)).   lit(3,1,c).    % 3 ==  -a|c   ==> 1
lit(4,1,n(a)).   lit(4,1,b).    % 4 ==  -a|b   ==> 1
```

Listing 2. Point of no return: domain declarations

```
% Identify atoms and literals
literal(L)    :- lit(_,_,L).
negative(n(A)) :- literal(n(A)).
atom(L)  :- literal(L), not negative(L).

% Determine arcs, nodes, and the start node
arc(X,Y) :- lit(X,Y,_).
node(X)  :- arc(X,_).        node(Y)  :- arc(_,Y).
start(N) :- node(N), N2 >= N: node(N2).
```

1. *there is a directed path* $s = n_1, n_2, ..., n_k = n$ *in* G,
2. *the set of clauses* $S(s,n) = \{cl(n_1, n_2), ..., cl(n_{k-1}, n_k)\}$ *is satisfiable, and*
3. *there is* **no** *directed return path* $n = m_1, m_2, ..., m_l = s$ *in* G *such that the set of clauses* $S(s,n) \cup \{cl(m_1, m_2), ..., cl(m_{l-1}, m_l)\}$ *is satisfiable.*

Our ASP encoding of this problem is given as four Clingo code snippets: (i) an example of a problem instance, (ii) some joint domain definitions, (iii) the main program, and (iv) the oracle. In Listing 1, we describe a minimal problem instance using a predicate lit/3 which associates for an arc $\langle n_1, n_2 \rangle$ one literal l involved in the labeling clause $cl(n_1, n_2)$ at a time. The function symbol n/1 is used to express negative literals. Assuming that 1 is the start node, then the node 4 is a point of no return: the set of clauses $\{a \vee b, \neg a \vee \neg b, a \vee \neg b\}$ is satisfiable while adding the final clause $\neg a \vee b$ will make it necessarily unsatisfiable. The other nodes are not points of no return due to the short-cutting arc from 3 to 1 enforcing the clause $\neg a \vee c$. The rules in Listing 2 define some joint domains involved in the problem. The names of predicates literal/1, atom/1, arc/2, and node/1 should be self-explanatory in this respect. Moreover, the predicate start/1 picks the smallest node as the start node for the whole input graph.

The main program, as given by Listing 3, deploys *choice rules* [32] with *bounds on cardinality* for the sake of conciseness. The path/2 predicate captures the path from the start node to a node acting as a candidate point of no return and eventually pointed out by predicate ponr/1. The recursive selection of the path is guided by the predicate reach/1 formalizing reachability from the start node along the path. Finally, predicate true/1 chooses a subset of atoms to be

Listing 3. Point of no return: main program

```
% Choose path and the point of no return
{ path(X,Y): arc(X,Y), not start(Y) } = 1 :- start(X).
{ path(X,Y): arc(X,Y), not start(Y) } <= 1 :- reach(X).

% The point of no return is the final node reached
reach(Y) :- path(X,Y).
ponr(X) :- reach(X), not path(X,Y): arc(X,Y).
:- not ponr(X): node(X).

% Check satisfiability along the chosen path
{ true(A) } :- atom(A).
true(n(A)) :- negative(n(A)), not true(A).
:- arc(X,Y), path(X,Y), not true(L): lit(X,Y,L).
```

true and the satisfaction of the clauses along the chosen path is enforced by the constraint in the end. The encoding for the required oracle is quite similar as can be seen from Listing 4. At first, the input predicates are declared using choice rules. Only them are made visible for translators. The choice of return path is analogous but formalized *backwards* from the start node toward the anticipated point of no return. The predicate reach/1 can be reused here since it will not be visible to the main program. The final satisfiability check is quite the same except that the clauses along both chosen paths ought to be satisfied. Assuming that the portions of code from Listings 1–4 are stored in files literals.lp, graph.lp, main.lp, and oracle.lp, respectively, we may invoke the following shell commands to solve the problem with Gringo and Clasp:

```
$ gringo --output smodels literals.lp graph.lp main.lp > main.sm
$ gringo --output smodels literals.lp graph.lp oracle.lp \
   | lp2normal2 | lp2acyc | lp2sat -b | unsat2lp > oracle.sm
$ lpcat main.sm oracle.sm | clasp
```

For backward compatibility, we use Gringo's option --output smodels. Notice how the instance and domain declarations are used when grounding the main program and the oracle in separation. Finally, they are linked together with LPCAT and fed as input for Clasp which accepts Smodels format as such.

7.2 Performance Analysis

To get an idea of the performance of our approach to implementing stable-unstable semantics, we carried out some preliminary experiments using the encodings from Listings 1–4. We used Gringo (v. 5.2.2) as the grounder and Clasp (v. 3.3.4) as the solver. All runs were executed on an Intel(R) Core i7-8750H CPU with a 2.20 GHz clock rate under Linux operating system.

Listing 4. Point of no return: oracle

```
% Input
{ path(X,Y) } :- arc(X,Y), not start(Y).
{ ponr(X) } :- node(X), not start(X).
#show path/2.
#show ponr/1.

% Choose return path
{ return(X,Y): arc(X,Y), not start(X) } = 1 :- reach(Y).
:- return(X,Y), path(X,Y).

% Check that the point of no return is reached
reach(X) :- start(X).
reach(X) :- return(X,Y), not ponr(X).
:- ponr(X), not return(X,Y): arc(X,Y).

% Check satisfiability along both paths
{ true(A) } :- atom(A).
true(n(A)) :- negative(n(A)), not true(A).
:- arc(X,Y), path(X,Y), not true(L): lit(X,Y,L).
:- arc(X,Y), return(X,Y), not true(L): lit(X,Y,L).
```

Since the existence of Hamiltonian paths in planar graphs has been previously investigated, we decided to generate such graphs using the PLANAR tool from the ASPTOOLS collection. The tool outputs a random planar graph with a given number of nodes. The graphs are directed and symmetric, i.e., arcs are provided in both directions. First, we check the performance of Clasp on unsatisfiable instances obtained from planar graphs with $n = 9 \ldots 18$ nodes and roughly from 40 to 85 arcs. By mapping arcs to a fixed atom a, all paths are consistent and no points of no return are feasible. The runtimes vary from 0.70 s to 16 000 s and the growth is clearly exponential in n that we verified using a logarithmic plot.

Based on the preliminary screening, we pick $n = 15$, for which a runtime of 390 s is initially obtained, for further study. Next, we map the arcs of the planar graphs to random literals based on v different atoms. Both the atom and its polarity are selected uniformly. As a result, arcs labeled with opposite literals become mutually exclusive. On the one hand, this is a significant source of complexity (see [22] for an analogous restriction) but, on the other hand, makes points of no return existent. When the number of atoms v is increased, the resulting instances are expected to become more demanding. To see the effect, we generate ten instances for each $v = 1 \ldots 40$. The runtime behavior is illustrated by the graph in Fig. 1 (left). The number of unsatisfiable instances starts to grow from $v = 31$, i.e., roughly 45% of the number of arcs when $n = 15$, and therefore, runtimes approach and settle around 400 s as observed for unsatisfiable instances earlier. Next, we select $v = n$ as the criterion for our final experiment and let n vary from 5 to 40 nodes. The runtimes are illustrated by the graph in Fig. 1 (right). By the logarithmic scale, runtimes tend to grow exponentially in n. The resulting instances are mostly satisfiable except for small values for n when finding a (satisfiable) path may become an obstacle (cf. Definition 10).

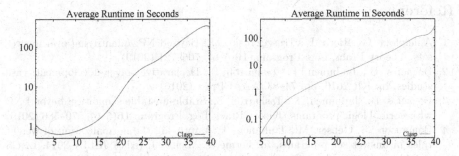

Fig. 1. Point of no return: runtime scaling for instances based on planar graphs

8   Discussion and Conclusion

In this work, we propose an alternative way to implement stable-unstable semantics of (normal) logic programs. In contrast with related approaches based on meta-programming [10, 13] and translations toward QBFs [2, 11], we encode oracles as stand-alone (effectively normal) programs, ground and translate them separately, and finally link them with the ground main program for solving. This makes our approach highly modular and enables the separation of concerns in case of multiple oracles, thus generalizing stable-unstable semantics in the first place. We anticipate that the saturation step is less error-prone when outsourced for a translator, relieving the programmer from a potentially intricate task and enabling the testing of oracles in separation. Moreover, in contrast with [1, 11] our approach counts on implicit quantification as put forth in original stable-unstable semantics. When modeling with stable-unstable semantics, we essentially seek solutions to problems whose particular subproblems have no solutions. Finally, our preliminary performance analysis suggests that computing points of no return will provide a challenging benchmark for answer set solvers.

As regards future work, we note that it is possible to change the translation $\mathrm{Tr_{SAT}}(P)$ from NLPs to SAT very easily, e.g., for improving performance. Although our approach enables more comprehensive modeling based on stable-unstable semantics, we still call for native implementations that support stable-unstable semantics directly rather than through the stable semantics of DLPs. Such implementations are expected to mimic the design of GnT [23] with interacting solvers, but use conflict-driven nogood learning (CDNL) [14] instead of traditional branch-and-bound search. Moreover, if solvers are integrated with each other recursively, following the original idea of *combined programs* from [3], the levels beyond the second one in polynomial hierarchy can also be covered.

Acknowledgments. The author wishes to thank the anonymous referees for comments and suggestions for improvement. The author has been partially supported by the Academy of Finland projects ETAIROS (327352) and AI-ROT (335718).

References

1. Amendola, G., Ricca, F., Truszczynski, M.: Beyond NP: quantifying over answer sets. Theory Pract. Log. Program. **19**(5–6), 705–721 (2019)
2. Bogaerts, B., Janhunen, T., Tasharrofi, S.: Declarative solver development: case studies. In: KR 2016, pp. 74–83. AAAI Press (2016)
3. Bogaerts, B., Janhunen, T., Tasharrofi, S.: Stable-unstable semantics: beyond NP with normal logic programs. Theory Pract. Log. Program. **16**(5–6), 570–586 (2016)
4. Bomanson, J., Gebser, M., Janhunen, T.: Improving the normalization of weight rules in answer set programs. In: Fermé, E., Leite, J. (eds.) JELIA 2014. LNCS (LNAI), vol. 8761, pp. 166–180. Springer, Cham (2014). https://doi.org/10.1007/978-3-319-11558-0_12
5. Bomanson, J., Janhunen, T., Niemelä, I.: Applying visible strong equivalence in answer-set program transformations. ACM Trans. Comput. Log. **21**(4), 33:1–33:41 (2020)
6. Brewka, G., Eiter, T., Truszczynski, M.: Answer set programming at a glance. Commun. ACM **54**(12), 92–103 (2011)
7. Clark, K.: Negation as failure. In: Logic and Data Bases, pp. 293–322. Plenum Press (1978)
8. Dix, J., Gottlob, G., Marek, V.W.: Reducing disjunctive to non-disjunctive semantics by shift-operations. Fundam. Informaticae **28**(1–2), 87–100 (1996)
9. Eiter, T., Gottlob, G.: On the computational cost of disjunctive logic programming: propositional case. Ann. Math. Artif. Intell. **15**(3–4), 289–323 (1995). https://doi.org/10.1007/BF01536399
10. Eiter, T., Polleres, A.: Towards automated integration of guess and check programs in answer set programming: a meta-interpreter and applications. Theory Pract. Log. Program. **6**(1–2), 23–60 (2006)
11. Fandinno, J., Laferrière, F., Romero, J., Schaub, T., Son, T.C.: Planning with incomplete information in quantified answer set programming. Theory Pract. Log. Program. **21**(5), 663–679 (2021)
12. Gebser, M., Janhunen, T., Rintanen, J.: Answer set programming as SAT modulo acyclicity. In: Proceedings of ECAI 2014, pp. 351–356. IOS Press (2014)
13. Gebser, M., Kaminski, R., Schaub, T.: Complex optimization in answer set programming. Theory Pract. Log. Program. **11**(4–5), 821–839 (2011)
14. Gebser, M., Kaufmann, B., Schaub, T.: Conflict-driven answer set solving: from theory to practice. Artif. Intell. **187**, 52–89 (2012)
15. Gelfond, M., Lifschitz, V.: The stable model semantics for logic programming. In: Proceedings of ICLP, pp. 1070–1080. MIT Press (1988)
16. Gelfond, M., Lifschitz, V.: Classical negation in logic programs and disjunctive databases. New Gener. Comput. **9**(3/4), 365–386 (1991). https://doi.org/10.1007/BF03037169
17. Janhunen, T.: Some (in)translatability results for normal logic programs and propositional theories. J. Appl. Non Class. Log. **16**(1–2), 35–86 (2006)

18. Janhunen, T.: Intermediate languages of ASP systems and tools. In: Proceedings of SEA 2007, The 1st International Workshop on Software Engineering for Answer Set Programming, pp. 12–25. University of Bath, Department of Computer Science, Report CSBU-2007-05 (2007)

19. Janhunen, T.: Modular equivalence in general. In: Proceedings of ECAI 2008, pp. 75–79 (2008)

20. Janhunen, T.: Modular construction of ground logic programs using LPCAT. In: The 3rd International Workshop on Logic and Search (LaSh 2010) (2010)

21. Janhunen, T.: Cross-translating answer set programs using the ASPTOOLS collection. Künstliche Intell. **32**(2–3), 183–184 (2018). https://doi.org/10.1007/s13218-018-0529-9

22. Janhunen, T., Niemelä, I.: The answer set programming paradigm. AI Mag. **37**(3), 13–24 (2016)

23. Janhunen, T., Niemelä, I., Seipel, D., Simons, P., You, J.: Unfolding partiality and disjunctions in stable model semantics. ACM Trans. Comput. Log. **7**(1), 1–37 (2006)

24. Janhunen, T., Oikarinen, E., Tompits, H., Woltran, S.: Modularity aspects of disjunctive stable models. J. Artif. Intell. Res. **35**, 813–857 (2009)

25. Lierler, Y., Truszczynski, M.: On abstract modular inference systems and solvers. Artif. Intell. **236**, 65–89 (2016)

26. Lifschitz, V., Razborov, A.: Why are there so many loop formulas? ACM Trans. Comput. Log. **7**(2), 261–268 (2006)

27. Lin, F., Zhao, J.: On tight logic programs and yet another translation from normal logic programs to propositional logic. In: Proceedings of IJCAI 2003, pp. 853–858 (2003)

28. Lin, F., Zhao, Y.: ASSAT: computing answer sets of a logic program by SAT solvers. In: Proceedings of AAAI 2002, pp. 112–118 (2002)

29. Lin, F., Zhao, Y.: ASSAT: computing answer sets of a logic program by SAT solvers. Artif. Intell. **157**(1–2), 115–137 (2004)

30. Marek, V., Truszczyński, M.: Autoepistemic logic. J. ACM **38**(3), 588–619 (1991)

31. Oikarinen, E., Janhunen, T.: A translation-based approach to the verification of modular equivalence. J. Log. Comput. **19**(4), 591–613 (2009)

32. Simons, P., Niemelä, I., Soininen, T.: Extending and implementing the stable model semantics. Artif. Intell. **138**(1–2), 181–234 (2002)

33. Tseitin, G.: On the complexity of derivation in the propositional calculus. Zapiski Nauchnykh Seminarov LOMI **8**, 234–259 (1968)

Smart Devices and Large Scale Reasoning via ASP: Tools and Applications

Kristian Reale[1,2]([✉]) [iD], Francesco Calimeri[1,2] [iD], Nicola Leone[1] [iD], and Francesco Ricca[1] [iD]

[1] Department of Mathematics and Computer Science,
University of Calabria, Rende, Italy
{reale,calimeri,leone,ricca}@mat.unical.it
[2] DLVSystem L.T.D., Via della Resistenza 19/C, Rende, Italy
{reale,calimeri}@dlvsystem.com

Abstract. In the last few years, we have been witnessing the spread of computing devices getting smaller and smaller (e.g., Smartphones, Smart Devices, Raspberry, etc.), and the production and availability of data getting bigger and bigger. In this work we introduce DLV Large Scale (DLV-LS), a framework based on Answer Set Programming (ASP) for performing declarative-based reasoning tasks over data-intensive applications, possibly on Smart Devices. The framework encompasses DLV Mobile Edition (DLV-ME), an ASP based solver for Android systems and Raspberry devices, and DLV Enterprise Edition (DLV-EE), an ASP-based platform, accessible by REST interfaces, for large-scale reasoning over Big Data, classical relational database systems, and NoSQL databases. DLV-LS enables Smart Devices to both locally perform reasoning over data generated by their own sensors and properly interact with DLV-EE when more computational power is needed for harder tasks, possibly over bigger centralized data. We present also a real-world application of DLV-LS; the use case consists of a tourist navigator that calculates the best routes and optimizes a tour of a tourist under custom-defined time constraints.

Keywords: Answer set programming · Large scale reasoning · Smart devices

1 Introduction

Answer Set Programming (ASP) [9,10,21] is an expressive [15] logic programming paradigm proposed in the area of non-monotonic reasoning that allows one to specify a complex computational problem in a fully declarative fashion. With ASP, a problem is encoded into a rule-based logic program whose intended models, called answer sets, correspond one-to-one to solutions; solutions can be actually computed by using ASP solvers, often called ASP systems [5,12,20,24]. The intrinsic declarative nature of ASP, coupled with its

This paper is partially supported by the DLVSystem organization.

J. Cheney and S. Perri (Eds.): PADL 2022, LNCS 13165, pp. 154–161, 2022.
https://doi.org/10.1007/978-3-030-94479-7_10

high expressive power fostered the development of supporting systems within the scientific community over the years; in turn, the availability of robust and reliable systems encouraged the development of a significant number of applications, both in academia and in industry, in several contexts and scenarios (e.g., Artificial Intelligence, Information Integration, Knowledge Management, Healthcare, Workforce Management, Diagnosis, Workflows, Optimization, and more) [2–4,8,14,17,18,25,28]. With the growth of the use of ASP in industry, also effective development tools have been introduced, capable of supporting programmers, knowledge engineers and organizations in managing complex projects in real-world domains [11,13,19,22,27]. Nevertheless, practical applications scenarios have been constantly evolving; in the latest years, we observed the availability of computing devices that are getting smaller and smaller along with the production and availability of heterogeneous data that are getting bigger and bigger.

In this paper, we present a novel advanced platform for the development of ASP-based applications in scalable data-intensive and mobile architectures, called *DLV Large Scale* (DLV-LS). The platform heavily relies on DLV [5,24], one of the most widespread ASP systems in industry, that has been engineered by the *DLVSystem* company and extended to obtain both an Enterprise server version of DLV, called *DLV Enterprise Edition* (DLV-EE), and a (light) version for mobile devices, called *DLV Mobile Edition* (DLV-ME). For the DLV-EE system, the existing functionalities of DLV were extended in order to optimize the evaluation techniques of ASP programs in a data-intensive environment and, moreover, the system was made capable to inter-operate with both relational DBMS and NoSQL technologies. DLV-EE provides also a service interface, based to the REST philosophy, allowing client environments (classic programs and/or Mobile Apps) to interact with DLV-EE. On the other hand, DLV-ME is a system for devices with low computational power and compatible with "mobile" technologies (Android based Smartphones and Raspberry). In such a way, Smart Devices are enabled to perform local reasoning over, for example, data provided by their own sensors, and, for more complex reasoning tasks requiring also a large amount of data that are generally available to clouds (think for example to Social Network data), the devices can delegate the reasoning to the DLV-EE by exploiting the REST services interface. The resulting DLV-LS system was also equipped by an Integrated Development Environment (IDE) consisting on the extension of the most comprehensive IDE for ASP called *ASPIDE* [19], a system that supports the entire life-cycle of ASP development, from program editing to application deployment, combining a cutting-edge editing tool with a collection of user-friendly graphical tools for program composition, debugging, testing, profiling, DBMS access, solver execution configuration and output-handling. Our extension of *ASPIDE* allows programmers to easy develop ASP solutions for both DLV-ME and DLV-EE systems.

In the following, we first introduce DLV-LS, by illustrating the System Architecture and providing the reader with a brief overview of the IDE; then, we present a practical use case application, that consists of a tourist navigator that computes the best routes and optimizes a tour of a tourist under custom-defined time constraints; eventually, we draw our conclusions.

2   The DLV-LS System

DLV-LS consists of different modules that work together for making the development of effective ASP based data-intensive solutions possible; in such scenarios, where different features need to be accessed and integrated, Integrated Development Environment (IDE) for DLV-LS is crucial. In this Section we describe the System Architecture of both DLV-LS and the corresponding IDE.

Architecture Description. The DLV-LS system consists of two components. The first component, named DLV-ME, is the mobile version of DLV that works on *Android* and *Raspberry* systems (Smart Devices). The second component, named DLV-EE, emerges from the integration of different versions of DLV exploiting all most recent and advanced features, and, moreover, interact with Big Data systems and external database systems (both relational and *NoSQL*).

The DLV-ME systems for *Android* and *Raspberry* can natively execute logic programs as long as the input is small and the complexity of the logic programs is not high. In particular, since the basic ASP language is able to express all problems belonging to the complexity classes Σ_2^p and Π_2^p, it is important to check which complexity (at most) the ASP programs should have in order to be executed to the devices. In such a way, to decide if a given reasoning task can be carried out on a smart device, we performed some experimental analysis in order to empirically set a "threshold"; in particular, we selected a set of ASP programs solving well-known problems belonging to the complexity classes P and NP, and we executed them on the smart devices by gradually increasing both the complexity of the programs and the input size. As a consequence, when the system needs to take advantage of greater computing power, DLV-EE Framework can be invoked using the REST services made available by the introduction of a REST Endpoint. In such a way, besides DLV-ME systems, also any other system that wants to use DLV-EE can do it my making REST invocations.

The Fig. 1a illustrates the DLV-LS architecture. In particular, on the top of the Figure we have DLV-ME for *Android* and *Raspberry* devices. They can, for example, read input data from their device sensors and execute a local ASP program for "stand alone" reasoning: consider for example the case of an Android ASP based navigator which can recalculate a path locally, or a *Raspberry* placed on a road that can make local reasoning for traffic control. In the case where the complexity of the local ASP program is too high or the input data is too big, the system can interact with DLV-EE by exploiting the REST interface in order to delegate more complex reasoning tasks. On the bottom of the Figure we have the architecture of DLV-EE. In particular, the Engine component is composed by following modules:

– a module for performing distributed reasoning over Big Data systems; in particular, DLV performs reasoning tasks using the *Apache Hadoop* system [6];

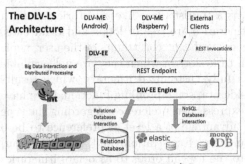
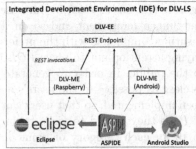

(a) Architecture of DLV-LS

(b) Integrated Development
Environments for DLV-LS.

Fig. 1. DLV-LS architecture and the integrated development environments for DLV-LS.

note that, in order to exploit the system, DLV uses the Hadoop middleware *Apache Hive* [7] that allows for managing Hadoop datasets using SQL, facilitating, in such a way, the mapping with datasets and ASP predicates;
- a module for performing reasoning tasks on Relational Database systems;
- a module for performing reasoning tasks on *NoSQL* database systems, using, in our case, the *Elasticsearch* [16] and *MongoDB* [26] systems.

Integrated Development Environments for DLV-LS. In order to develop DLV-LS based solutions, our idea consisted of making a synergy of multiple Integrated Development Environments (IDEs) suitably adapted for our purpose (see Fig. 1b).

In particular, for the development of DLV-ME based solutions for *Android*, we implemented a synergy between the *ASPIDE* environment (for the definition of logic programs) [19] and the *Android Studio* environment [23] (for the development of software solutions based on *Android*). On the other hand, for the development of DLV-ME based solutions for *Raspberry*, we implemented a synergy between the Eclipse environment (for implementing *Raspberry* solutions) and the *ASPIDE* environment (for the definition of ASP programs).

Finally, for the development of solutions that directly exploit DLV-EE, on the one hand it is possible to develop software tools that make use of DLV-EE by accessing the REST services directly, on the another we extended the *ASPIDE* environment in order to exploit the REST services for developing ASP programs that make use of DLV-EE.

3   A Use Case Application of DLV-LS

DLVNavigator is a web service that can automatically generate scheduled tourist itineraries. In particular, the system provides the user with a planned itinerary with information regarding the location and the visiting time of the points of interest (*POIs*). A *POI*, in our case, is a tourist place like a historic square, a museum, a monument and so on. Itineraries are free of loops and dead ends, ensuring compliance with the preferences and time constraints of the user, while paying attention not to place *POIs* in time slots in which they are not available to the public. In order to generate a fully customized itinerary, which results as close as possible to the users's desiderata, some profiling functionalities have been implemented, so that users can express their preferences regarding the type of *POIs* they intend to visit, taking advantage of a level of preference to be 0 to 10 for each category of point of interest. Registration (and authentication) functions have been made available to the user in order to associate itineraries and profiles to a specific user account. The web service can be easily accessible from multiple clients (browsers and smartphones included) exploiting a *RESTful* architecture that exposes *APIs* capable of providing all the services described above.

Finally, an Android App was created for allowing the user to exploit the services in order to generate scheduled tourist itineraries. For the generation of scheduled tourist itinerary (we call it a *tour*), a proper ASP program has been implemented to be executed by exploiting DLV-EE. The ASP program is composed by two layers; we report next some details. The first layer basically consists of the following rules:

```
1. n(1..14).
2. n_category(C,N) :- category(C), #count{ID: poi(ID,_,_,_,_,_,_,
   C,_,_)} = N.
3. {n_chosen_category(C, N) : n(N), N <= X, n_category(C, X)} = 1
   :- category(C).
4. node(ID,C,DT) :- start(ID), poi(ID,_,_,_,_,DT,_,C,_,_).
5. node(ID,C,DT) :- poi(ID,_,_,_,_,DT,_,C,_,P),
   n_chosen_category(C,N).
6. :~ category(CODE), #count{ID: node(ID,CODE,_)} = X,
   partition(CODE,Y), X < Y, Z = Y - X. [Z@2]
7. :~ poi(ID,_,_,_,_,DT,_,C,_,P), node(ID,C,DT). [P@1]
```

The facts in Rule 1 specify how many *POIs* a user can visit in a tour, at most. Rule 2 defines the extension of predicate *n_category*, collecting the number of existing *POIs* for each category. Choice Rule 3 guesses, for each category, a number of *POIs* to visit that does not exceed a given maximum (specified by Rule 1). Predicate *node* is the output predicate that collects the candidate *POIs* of the final tour. A starting *POI* is specified in input and will be part of the tour (see Rule 4); subsequent *POIs* will be chosen by considering the same choosen category (see Rule 5). The first Weak Constraint (Rule 6) ensures that the chosen nodes respects, as much as possible, the user preference summarized by predicate *partition*, where the first attribute represents a category and the second attribute is a preference value containing the number of nodes that a user would like to visit for that category. In such a way, the Weak Constraint states that the number of nodes of the tour, preferably, should match the value of the partition. The second Weak Constraint (Rule 7), specify to minimize, with lower priority, the cost for visiting the *POIs*.

The second layer consists of following ASP rules:

```
1. slot(X,IN,OUT) :- start(X), node(X,_,DT), poi(X,IN,_,_,
   _,_,_,_,_,_), OUT=IN+DT, budget(B), OUT<B.
2. slot(Y,IN,OUT) :- slot(X,_,OUTP), inPath(X,Y,TT,_),
   node(Y,_,DT), budget(B), IN=OUTP+TT, OUT=IN+DT, OUT<B.
```

The answers sets of this program represent the final tour for the user via predicate *slot*. The attributes of the predicate represent, respectively, the place (node) to visit, the entry time and the exit time. Rule 1 states that, for a given node of the candidate *POIs*, get the entry time and the exit time of the place being careful to not exceed the temporal budget of the user. Rule 2 is a recursive rule that builds the tour by considering subsequent entry/exit time and the available time budget. The predicate *inPath* of the rule is determined using a variant of the well known *Hamiltonian Path problem* ASP encoding [1], that, in our case, is used to minimize the distance between single locations.

We briefly describe next the usage of the Android app that exploits, using REST invocations, *DLVNavigator* for the generation of a tour for the specific user; some screenshots that ease the presentation of the mobile app can be found at https://www.mat.unical.it/ricca/aspide/dlvls. The main section of the app consists of a Map with the current user position; the user can easily edit her preferences and setting her degree of interest for each available *POI*. Upon the request for a new tour, the user is asked to choose *time duration, budget* and *mode (on foot, by car)*. *DLVNavigator* is invoked in order to plan the tour, and the result is displayed: the list of suggested *POIs* with estimated duration, check-in/out times and estimated cost is reported. The user can reject the proposal and ask for a new one; once she is satisfied, she can start the tour: the app will then show the Map displaying the individual *POIs* featured by the accepted tour and the current position of the user. When the user physically reaches a *POI*, a countdown is started reporting the remaining suggested allotted time for the current place, along with the remaining time to finish the entire tour. Textual pieces of information can be displayed, namely: distance from the user, minimum stop time, maximum and recommended stop and check-in/check-out times recorded by the movements on the map. If the stop at a *POI* lasts longer than expected, the system proposes a rescheduling of the tour taking into account the remaining time and user preferences.

4   Conclusion

In this paper we presented DLV-LS, an ASP-based Framework for performing declarative-based reasoning tasks over data-intensive applications. The Framework exploits DLV-ME for local reasoning over Smart Devices, and DLV-EE for more complex reasoning tasks over Big Data, classical relational database systems, and NoSQL databases. Moreover, an Integrated Development Environment for DLV-LS was proposed thus equipping the Framework with an Environment for developing ASP-based data-intensive applications. The entire system can be downloaded from https://www.mat.unical.it/ricca/aspide/dlvls.

The use case herein reported is just a simple (yet real) application of our Framework; more complex usages can be defined thanks to the possibility of performing reasoning tasks over smart devices, that are generally connected to internet: in such a way, distributed reasoning can also be implemented, for instance in the Smart Cities context. Just as example, a traffic-control application relying on a series of Raspberries is currently under consideration.

As far as future work is concerned, we plan to extend both the DLV-LS system and the IDE, to deal with more data sources, both relational and NoSQL, and to further improve performance in data-intensive contexts.

Acknowledgments. This work has been partially supported by : (i) POR CALABRIA FESR-FSE 2014–2020, project "DLV Large Scale: un sistema per applicazioni di Intelligenza Artificiale in architecture data-intensive e mobile", CUP J28C17000220006; (ii) PRIN PE6, Title: "Declarative Reasoning over Streams", funded by the Ital-ian Ministero dell'Universit'a, dell'Istruzione e della Ricerca (MIUR), CUP:H24I17000080001; (iii) PON-MISE MAP4ID, Title: "Multipurpose Analytics Platform 4 IndustrialData", funded by the Italian Ministero dello Sviluppo Economico (MISE), CUP: B21B19000650008; (iv) PON-MISE S2BDW, Title: "Smarter Solution in the Big Data World", funded by the Italian Ministero dello Sviluppo Economico (MISE), CUP: B28I17000250008.

References

1. HPP DLV encoding. https://asparagus.cs.uni-potsdam.de/encoding/show/id/3491
2. Abels, D., Jordi, J., Ostrowski, M., Schaub, T., Toletti, A., Wanko, P.: Train scheduling with hybrid answer set programming. CoRR abs/2003.08598 (2020). https://arxiv.org/abs/2003.08598
3. Abseher, M., Gebser, M., Musliu, N., Schaub, T., Woltran, S.: Shift design with answer set programming. Fundam. Inf. **147**, 1–25 (2016)
4. Adrian, W.T., et al.: The ASP system DLV: advancements and applications. KI - Künstl. Intell. **32**, 177–179 (2018). https://doi.org/10.1007/s13218-018-0533-0
5. Alviano, M., Calimeri, F., Dodaro, C., Fuscà, D., Leone, N., Perri, S., Ricca, F., Veltri, P., Zangari, J.: The asp system dlv2. In: Balduccini, M., Janhunen, T. (eds.) Logic Program. Nonmonotonic Reason., pp. 215–221. Springer International Publishing, Cham (2017)
6. Apache Software Foundation: Hadoop. https://hadoop.apache.org
7. Apache Software Foundation: Hive. https://hive.apache.org
8. Bobda, C., Yonga, F., Gebser, M., Ishebabi, H., Schaub, T.: High-level synthesis of on-chip multiprocessor architectures based on answer set programming. J. Parall. Distrib. Comput. **117**, 161–179 (2018)
9. Brewka, G., Eiter, T., Truszczyński, M.: Answer set programming at a glance. Commun. ACM **54**(12), 92–103 (2011)
10. Calimeri, F., et al.: Asp-core-2 input language format. Theor. Practice Logic Program. **20**(2), 294–309 (2020). https://doi.org/10.1017/S1471068419000450

11. Calimeri, F., Fuscà, D., Germano, S., Perri, S., Zangari, J.: Fostering the Use of Declarative Formalisms for Real-World Applications: The EmbASP Framework. New Generation Computing **37**(1), 29–65 (2018). https://doi.org/10.1007/s00354-018-0046-2

12. Calimeri, F., Gebser, M., Maratea, M., Ricca, F.: Design and results of the fifth answer set programming competition. Artif. Intell. **231**, 151–181 (2016)

13. Calimeri, F., Germano, S., Palermiti, E., Reale, K., Ricca, F.: Developing ASP programs with ASPIDE and *L* oIDE. KI - Künstl. Intell. **1**, 185–186 (2018). https://doi.org/10.1007/s13218-018-0534-z

14. De Bortoli, M., Steinbauer, G., Fabricius, F., Selmair, M., Reip, M., Gebser, M.: Towards asp-based scheduling for industrial transport vehicles. In: Joint Austrian Computer Vision and Robotics Workshop, pp. 34–41 (2020)

15. Eiter, T., Gottlob, G., Mannila, H.: Disjunctive datalog. ACM Trans. Database Syst. **22**(3), 364–418 (1997)

16. Elastic: Elasticsearch. https://www.elastic.co/elasticsearch/

17. Erdem, E., Gelfond, M., Leone, N.: Applications of answer set programming. AI Mag. **37**(3), 53–68 (2016)

18. Falkner, A.A., Friedrich, G., Schekotihin, K., Taupe, R., Teppan, E.C.: Industrial applications of answer set programming. KI - Künstl. Intell. **32**, 165–176 (2018)

19. Febbraro, O., Reale, K., Ricca, F.: Aspide: Integrated development environment for answer set programming. In: Delgrande, J.P., Faber, W. (eds.) Logic Programming and Nonmonotonic Reasoning, pp. 317–330. Springer, Berlin Heidelberg, Berlin, Heidelberg (2011)

20. Gebser, M., Kaminski, R., Kaufmann, B., Schaub, T.: Multi-shot ASP solving with clingo. CoRR abs/1705.09811 http://arxiv.org/abs/1705.09811 (2017)

21. Gelfond, M., Lifschitz, V.: Classical negation in logic programs and disjunctive databases. New Generation Computing 9, 365–385 (1991), http://www.cs.utexas.edu/users/ai-lab?gel91b

22. Germano, S., Calimeri, F., Palermiti, E.: Loide: a web-based IDE for logic programming - preliminary technical report. CoRR abs/1709.05341 http://arxiv.org/abs/1709.05341 (2017)

23. Google, JetBrains: Android studio, https://developer.android.com/studio

24. Leone, N., et al.: The dlv system for knowledge representation and reasoning. ACM Trans. Comput. Logic **7**(3), 499–562 (2006). https://doi.org/10.1145/1149114.1149117

25. Leone, N., Ricca, F.: Answer set programming: a tour from the basics to advanced development tools and industrial applications. In: Faber, W., Paschke, A. (eds.) Reasoning Web 2015. LNCS, vol. 9203, pp. 308–326. Springer, Cham (2015). https://doi.org/10.1007/978-3-319-21768-0_10

26. MongoDB: Mongodb. https://www.mongodb.com

27. Oetsch, J., Pührer, J., Tompits, H.: The sealion has landed: an IDE for answer-set programming–preliminary report. CoRR abs/1109.3989 http://arxiv.org/abs/1109.3989 (2011)

28. Ricca, F., et al.: Team-building with answer set programming in the Gioia-Tauro seaport. Comput. Res. Reposit - CORR **12**(3), 361–381 (2011). https://doi.org/10.1017/S147106841100007X

Declarative Solutions

Decomposition-Based Job-Shop Scheduling with Constrained Clustering

Mohammed M. S. El-Kholany[1,3] , Konstantin Schekotihin[1] ,
and Martin Gebser[1,2(✉)]

[1] Alpen-Adria-Universität Klagenfurt, Klagenfurt, Austria
{mohammed.el-kholany,konstantin.schekotihin,martin.gebser}@aau.at
[2] Technische Universität Graz, Graz, Austria
[3] Cairo University, Cairo, Egypt

Abstract. Scheduling is a crucial problem appearing in various domains,
such as manufacturing, transportation, or healthcare, where the goal is
to schedule given operations on available resources such that the operations are completed as soon as possible. Unfortunately, most scheduling problems cannot be solved efficiently, so that research on suitable
approximation methods is of primary importance. This work introduces a
novel approximation approach based on problem decomposition with data
mining methodologies. We propose a constrained clustering algorithm to
group operations into clusters, corresponding to time windows in which
the operations must be scheduled. The decomposition process consists of
two main phases. First, features are extracted, either from the problem
itself or from solutions obtained by heuristic methods, to predict the execution sequence of operations on each resource. The second phase deploys
our constrained clustering algorithm to assign each operation into a time
window. We then schedule the operations by time windows using Answer
Set Programming. Evaluation results show that our proposed approach
outperforms other heuristic schedulers in most cases, where incorporating features like *Remaining Processing Time*, *Machine Load*, and *Earliest
Starting Time* significantly improves the solution quality.

Keywords: Job-shop Scheduling Problem · Constrained clustering ·
Time windows · Answer Set Programming

1 Introduction

Scheduling is one of the most crucial problems in various industrial, transportation, or healthcare applications [10,12,24,30,32,34,43]. Such applications result
in different scheduling problem definitions, with the Job-shop Scheduling Problem (JSP) [38] being one if not the most well-known variant. In JSP, operations of

---

This work was partially funded by KWF project 28472, cms electronics GmbH, Fun-
derMax GmbH, Hirsch Armbänder GmbH, incubed IT GmbH, Infineon Technologies Austria AG, Isovolta AG, Kostwein Holding GmbH, and Privatstiftung Kärntner
Sparkasse.

J. Cheney and S. Perri (Eds.): PADL 2022, LNCS 13165, pp. 165–180, 2022.
https://doi.org/10.1007/978-3-030-94479-7_11

given jobs must be scheduled on available machines in an optimal way wrt. some predefined criteria. The latter include, for instance, minimization of makespan, i.e., the latest completion time of any job, or tardiness, i.e., the sum of delays over all jobs completed after their deadlines.

However, JSP is an NP-hard combinatorial optimization problem [20,37] for which no efficient algorithms are known. Therefore, searching for an optimal solution with state-of-the-art solvers for Answer Set Programming (ASP), Mixed Integer Programming, or Constraint Programming [3,11,16,28] often takes too much computation time, even for seemingly small instances. Practical applications instead necessitate solving JSP instances of large scale with thousands of operations [46]. As a result, much research work focuses on efficient methods for finding high-quality approximations of optimal schedules, including dispatching rules and other heuristic approaches [8] as well as stochastic optimization techniques [9,41]. The main issue of these approaches is that they require manual parametrization for a particular scheduling problem, which is tedious and error-prone. For instance, adapting heuristic methods might involve the development of new dispatching rules or specific combinations of existing ones. Similarly, merely utilizing default parameters for stochastic techniques might lead to mediocre schedules. In view of these challenges, recent research interest lies on the automatic parametrization of approximation methods using machine learning methodologies [7].

In this work, we introduce a method based on clustering to automatically decompose a JSP instance into several time windows that are small enough for optimization by an ASP solver. General clustering algorithms are unsupervised learning methods that partition a given set of objects into disjoint clusters, where each cluster comprises close objects wrt. some distance measure. In scheduling settings, however, clusters must satisfy additional constraints implied by the precedence relation between operations of a job. Standard constrained clustering algorithms are not readily applicable to scheduling scenarios either, as they are limited to disjointness constraints specifying objects that must not appear together in a cluster [14,42,45]. Therefore, our clustering method implements a novel type of constraints that *(i)* prevent the assignment of an operation to a cluster if its preceding operation is not yet assigned to the same or a previous cluster and *(ii)* ensure balancing between clusters according to the target number of operations per cluster. Further contributions of our work can be summarized as follows:

- Since a typical JSP instance describing jobs, their operations, and available machines does not provide sufficient information by itself for finding some promising decomposition by a clustering algorithm, we incorporate heuristic approaches like *First-In-First-Out* and *Machine Load* to extract features from their solutions.
- We implement the proposed constrained clustering algorithm and combine it with the forward selection of features, which is an automatic method for identifying a subset of features allowing the clustering method to compute decompositions resulting in best-quality schedules.

– The evaluation of our approach on Taillard's and Demirkol's benchmark instances [13,38] shows that it significantly outperforms baseline heuristic methods and pure ASP optimization wrt. the makespan optimization criterion within a short solving time limit of 10 min.

The rest of this paper is organized as follows. Section 2 introduces JSP along with a running example. In Sect. 3, we describe the feature extraction, including heuristic methods to obtain corresponding reference solutions. Section 4 presents our proposed constrained clustering algorithm. In Sect. 5, we empirically evaluate our approach and compare it to baseline heuristic methods as well as pure ASP optimization. Section 6 then surveys related work, followed by conclusions and future work in Sect. 7.

2   Job-Shop Scheduling Problem

The Job-shop Scheduling Problem (JSP) is one of the most well-known scheduling problems [4,27,38]. A JSP instance comprises a set $J = \{J_1, J_2, \ldots, J_n\}$ of jobs and a set $M = \{M_1, M_2, \ldots, M_m\}$ of machines. Each job J_i consists of a sequence $(O_{i,1}, O_{i,2}, \ldots, O_{i,m})$ of operations that must be processed in the given order. Each machine M_i executes one operation per job with a predefined, fixed processing time. Once the execution of an operation is started, it cannot be interrupted, and each machine can perform at most one operation at a time. The main objective of JSP solving algorithms is to find a schedule that minimizes optimization criteria, where we focus on the makespan, i.e., the latest completion time of any job.

Let us illustrate the problem on the small JSP instance specified in Table 1, which provides parameters for 3 jobs and 3 machines. The rows list operations along with their respective machines and processing times, e.g., the third operation of the first job, $O_{1,3}$, takes 5 time units for execution by machine 1. The minimum makespan happens to be 20, which matches the sum $9 + 6 + 5$ of processing times for the operations $O_{1,1}$, $O_{2,2}$, and $O_{3,3}$ executed by machine 2. While there are plenty, i.e., 234, optimal schedules with makespan 20, they agree on the execution orders $(O_{3,1}, O_{1,3}, O_{2,3})$ and $(O_{1,1}, O_{2,2}, O_{3,3})$ of operations processed by machine 1 or 2, respectively. The two feasible execution orders for machine 3 are $(O_{2,1}, O_{3,2}, O_{1,2})$ and $(O_{2,1}, O_{1,2}, O_{3,2})$. In both cases, the earliest eligible starting times for the operations $O_{1,1}$, $O_{1,2}$, and $O_{1,3}$ of job J_1 are 0, 9, and 12, as well as 0, 9, and 17 for $O_{2,1}$, $O_{2,2}$, and $O_{2,3}$ belonging to the job J_2. Regarding the operations of J_3, the earliest starting time for $O_{3,1}$ is 0, $O_{3,3}$ can only be started at time 15 because its machine 1 is occupied before, while either 4 or 12 is the earliest eligible starting time for $O_{3,2}$, depending on whether it is processed directly after completing $O_{3,1}$ (and $O_{2,1}$ on its machine 3) or waits for the completion of $O_{1,2}$ on machine 3. The latter option lets machine 3 idle unnecessarily and may seem less attractive, yet it does not stretch the resulting makespan beyond time 20.

Since JSP is NP-hard [20,37] and no efficient solving algorithms are known, even state-of-the-art optimization methods can often not find (near-)optimal solutions in reasonable time, already for instances with a seemingly small number of

Table 1. A sample JSP instance.

Operation	Machine	Processing time
$O_{1,1}$	2	9
$O_{1,2}$	3	3
$O_{1,3}$	1	5
$O_{2,1}$	3	4
$O_{2,2}$	2	6
$O_{2,3}$	1	2
$O_{3,1}$	1	4
$O_{3,2}$	3	3
$O_{3,3}$	2	5

Table 2. Possible decomposition.

Operation	Time Window
$O_{1,1}$	1
$O_{1,2}$	1
$O_{2,1}$	1
$O_{2,2}$	1
$O_{3,1}$	1
$O_{1,3}$	2
$O_{2,3}$	2
$O_{3,2}$	2
$O_{3,3}$	2

operations. As the number of operations in real-life applications can easily reach tens of thousands [46], approximation methods have attracted particular research interest. One such approach is decomposition into easier to optimize parts, which can be solved separately and whose partial solutions are eventually combined into a joint schedule for the entire problem instance. While various decomposition strategies have been proposed in the literature [31,36,40,44], none of them can provide solution quality guarantees or strictly dominates over heterogeneous JSP instances.

For our example in Table 1, there are 9 operations and 3 machines. Assume that we aim to split the operations into two parts to be scheduled separately such that the precedence between operations belonging to the same job is preserved. That is, we should not assign a successor operation to an earlier Time Window (TW) than its predecessor. Table 2 shows one feasible decomposition that we may like to generate. The operations $\{O_{1,1}, O_{1,2}, O_{2,1}, O_{2,2}, O_{3,1}\}$ are here assigned to TW 1, and the remaining operations to TW 2. Given this decomposition, a multi-shot optimization approach, as offered by ASP [21], can first optimize a schedule (wrt. the makespan) for the operations in TW 1, and then extend the first part by additionally scheduling the operations in TW 2 in an optimal way. However, considering that the operation $O_{3,2}$ belongs to TW 2 and should be executed later than $O_{1,2}$ of TW 1, the decomposition is incompatible with the execution order $(O_{2,1}, O_{3,2}, O_{1,2})$ for machine 3 and thus discards optimal schedules.

In this work, we introduce and deploy a constrained clustering algorithm to decompose JSP instances into time windows, where we extract some features from the problem itself and others from solutions obtained by heuristic methods. The features we consider for the decomposition process are explained in detail in the next section.

3   Feature Extraction

The application of machine learning methods to scheduling problems requires a careful selection of data describing the hidden dependencies between operations

Table 3. Features extracted from the sample problem instance in Table 1.

Operation	RPT	EST	ML	ST_FIFO	WT_FIFO
$O_{1,1}$	17	0	20	0	0
$O_{1,2}$	8	9	3	9	0
$O_{1,3}$	5	12	5	12	0
$O_{2,1}$	12	0	10	0	0
$O_{2,2}$	8	4	11	9	5
$O_{2,3}$	2	10	7	17	2
$O_{3,1}$	12	0	11	0	0
$O_{3,2}$	8	4	6	4	0
$O_{3,3}$	5	7	5	15	8

of different jobs [23, 29]. Clustering methods, which we intend to apply in our approach, are not an exception to this. That is, a clustering method requires an informative set of features characterizing the jobs, their operations, and machines of a problem instance to identify patterns resulting in a beneficial decomposition of the operations into time windows.

Methods suggested in the literature [2, 22, 23, 26, 29, 35] characterize instances of scheduling problems based on the following features: priority, processing time, remaining processing time, machine load, and sequence position. Most of these approaches convert the quantitative feature values into qualitative attributes in order to obtain generic dispatching rules that remain applicable to instances of different size. In this work, we propose a method that can be applied to feature values directly and does not require any problem-specific transformations. However, our clustering method for JSP instance decomposition requires all features to have numerical values, which permit the calculation of distance measures for estimating (dis)similarities between operations.

In detail, we consider the following features of jobs, operations, and machines:

Operation (OP) is the ordinal value for the position of an operation in its job.

Processing Time (PT) is the time for executing an operation on its machine. This feature is part of a JSP instance, such as the sample instance specified in Table 1.

Remaining Processing Time (RPT) provides the total processing time for pending operations until the completion of a job. For example, Table 3 lists *RPT* values for operations of the sample instance in Table 1. The job J_1 consists of 3 operations with a total processing time of 17, which matches *RPT* for the first operation $O_{1,1}$. The *RPT* for $O_{1,2}$ is obtained by subtracting the processing time of $O_{1,1}$, i.e., $17 - 9 = 8$, and it corresponds to the processing time 5 for the last job $O_{1,3}$.

Time Length of a Job (TLJ) is the total processing time for operations of a job, which coincides with the *RPT* value of the job's first operation and is more coarse-grained than the operation-specific *RPT* feature.

Earliest Starting Time (EST) represents the earliest possible time for executing an operation, given by the total processing time for the predecessor operations in its job. For the first operation of each job, the EST value defaults to 0.

Machine Load (ML) is a property describing how much time it takes to execute the operations assigned to a machine. Initially, ML corresponds to the total processing time for all operations to be executed by a machine. Then the assumption is that the operations are processed in increasing order of their EST values, and ML is thus reduced by the processing times of preceeding operations. For example, the EST for the operations $O_{2,1}$, $O_{3,2}$, and $O_{1,2}$ assigned to machine 3 is 0, 4, or 9, respectively. Proceeding in this execution order, ML is the total processing time 10 for $O_{2,1}$, reduced by the processing time of $O_{2,1}$ to $10 - 4 = 6$ for $O_{3,2}$, and then we obtain the execution time 3 for the last operation $O_{1,2}$.

Starting Time (ST) is a family of features providing the starting times of operations obtained by scheduling them with heuristic greedy search methods. In our work, we consider Earliest Starting Time (ST_EST), First-In-First-Out (ST_FIFO), and Most Total Work Remaining (ST_MTWR) as heuristics for the greedy operation allocation; see [25] for an overview of such techniques. At each step, a simple greedy algorithm [16] selects some pending operation whose machine is available according to the heuristic and schedules it. In the case of ST_FIFO, the algorithm selects an operation waiting longest for its machine to become available. For example, the first operations $O_{1,1}$, $O_{2,1}$, and $O_{3,1}$ are all scheduled at time 0 (on different machines), then $O_{2,2}$ waits from time 4 for its machine 2 to get available, while $O_{3,2}$ is started on machine 3 at time 4, so that $O_{3,3}$ also waits for machine 2 from time 7. When the machine 2 is at time 9 ready to start another operation, the ST_FIFO heuristic thus selects the operation $O_{2,2}$, which waits for longer, to be executed next. With the ST_EST and ST_MTWR heuristics, the selection of the next operation is based on smaller EST or greater RPT values, respectively, which in view of the attributes in Table 3 also leads to the result that $O_{2,2}$ is processed before $O_{3,3}$.

Waiting Time (WT) is also a family of features, where variants denoted by WT_EST, WT_FIFO, and WT_MTWR rely on schedules obtained with the corresponding ST heuristic, i.e., ST_EST, ST_FIFO, or ST_MTWR. Given a schedule computed by the greedy algorithm, the waiting time of an operation is determined by the difference between its starting time and the time of completing the predecessor operation, or simply the starting time for the first operation of each job. For instance, the starting times with ST_FIFO listed in Table 3 yield the waiting times given in the WT_FIFO column. In fact, $O_{2,2}$ waits for 5 time units for its machine 2 to get available, its processing time is included in the waiting time 8 of $O_{3,3}$, and $O_{2,3}$ also needs to wait 2 time units for the completion of $O_{1,3}$ before its execution by machine 1.

We extract all of the features described above from a given JSP instance and can thus use them as inputs to our decomposition method presented in the next section.

4   Constrained Clustering Algorithm

Our approximation approach comprises two main phases: *(i)* first, we decompose a problem instance into a sequence of sub-problems, called *time windows*, and *(ii)* second, the time windows are solved one after another, where optimized solutions for preceding time windows are taken as input for solving the next. As a result, the solution obtained for the last time window provides a complete schedule for the given JSP instance. The computational efficiency of this approach and the quality of obtained schedules rely on the decomposition performed in the first phase [44, 46]. Our approach incorporates a novel constrained clustering method for the favorable decomposition of JSP instances based on features of their comprised operations. Each cluster represents a time window, i.e., a subset of operations to be scheduled in one go of an iterative solving algorithm.

Clustering algorithms are unsupervised learning methods whose goal is to partition a set of data objects into (disjoint) clusters such that each cluster gathers objects of high similarity. Such similarity is determined by some measure, e.g., Euclidean distance, based on features of each object, like the features of operations described in the previous section. However, the direct application of common clustering algorithms, such as K-Means [17], to scheduling problems is impractical since the partitioning does not take the sequence of operations in a job into account. For instance, a clustering algorithm may put $O_{1,1}$ and $O_{1,3}$ into the same and $O_{1,2}$ into another cluster. As a result, the sequence of time windows becomes inconsistent, and no compatible schedule exists.

We thus propose a constrained clustering algorithm that preserves sequences of operations by considering their order in the assignment to clusters. That is, the predecessors of an operation to be put into the nth cluster must be assigned within the clusters $1, \ldots, n$. Also considering that our approach involves cluster-wise combinatorial optimization, the generation of large clusters risks to deteriorate the solving performance significantly. In the extreme case, all operations could be put into a single cluster representing the entire problem instance. Hence, in addition to the similarity of operations, our decomposition method also aims at balancing the number of operations per cluster.

Algorithm 1 provides a pseudocode description of our constrained clustering algorithm. Similar to K-Means, we assume that the algorithm gets the target number of clusters into which the operations shall be partitioned as input. The cluster capacity, used for balancing the operations per cluster, is then obtained by dividing the total number of operations by the number of clusters. Moreover, the clustering algorithm takes care of generating one initial centroid per cluster, given by randomly selected operations that are compatible with the precedence relation. For example, when each job consists of 15 operations and the target number of clusters is 3, the first centroid will be an operation at the first to

Algorithm 1. Constrained Clustering Algorithm

Input: *operations, num_clusters*

    $cluster\_capacity \leftarrow \left\lceil \frac{|operations|}{num\_clusters} \right\rceil$

    Generate *num_clusters* many centroids

    for $n = 1$ **to** *num_clusters* **do**

        $clusters[n] \leftarrow \emptyset$

        $current\_capacity \leftarrow cluster\_capacity$

        while $0 < current\_capacity$ **do**

            Calculate distance between data objects and nth centroid ▷ Using Euclidean distance

            $O_{i,j} \leftarrow$ Nearest data object from *operations*

            repeat

                $current\_capacity \leftarrow current\_capacity - 1$

                $operations \leftarrow operations \setminus \{O_{i,j}\}$

                $clusters[n] \leftarrow clusters[n] \cup \{O_{i,j}\}$ ▷ Assigning operation $O_{i,j}$ to nth TW

                $j \leftarrow j - 1$

            until $O_{i,j} \notin operations$ ▷ Satisfying the precedence constraint

            Update the nth centroid

        end while

    end for

---

fifth place of its job, the second an operation from place six to ten, and the third an operation at the eleventh or later place. In order to populate each cluster, the algorithm inspects features to determine the Euclidean distance of each yet unassigned operation to the centroid of the current cluster and assigns the nearest operation to the cluster. To also preserve the precedence between operations, we additionally include any yet unassigned predecessor operations in the current cluster, and then update its centroid with the features of newly assigned operations. Whenever the cluster capacity is reached, the algorithm proceeds to the next cluster, and this decomposition process continues until all operations are assigned to clusters.

In order to identify the most promising features for distance calculation among those introduced in the previous section, we suggest the following forward selection principle: start with a small set of features, perform decomposition by Algorithm 1, and iteratively solve JSP instances. Then, we evaluate the possible extensions by one more feature, compare the quality of resulting schedules, and pick the best set of features. This process continues until either *(i)* all features are selected, or *(ii)* any extension by another feature leads to solutions of lower quality.

5   Evaluation Results

We use randomly generated JSP instances with 50 jobs, 15 machines, and $50 \times 15 = 750$ operations, part of which are known to be challenging for greedy and stochastic optimization techniques, from Taillard's and Demirkol's benchmark suites [13,38] for the empirical evaluation of our approach.[1] For each instance, we extracted the 12 features described in Sect. 3. In order to assess their impact on the clustering and, consequently, the quality of schedules, we make fix use of the features ST_FIFO, ST_MTWR, and ST_EST, which provide the starting times of operations obtained by heuristic greedy search methods, as these three features promised to be informative in preliminary experiments. In contrast to that, considering the position of operations in jobs (OP), processing times (PT), and jobs' time length (TLJ) turned out to be counterproductive in our preliminary investigation, so that we disregard such features in the following. The six leftover features, i.e., remaining processing time (RPT), earliest starting time (EST), machine load (ML) as well as the waiting times WT_FIFO, WT_MTWR, and WT_EST based on schedules computed by corresponding greedy algorithms, are added and combined to feature sets as follows:

$F1 \rightarrow$ { ST_FIFO, ST_MTWR, ST_EST }
$F2 \rightarrow$ { ST_FIFO, ST_MTWR, ST_EST, RPT }
$F3 \rightarrow$ { ST_FIFO, ST_MTWR, ST_EST, EST }
$F4 \rightarrow$ { ST_FIFO, ST_MTWR, ST_EST, ML }
$F5 \rightarrow$ { ST_FIFO, ST_MTWR, ST_EST, RPT, EST }
$F6 \rightarrow$ { ST_FIFO, ST_MTWR, ST_EST, RPT, ML }
$F7 \rightarrow$ { ST_FIFO, ST_MTWR, ST_EST, EST, ML }
$F8 \rightarrow$ { ST_FIFO, ST_MTWR, ST_EST, RPT, EST, ML }
$F9 \rightarrow$ { ST_FIFO, ST_MTWR, ST_EST, WT_FIFO, WT_MTWR, WT_EST }
$F10 \rightarrow$ { ST_FIFO, ST_MTWR, ST_EST, WT_FIFO, WT_MTWR, WT_EST, RPT }
$F11 \rightarrow$ { ST_FIFO, ST_MTWR, ST_EST, WT_FIFO, WT_MTWR, WT_EST, EST }
$F12 \rightarrow$ { ST_FIFO, ST_MTWR, ST_EST, WT_FIFO, WT_MTWR, WT_EST, ML }
$F13 \rightarrow$ { ST_FIFO, ST_MTWR, ST_EST, WT_FIFO, WT_MTWR, WT_EST, RPT, EST }
$F14 \rightarrow$ { ST_FIFO, ST_MTWR, ST_EST, WT_FIFO, WT_MTWR, WT_EST, RPT, ML }
$F15 \rightarrow$ { ST_FIFO, ST_MTWR, ST_EST, WT_FIFO, WT_MTWR, WT_EST, EST, ML }
$F16 \rightarrow$ { ST_FIFO, ST_MTWR, ST_EST, WT_FIFO, WT_MTWR, WT_EST, RPT, EST, ML }

We utilized the above feature sets for partitioning the operations of JSP instances into 3 clusters or time windows, respectively, and then ran the multi-shot optimization approach introduced in [16] for 10 min in total, i.e., 200 s per time window, on an Intel® Core™ i7-8650U CPU Dell Latitude 5590 machine under Windows 10. The resulting quality of schedules in terms of the achieved makespan for each instance is reported in Table 4 and Table 5, where the first four rows include the greedy FIFO and MTWR search methods supplied by the environment in [39] as well as single-shot and multi-shot pure ASP optimization, the latter taking earliest starting times instead of clustering for the decomposition into 3 time windows, for reference. Regarding these reference methods, FIFO and MTWR are more or less on par, with a slight advantage of FIFO on Taillard's instances and an edge for MTWR on Demirkol's instances, indicated by the average makespans given in the last column of each table. While combinatorial optimization by neither single- nor multi-shot ASP solving is able to keep step within the time limit and leads to greater averages over all instances, the multi-shot pure ASP optimization approach turns out to be comparably robust on half of the instances from Demirkol's benchmark suite, which points out the critical impact of instance patterns.

---

[1] The benchmarks and our implementation are available at: https://github.com/Sa3doun13/PADL-2022.

Table 4. Solution quality comparison for different feature sets (Taillard's instances).

Approach	TA51	TA52	TA53	TA54	TA55	TA56	TA57	TA58	TA59	TA60	AVG
FIFO	3549	3339	**3160**	**3218**	3291	3325	3654	**3299**	**3344**	3129	**3331**
MTWR	**3364**	**3304**	3168	3494	**3237**	**3287**	**3633**	3591	3394	3257	3373
Single-shot	3632	3615	3481	3462	3552	3610	3778	3718	3613	3550	3601
Multi-shot	3506	3773	3478	3497	3482	3605	3753	3731	3398	3247	3547
F1	3506	3277	3382	3414	3308	3353	3605	3352	3453	3483	3413
F2	3362	3318	3585	3425	3441	3380	3573	3412	3416	**3315**	3423
F3	3324	3330	3347	3425	3424	3548	3601	3370	3301	3617	3429
F4	3360	3286	3543	3503	3319	3270	3583	3509	3339	3563	3428
F5	3346	3243	3517	3397	3355	3383	3650	3707	3508	3591	3470
F6	**3294**	3275	3250	3265	3386	3366	**3480**	**3324**	3430	3327	**3340**
F7	3328	3226	3338	3353	3301	3564	3592	3496	3352	3399	3395
F8	3330	3273	3277	3492	3375	3469	3760	3410	3485	3573	3444
F9	3588	3397	3251	3563	3498	**3229**	3621	3517	3258	3374	3430
F10	3588	3373	3522	3443	3385	3306	3543	3716	3381	3526	3475
F11	3568	3533	3373	3386	3530	3362	3608	3644	3402	3637	3504
F12	3514	3256	3585	3352	3365	3344	3670	3611	**3145**	3425	3427
F13	3682	3494	**3143**	3270	3309	3332	3632	3471	3250	3676	3426
F14	3624	3505	3427	3236	3370	3338	3749	3437	3253	3659	3460
F15	3554	3373	3524	**3232**	3385	3483	3573	3365	3284	3767	3454
F16	3509	**3184**	3380	3289	**3218**	3389	**3480**	3481	3290	3569	3379
Virtual Best	**3294**	**3184**	**3143**	**3232**	**3218**	**3229**	**3480**	**3324**	**3145**	**3315**	**3256**

Table 5. Solution quality comparison for different feature sets (Demirkol's instances).

Approach	DE31	DE32	DE33	DE34	DE35	DE71	DE72	DE73	DE74	DE75	AVG
FIFO	**6817**	6318	**6029**	**6395**	**6409**	9678	10349	9617	9847	9479	8094
MTWR	7155	**6042**	6819	6570	6881	7764	8407	8411	8321	7893	**7426**
Single-shot	10370	10214	10064	10682	10203	6848	28369	32954	35325	6992	16202
Multi-shot	10318	9522	9785	10775	10398	**6492**	**6935**	**7202**	**7128**	**6243**	8480
F1	8488	8325	7831	8356	8088	8593	7188	7826	6611	7662	7897
F2	8440	8298	**7663**	8479	7986	6994	7606	7209	6627	7069	7637
F3	8234	8401	8037	8444	7780	**6590**	7785	7302	6690	7051	7631
F4	7991	8589	7996	8471	8207	8091	7834	6972	6708	6859	7771
F5	8164	8103	7835	8482	7802	6807	8357	7328	6774	7192	7684
F6	**7709**	8265	7795	8475	**7678**	6611	6708	7030	6569	6867	7371
F7	8268	8553	7892	8359	8032	7603	6855	7223	6609	7200	7659
F8	8873	8879	8201	9126	7982	6843	7971	7106	7545	6970	7950
F9	8500	8185	8533	8772	8535	6726	6518	7130	6592	7262	7675
F10	8322	8119	8433	8910	8233	6868	6764	7183	6267	7459	7656
F11	8617	8383	8614	8755	7969	7587	**6512**	**6762**	6505	7376	7708
F12	8400	8124	8043	**8185**	8799	7849	6618	6876	6397	7746	7704
F13	8916	8343	8441	8331	8153	7464	6757	6994	6434	6961	7679
F14	8392	**7937**	7943	8375	8049	7310	7703	6827	**6126**	6893	7555
F15	8412	8210	8117	8563	9068	7853	6968	6909	6350	7011	7746
F16	8184	8150	8295	8721	8003	6997	7156	6991	6355	**6584**	7544
Virtual Best	**7709**	**7937**	**7663**	**8185**	**7678**	**6590**	**6512**	**6762**	**6126**	**6584**	**7175**

Among our feature sets for clustering, in preparation of multi-shot optimization by ASP, we do not identify any clear winner dominating over all instances. However, the feature sets **F2**, **F6**, **F11**, **F12**, **F13**, **F14**, and **F16** yield significant makespan improvements relative to the other alternatives on particular instances. This means that considering the features *RPT*, *EST*, *ML*, or *WT_FIFO*, *WT_MTWR*, and *WT_EST* in addition to starting times *ST_FIFO*, *ST_MTWR*, and *ST_EST* by greedy algorithms is beneficial, while the particular combination of features achieving best schedules varies. Moreover, our clustering method for JSP instance decomposition outperforms (multi-shot) pure ASP optimization, and specific feature sets are ahead of the greedy FIFO and MTWR algorithms on seven out of ten Taillard's instances as well as half of Demirkol's instances, as indicated by the virtual best clustering results in the last row of Table 4 and Table 5. Notably, the feature set **F6** leads to the shortest average makespans for our cluster-wise JSP solving approach on both kinds of instances, comes close to FIFO on Taillard's and is most robust on Demirkol's instances, but the virtual best clustering results still improve significantly. We thus conclude that the instance decomposition by clustering can empower iterative combinatorial optimization to find better schedules than greedy algorithms in a short amount of time, where alternative feature sets deserve attention and trying several of them in parallel seems advisable.

6   Related Work

Data mining approaches [23] have been extensively proposed and applied to generate dispatching rules [8] for scheduling problems. Unlike combinatorial and stochastic optimization methods, dispatching rules do not take complete schedules into account, but address the prioritization of operations for making local allocation decisions by greedy scheduling algorithms. In addition to Earliest Starting Time (EST), First-In-First-Out (FIFO), and Most Total Work Remaining (MTWR), which we also use for obtaining starting times as features, common dispatching rules include Last-In-First-Out (LIFO) and policies incorporating Job Length (JL) in terms of the number of operations as well as further features like those described in Sect. 3: Operation Position (OP), Processing Time (PT), Remaining Processing Time (RPT), Time Length of a Job (TLJ), and Machine Load (ML). While dispatching rules enable an efficient operation allocation, even under real-time conditions, the quality of their decisions heavily depends on the problem instances under consideration, where data mining techniques come in to improve over tedious and ad hoc manual tuning.

The approach of [26] incorporates data mining methods, using OP, PT, RPT, and ML as features, for generating dispatching rules that approximate operation priorities found in schedules optimized by means of a genetic algorithm. On randomly generated test instances of comparably small size, i.e., 36 operations per instance, the generated dispatching rules were shown to outperform greedy search with shortest PT as a rigid criterion for making allocation decisions. Genetic algorithms are also utilized in [22] to obtain promising solutions for JSP instances and extract features to consider for the construction of dispatching rules. The specifically generated three-tiered policy comprises shortest PT, smallest JL, and longest RPT as dispatching criteria in the order of significance. Note that such a composite dispatching rule needs to reconstructed from scratch when new features or problem instances are analyzed, while our constrained clustering method can readily be applied to different instance or feature sets, respectively.

Beyond static scheduling, dynamic JSP [19] deals with events, such as the release of new jobs or sudden machine breakdowns, along with rescheduling or updating dispatching rules, respectively. In analogy to the static setting, the processing approach of [35] applies tabu search to training instances and generates allocation policies approximating the optimized complete schedules based on features like EST, PT, and RPT of operations. Applied in the dynamic JSP setting, the dispatching rules obtained by means of data mining were shown to yield better or comparable performance to rigid allocation strategies from the literature. A rescheduling approach combining Variable Neighborhood Search (VNS) with K-Means clustering is presented in [2], where clusters are updated to reconfigure the VNS on each event. The performance of this combined rescheduling strategy in the dynamic JSP setting turned out to be better than pure VNS and greedy algorithms with the FIFO, LIFO, or shortest PT allocation policy.

The integration of dispatching rules generated with data mining techniques into stochastic optimization in [29] works by running a greedy algorithm called "assignment procedure" to obtain promising JSP solutions and mine dispatching rules approximating them. But instead of relying on the dispatching rules alone for computing optimized schedules or performing efficient operation allocation on new instances, the high-quality draft solutions from greedy search with the dispatching rules are taken as inputs to population-based stochastic optimization. This metaheuristic optimization was shown to yield improved outcomes when launched with schedules generated by means of suitable dispatching rules rather than with a randomly generated initial population.

Similarities of our cluster-wise JSP solving approach to the discussed methods include that we apply (fixed) dispatching rules to extract the starting times of operations in corresponding schedules as instance features. Notably, the constrained clustering algorithm in Sect. 4 can readily be applied to arbitrary feature sets for decomposing the operations of JSP instances into balanced time windows, i.e., our clustering method does not presuppose tuning to specific instance or feature sets under consideration. The iterative combinatorial optimization by time windows can be viewed as a trade-off between efficient dispatching rules, aiming to optimize local allocation decisions by prioritizing operations, and the stochastic or combinatorial optimization of complete schedules for problem instances. While instance size and complexity can make the search for optimal solutions with state-of-the-art solvers for ASP, Mixed Integer Programming, or Constraint Programming prohibitive [11,46], successful application areas in scheduling include, e.g., industrial printing [5], team-building [33], shift design [1], course timetabling [6], lab resource allocation [18], and medical treatment planning [15].

7   Conclusions

Data mining and machine learning are of wide interest in scientific, business, and further fields. Our work investigates data mining and clustering methods to optimize solutions for the Job-shop Scheduling Problem within short solving times. The idea is to associate clusters of operations with time windows subject to iterative combinatorial optimization, eventually leading to a complete schedule. In contrast to usual clustering tasks, however, the time windows need to take the sequence of operations in a job into account, and the number of operations per cluster should also be balanced for partitioning a given problem instance into time windows of roughly similar solving complexity. We have thus devised a novel constrained clustering method that takes both concerns into account for gathering operations with similar feature values in a consistent and balanced way. Our experiments show that the decomposition into time windows obtained by clustering usually leads to significantly improved outcomes of multi-shot ASP solving in comparison to taking earliest starting times as simple (and consistent) partitioning criterion. While no single feature set for clustering turns out to be strictly more successful than greedy search with FIFO or MTWR allocation policy, schedules of comparable or better quality can be found with some feature set in the given solving time for most instances. Moreover, the iterative combinatorial optimization by time windows helps to increase the robustness of schedules obtained for different kinds of instances.

While search for optimal solutions is beyond reach due to the size and complexity of practical scheduling applications, reliably computing high-quality approximations is an important subject of future work. This includes automatic methods for deciding about the features to consider for partitioning operations into clusters, i.e., determining whether an eligible feature is informative or noisy, respectively. As we can hardly expect that even moderately sized time windows can be solved to optimality in a short amount of time or eventual optimization criteria values be accurately predicted from solutions for sub-problems, it can still be worthwhile to incorporate measures allowing for corrections of partitioning decisions, which could consist of overlapping time windows to enable revisions or dynamically relaunching the clustering algorithm wrt. computed partial schedules. Instead of obtaining features by greedy search methods only, we may also take the outcomes of one or several multi-shot optimization runs into account as features for another clustering and solving round until a fixpoint without further improvement is reached. That is, there are various opportunities to extend our approach in the future, where going beyond the classical Job-shop Scheduling Problem, e.g., by considering flexible resource allocations or partially ordered operations, can also be of interest for practical application scenarios.

References

1. Abseher, M., Gebser, M., Musliu, N., Schaub, T., Woltran, S.: Shift design with answer set programming. Fundam. Inform. **147**(1), 1–25 (2016)
2. Adibi, M., Shahrabi, J.: A clustering-based modified variable neighborhood search algorithm for a dynamic job shop scheduling problem. Int. J. Adv. Manuf. Technol. **70**(9–12), 1955–1961 (2014)
3. Al-Ashhab, M., Munshi, S., Oreijah, M., Ghulman, H.: Job shop scheduling using mixed integer programming. Int. J. Mod. Eng. Res. **7**(3), 2:23–2:29 (2017)
4. Baker, K.: Introduction to Sequencing and Scheduling. John Wiley & Sons, New York (1974)
5. Balduccini, M.: Industrial-size scheduling with ASP+CP. In: Proceedings of the Eleventh International Conference on Logic Programming and Nonmonotonic Reasoning (LPNMR'11), pp. 284–296. Springer-Verlag (2011). https://doi.org/10. 1007/978-3-642-20895-9
6. Banbara, M., Inoue, K., Kaufmann, B., Okimoto, T., Schaub, T., Soh, T., Tamura, N., Wanko, P.: teaspoon: solving the curriculum-based course timetabling problems with answer set programming. Ann. Oper. Res. **275**(1), 3–37 (2019)
7. Bengio, Y., Lodi, A., Prouvost, A.: Machine learning for combinatorial optimization: a methodological tour d'horizon. Eur. J. Oper. Res. **290**(2), 405–421 (2021)
8. Blackstone, J., Phillips, D., Hogg, G.: A state-of-the-art survey of dispatching rules for manufacturing job shop operations. Int. J. Prod. Res. **20**(1), 27–45 (1982)
9. Çalis, B., Bulkan, S.: A research survey: review of AI solution strategies of job shop scheduling problem. J. Intell. Manuf. **26**(5), 961–973 (2015)
10. Chaudhry, I., Khan, A.: A research survey: review of flexible job shop scheduling techniques. Int. Trans. Oper. Res. **23**(3), 551–591 (2016)
11. Da Col, G., Teppan, E.C.: Industrial size job shop scheduling tackled by present day CP solvers. In: Schiex, T., de Givry, S. (eds.) CP 2019. LNCS, vol. 11802, pp. 144–160. Springer, Cham (2019). https://doi.org/10.1007/978-3-030-30048-7_9
12. Demirbilek, M., Branke, J., Strauss, A.: Dynamically accepting and scheduling patients for home healthcare. Health Care Manag. Sci. **22**(1), 140–155 (2019)
13. Demirkol, E., Mehta, S., Uzsoy, R.: Benchmarks for shop scheduling problems. Eur. J. Oper. Res. **109**(1), 137–141 (1998)
14. Ding, H., Xu, J.: A unified framework for clustering constrained data without locality property. Algorithmica **82**(4), 808–852 (2020)
15. Dodaro, C., Galatà, G., Grioni, A., Maratea, M., Mochi, M., Porro, I.: An ASP-based solution to the chemotherapy treatment scheduling problem. Theory Pract. Logic Program. First View 1–17 (2021). https://doi.org/10.1017/ S1471068421000363
16. El-Kholany, M., Gebser, M.: Job shop scheduling with multi-shot ASP. In: Proceedings of the Fourth Workshop on Trends and Applications of Answer Set Programming (TAASP2020) (2020). http://www.kr.tuwien.ac.at/events/taasp20/papers/ TAASP_2020_paper_4.pdf
17. Forgy, E.: Cluster analysis of multivariate data: efficiency versus interpretability of classifications. Biometrics **21**, 768–769 (1965)
18. Francescutto, G., Schekotihin, K., El-Kholany, M.: Solving a multi-resource partial-ordering flexible variant of the job-shop scheduling problem with hybrid ASP. In: Proceedings of the Seventeenth European Conference on Logics in Artificial Intelligence (JELIA 2021), pp. 313–328. Springer-Verlag (2021)

19. French, S.: Sequencing and Scheduling: An Introduction to the Mathematics of the Job-shop. John Wiley & Sons, New York (1982)
20. Garey, M., Johnson, D., Sethi, R.: The complexity of Flowshop and Jobshop scheduling. Math. Oper. Res. **1**(2), 117–129 (1976)
21. Gebser, M., Kaminski, R., Kaufmann, B., Schaub, T.: Multi-shot ASP solving with clingo. Theory Pract. Logic Program. **19**(1), 27–82 (2019)
22. Harrath, Y., Chebel-Morello, B., Zerhouni, N.: A genetic algorithm and data mining based meta-heuristic for job shop scheduling problem. In: Proceedings of the IEEE International Conference on Systems, Man and Cybernetics (SMC 2002). IEEE (2002)
23. Ismail, R., Othman, Z., Bakar, A.: A production schedule generator framework for pattern sequential mining. In: Proceedings of the Seventh International Conference on Computing and Convergence Technology (ICCCT 2012), pp. 784–788. IEEE (2012)
24. Janakbhai, N., Saurin, M., Patel, M.: Blockchain-based intelligent transportation system with priority scheduling. In: Data Science and Intelligent Applications, pp. 311–317. Springer-Verlag, Singapore (2021). https://doi.org/10.1007/978-981-15-4474-3
25. Jones, A., Rabelo, L., Sharawi, A.: Survey of job shop scheduling techniques. National Institute of Standards and Technology Encyclopedia of Electrical and Electronics Engineering (1998). https://tsapps.nist.gov/publication/get_pdf.cfm?pub_id=821200
26. Koonce, D., Tsai, S.: Using data mining to find patterns in genetic algorithm solutions to a job shop schedule. Comput. Ind. Eng. **38**(3), 361–374 (2000)
27. Lenstra, J., Rinnooy Kan, A.: Computational complexity of discrete optimization problems. Ann. Discrete Math. **4**, 121–140 (1979)
28. Meng, L., Zhang, C., Ren, Y., Zhang, B., Lv, C.: Mixed-integer linear programming and constraint programming formulations for solving distributed flexible job shop scheduling problem. Comput. Ind. Eng. **142**, Article 106347 (2020)
29. Nasiri, M., Salesi, S., Rahbari, A., Meydani, N., Abdollai, M.: A data mining approach for population-based methods to solve the JSSP. Soft Comput. **23**(21), 11107–11122 (2019)
30. Nouiri, M., Bekrar, A., Jemai, A., Niar, S., Ammari, A.: An effective and distributed particle swarm optimization algorithm for flexible job-shop scheduling problem. J. Intell. Manuf. **29**(3), 603–615 (2018)
31. Ovacik, I., Uzsoy, R.: Decomposition Methods for Complex Factory Scheduling Problems. Kluwer Academic Publishers, Boston (1997). https://doi.org/10.1007/978-1-4615-6329-7
32. Pezzella, F., Morganti, G., Ciaschetti, G.: A genetic algorithm for the flexible job-shop scheduling problem. Comput. Oper. Res. **35**(10), 3202–3212 (2008)
33. Ricca, F., et al.: Team-building with answer set programming in the Gioia-Tauro seaport. Theory Pract. Logic Program. **12**(3), 361–381 (2012)
34. Schoenfelder, J., Bretthauer, K., Wright, D., Coe, E.: Nurse scheduling with quick-response methods: Improving hospital performance, nurse workload, and patient experience. Eur. J. Oper. Res. **283**(1), 390–403 (2020)
35. Shahzad, A., Mebarki, N.: Discovering dispatching rules for job shop scheduling problem through data mining. In: Proceedings of the Eighth International Conference of Modeling and Simulation (MOSIM 2010) (2010). https://www.academia.edu/3068769/DISCOVERING_DISPATCHING_RULES_FOR_JOB_SHOP_SCHEDULING_PROBLEM_THROUGH_DATA_MINING

36. Singer, M.: Decomposition methods for large job shops. Comput. Oper. Res. **28**(3), 193–207 (2001)
37. Sotskov, Y., Shakhlevich, N.: NP-hardness of shop-scheduling problems with three jobs. Discrete Appl. Math. **59**(3), 237–266 (1995)
38. Taillard, E.: Benchmarks for basic scheduling problems. Eur. J. Oper. Res. **64**(2), 278–285 (1993)
39. Tassel, P., Gebser, M., Schekotihin, K.: A reinforcement learning environment for job-shop scheduling. In: Proceedings of the ICAPS 2021 Workshop on Planning and Reinforcement Learning (PRL 2021) (2021). https://prl-theworkshop.github.io/prl2021/papers/PRL2021_paper_9.pdf
40. Uzsoy, R., Wang, C.: Performance of decomposition procedures for job shop scheduling problems with bottleneck machines. Int. J. Prod. Res. **38**(6), 1271–1286 (2000)
41. Vaessens, R., Aarts, E., Lenstra, J.: Job shop scheduling by local search. INFORMS J. Comput. **8**(3), 302–317 (1996)
42. Wagstaff, K., Cardie, C., Rogers, S., Schrödl, S.: Constrained k-means clustering with background knowledge. In: Proceedings of the Eighteenth International Conference on Machine Learning (ICML 2001), pp. 577–584. Morgan Kaufmann, San Francisco (2001)
43. Wang, H.: Routing and scheduling for a last-mile transportation system. Transp. Sci. **53**(1), 131–147 (2019)
44. Zhai, Y., Liu, C., Chu, W., Guo, R., Liu, C.: A decomposition heuristics based on multi-bottleneck machines for large-scale job shop scheduling problems. J. Ind. Eng. Manag. **7**(5), 1397–1414 (2014)
45. Zhang, H., Basu, S., Davidson, I.: A framework for deep constrained clustering - algorithms and advances. In: Brefeld, U., et al. (eds.) ECML PKDD 2019. LNCS (LNAI), vol. 11906, pp. 57–72. Springer, Cham (2020). https://doi.org/10.1007/978-3-030-46150-8_4
46. Zhang, R., Wu, C.: A hybrid approach to large-scale job shop scheduling. Appl. Intell. **32**(1), 47–59 (2010)

Modeling and Verification of Real-Time Systems with the Event Calculus and s(CASP)

Sarat Chandra Varanasi[1(✉)], Joaquín Arias[2], Elmer Salazar[1], Fang Li[1], Kinjal Basu[1], and Gopal Gupta[1]

[1] The University of Texas at Dallas, Richardson, USA
{sxv153030,ees101020,fang.li,kinjal.basu,gupta}@utdallas.edu
[2] CETINIA, Universidad Rey Juan Carlos, Madrid, Spain
joaquin.arias@urjc.es

Abstract. Modeling a cyber-physical system's requirement specifications makes it possible to verify its properties w.r.t. the expected behavior. Standard modeling approaches based on automata theory model these systems at the *system architecture level*, as they have to explicitly encode the notion of states and define explicit transitions between these states. Event Calculus encoding using Answer Set Programming (ASP) allows for elegant and succinct modeling of these dynamic systems at the *requirements specification level*, thanks to the near-zero semantics gap between the system's requirement specifications and the Event Calculus encoding. In this work we propose a framework that uses the EARS notation to describe the system requirements, and an Event Calculus reasoner based on s(CASP), a goal-directed Constraint Answer Set Programming reasoner over the rationals/reals, to *directly* model these requirements. We evaluate our proposal by (i) modeling the well-known Train-Gate-Controller system, a railroad crossing problem, using the EARS notation and Event Calculus, (ii) translating the specifications into s(CASP), and (iii) checking safety and liveness of the system.

1 Introduction

Cyber-physical systems are ever increasing in their prominence in our day-to-day lives. Much research has been published towards modeling and verifying properties of these systems. Primarily, timed-automata approaches have been studied and used on industrial scale applications [1,7]. Timed-automata approaches require an explicit notion of state and transitions between states using clock variables [2]. Timed automata have also been modeled as constraint logic programs, where there is little semantic gap between the logic programs and the intended cyber-physical system that is modeled [10]. Techniques based on co-inductive constraint logic programming (Co-CLP) have also been applied in verifying properties of timed-automata [16,17]. The Co-CLP techniques to study timed systems culminated in the development of Goal-directed Answer Set Programming [6]. More recently, the well-known Event Calculus (EC) formalism has been used [4] along

© Springer Nature Switzerland AG 2022
J. Cheney and S. Perri (Eds.): PADL 2022, LNCS 13165, pp. 181–190, 2022.
https://doi.org/10.1007/978-3-030-94479-7_12

with powerful reasoning supported in Answer Set Programming. Additionally, the work of Arias et al. [3] extends prior work on Co-CLP to support natural reasoning over hybrid systems, in the language of Event Calculus. Theirs is the first work to use the s(CASP) system to model Event Calculus along with abductive reasoning supported in Answer Set Programming. The s(CASP) system has also been used in knowledge-based methods that analyze faulty requirements in simple avionics software systems modeled with a single automata [11]. In this paper we model more complex cyber physical systems that involve multiple automata (for example, the well-known Train-Gate-Controller system) in Event Calculus. We *start with the requirements specification* written succinctly and concisely in the EARS notation [14] and *model them directly in the Event Calculus*. We use the Event Calculus encoding in Answer Set Programming along with real-time constraints that can be directly run on the s(CASP) system. Thus, the entire system can be modeled in s(CASP). Simulation runs can be executed and safety and liveness of the system automatically checked, with prior knowledge of the physical properties such as train speed, system response time, and the rate at which the gate rotates.

The Event Calculus encoding in s(CASP) is obtained *directly* from the requirements specification written in EARS [14]. The main advantage of this approach is that design decisions do not "creep" into the encoding. This is in contrast to automata theoretic approaches (such as those based on timed automata) where some design decisions have to be made in order to obtain the timed automata encoding (for example, decisions regarding how to split the system into subsystems for each of which an automaton will be designed; what states and transitions these automata will have, etc.). Thus, verification performed at the level of timed automata verifies the requirements as rendered in the design realized in the automata, rather than at the level of requirements specification itself. In our approach, verification of safety and liveness is performed at the level of requirements specification. Thus, we can ensure that requirements are consistent and robust and permit a design that satisfies safety and liveness.

The methods developed in this paper allow us generate simulation runs of the system as well as check the correctness of its requirements specification. These experiments allow the user to refine/correct the system requirement specifications. Errors in specifications are a major source of flaws in software implementations. The later a defect is discovered in requirements specification, the costlier it is to fix. Thus, the ability to faithfully model requirements specification of a system can lead to significant benefits. The main contribution of the paper is the following:

- We show how requirements specification for a cyber-physical system can be directly modeled in the Event Calculus using ASP. This Event Calculus coding of requirement specifications can then be directly executed in s(CASP). The encoding can be used for generating simulation runs and for verification, for example, of safety and liveness properties.
- Use of the Event Calculus, ASP, and s(CASP) for modeling real-time systems has been limited to very simple examples. We present the encoding of a complex system, namely, the canonical Train-Gate-Controller system that has been widely discussed in the literature [2].

Ubiquitous: always active.   The `<system name>` shall `<system response>`

State Driven: active as long as the specific state remains true.
   WHILE `<precondition(s)>`,   the `<system name>` shall `<system response>`

Event Driven: specify how a system must respond when a triggering event occurs.
   WHEN `<trigger>`,   the `<system name>` shall `<system response>`

Unwanted Behavior: specify the required system response to undesired situations.
   IF `<trigger>`, THEN   the `<system name>` shall `<system response>`

Complex Behavior: specify requirements for richer system behaviour.
   WHILE `<precondition(s)>`, WHEN `<trigger>`,
                             the `<system name>` shall `<system response>`

Fig. 1. Generic EARS syntax

2   Background

2.1   Easy Approach to Requirement Syntax (EARS)

The Easy Approach to Requirement Syntax (EARS) [13,14] is a pragmatic approach to specifying requirements for cyber-physical systems based on using five structured templates and keywords popular in the avionics industry. Keywords 'WHEN', 'WHILE' and 'IF'-'THEN' are used in these templates and play a major role (see Fig. 1). Studies have shown the use of EARS to reduce requirements errors while improving requirement quality and readability [14]. For cyber-physical real-time systems, response times are important, hence formally budgeting the allocation of time throughout the levels of function & temporal decomposition are primary concerns. An example requirement specification in EARS style is given: **WHEN** the `train_position` reaches 10 feet, the `Train-gate-Controller` **SHALL** trigger `gate_closure within 1 s`.

System response and trigger are typically time constrained events. In Sect. 3 we explain how requirement specifications written in EARS can be directly modeled in Event Calculus.

2.2   Basic Event Calculus (BEC)

Event Calculus (presented at length elsewhere [15]) is a formalism for reasoning about events and change, of which there are several axiomatizations. In this paper we use the Basic Event Calculus (BEC) formulated by [18]. There are three fundamental, mutually related, concepts in EC: *events*, *fluents*, and *time points*. An event is an action or incident that may occur in the world: for instance, a person dropping a glass is an event. A fluent is a time-varying property of the world, such as the altitude of a glass. A time point is an instant in time. Events may happen at a time point; fluents have a truth value at any time point or over an interval, and their truth values are subject to change, upon the occurrence of an event. In addition, fluents may by associated with (continuous) physical quantities that change over time. For example, rolling a ball on the floor can be described by two *fluents*: one *fluent* that states that the ball itself is *rolling*, while another *fluent* captures *movement* of the ball in some metric unit, changing at a certain rate, over time. The *event* of setting the ball to roll *initiates rolling* and also determines the change in position from a starting point. Likewise, the event of stopping the ball *terminates* rolling of the ball and the ball is now stationary in its last position. An EC description consists of a *domain narrative* and a *universal theory*. The domain narrative consists of the causal laws of the domain, the known events, and the fluent properties, and the universal theory is a conjunction of EC axioms that encode, for example, the commonsense laws of inertia. In Sect. 3 we show how EC descriptions can be translated and evaluated using an EC-reasoner implemented using s(CASP) [5].

2.3   Goal-Directed Answer Set Programming

Our framework relies on Answer Set Programming (ASP) [9] to encode system requirements. In particular, we use the goal-directed s(CASP) [3] system. The top-down query-driven execution strategy of s(CASP) has three major advantages w.r.t. traditional ASP system: (a) it does not require to ground the programs; (b) its execution starts with a query and the evaluation only explores the parts of the knowledge base relevant to the query. Hence relying on a strategy not based on grounding, makes s(CASP) scalable for cyber physical domains using dense real-valued time. Additionally, s(CASP) can output the justification tree for issued queries and provide an easily visualizable HTML version of the same tree. The predicates used in the modelling can be mapped to their intended English language meanings to make the justifications more readable. These justifications make it possible to understand the behavior of the cyber-physical system, when its properties hold and when they do not hold.

In Sect. 4 we show that the safety and liveness properties of a CPS can be checked using s(CASP) queries. The direct mapping of EC Axioms in [5] is possible due to s(CASP) capability to support continuous time. To the best of our knowledge, s(CASP) is the only logic programming system that encodes EC with dense time. This is to be distinguished from grounding-based ASP solvers that can only reason over discretized time [12].

3   Modeling and Verifying Cyber Physical Systems in EC

The Train-Gate-Controller (TGC) is a cyber-physical system commonly used to study modeling and verification of properties of such systems [10]. The system consists of a set of sensors and actuators that automatically open and close a railway gate upon detecting the arrival or departure of a train. The system should signal gate closure in a timely fashion.

Let us consider the specifications of the Train-Gate-Controller system described in [2]:[1] *The train signals its approach and exit. Events in and*

---

[1] We have made some minor (and inconsequential) changes to the Train-Gate-Controller system to simplify the illustration.

out signal the entry and exit of the train from the gate area. *The train should signal* **approach** *at least* 2 min *before entering gate area. This forces the minimum delay between* **approach** *and* **in** *to be* 2 min. *The maximum delay between* **approach** *and* **exit** *is* 5 min. We make the train's approach more tangible by considering actual movement of the train on a track. We set markers for the entry point and exit point of the gate area. When the trains position hits these points, then correspondingly, the train has entered or exited the gate area. Therefore, the minimum 2 min delay is ignored. Further, we consider if the gate is eventually closed, ignoring the 5 min delay. We assume that the train changes its position uniformly at a rate of 10 units per second. The gate area is at position 10. Once the train reaches the gate area, we consider the train being *in* the gate area. Initially, the gate is open and is inclined vertically at an angle of zero degrees. The system should signal the *closing* of the gate before the train is in the gate area. The gate also uniformly changes its angle of inclination when it is in motion. When the *gate angle* becomes 90°, the gate is closed and inclined horizontally.

3.1   Train-Gate-Controller in EARS

In this section we translate the TGC requirements into EARS notation.

R1   **WHEN** the train reaches a position of 10 units, **the** system **shall** signal the train to be in the gate area

R2   **WHEN** the train reaches a position of 5 units, **the** system **shall** signal lowering of the gate

R3   **WHEN** the gate angle reaches vertical angle of 90° from below, **the** system **shall** signal gate closure

R4   **WHEN** the gate angle reaches a vertical angle of 0° from above, **the** system **shall** signal the gate to be open

R5   **WHEN** the train starts leaving the gate area, **the** system **shall** signal raising of the gate

R6   **WHEN** the train reaches a position of 20 units, **the** system **shall** signal the train to be exiting the gate area

R7   **The** system **shall** ensure the gate is closed when the train is passing through the gate area

R8   **The** Gate **shall** be open after train has exited the gate area

3.2   Train-Gate-Requirements in EC Using s(CASP)

We first identify the fluents (sensor triggered) and events (actuator triggered). For clarity in the code below, fluent & event names have been made more descriptive (e.g., **in** has been renamed **train_in**).

```
fluent(passing).      % Train is passing through the gate area
fluent(leaving).      % Train is leaving form the gate area
fluent(position(X)).  % Train is at some position X
```

```
fluent(gate_angle(A)). % Gate is vertically inclined with an angle A
fluent(opened).        % The gate is completely opened
fluent(closed).        % The gate is completely closed
fluent(lowering).      % The gate is being lowered
fluent(rising).        % The gate is being raised
event(train_in).       % The train enters the gate area
event(signal_lower).   % The system signals gate lowered
event(signal_raise).   % The system signals gate raised
event(gate_close).     % The gate closes
event(gate_open).      % The gate opens
event(train_exit).     % The train exits the gate area
```

The causal effects of the events in the system follow straightforwardly:

```
initiates(train_in,passing,T).          terminates(signal_lower,opened,T).
initiates(signal_lower,lowering,T).     terminates(gate_close,lowering,T).
initiates(gate_close,closed,T).         terminates(train_exit,passing,T).
initiates(train_exit,leaving,T).        terminates(signal_raise,closed,T).
initiates(raise,rising,T).              terminates(gate_open,rising,T).
initiates(gate_open,opened,T).
```

Next, `train_speed(S)`, `angle_lower_rate(L)`, `angle_rise_rate(R)` denote, respectively, that the speed of the train is S, the rate at which the gate lowers is L and rises is R. We now describe the conditions under which various events happen. The motion of the train itself is modeled as a trajectory. Similarly, the change in inclination of the gate angle is also modeled as a trajectory, depending upon whether `event(signal_lower)` or `event(signal_raise)` happen. If the gate is lowering (rising), then the gate inclination steadily decreases (increases)[2].

```
trajectory(started, T1, position(X), T2) :-
    train_speed(S), T2 #> T1, X #= (T2 - T1) * S.
```

```
1    gate_angle_lower(A, T2) :-       6    gate_angle_rise(A, T2):-
2        happens(signal_lower,T),     7        happens(signal_raise,T),
3        angle_lower_rate(L),         8        angle_rise_rate(R),
4        T2 #> T,                     9        T2 #> T,
5        A #= (T2-T1)*L.             10        A #= 90 - (T2-T1)*R.
```

The events mentioned previously happen when the fluents cross a certain threshold. For example, we consider train to be in the gate area when it has reached a position value = 10. Similarly, the system signals lower_gate when the train position crosses value = 5. All transitions in the train position, gate angle are resolved at a sampling window of 0.1 time unit. That is, the system

---

[2] We treat `gate_angle_lower` and `gate_angle_rise` as derived fluents. They can also be modeled as trajectories.

can detect changes in continuous quantities at a temporal precision of 0.1 time unit. This is a reasonable assumption to make the system behave realistically. If we used a temporal precision of 0, then the system can detect instantaneous changes in continuous values, which is impossible in a real-world system. We use the infimum on the 0.1 s interval, to signify the precise instance when the transition of train position or gate angle crosses a threshold. Note that any arbitrarily small (positive) value can be chosen for this temporal precision.

```
1   happens(train_in, T) :-
2       holdsAt(position(X1),T1),
3       holdsAt(position(X2),T2),
4       X1 #< 10, X2 #>= 10,
5       sampling_window(W),
6       T2 #< T1 + W, T2 #> T1,
7       infimum(T2, T).
8   happens(signal_lower, T) :-
9       holdsAt(position(X1),T1),
10      holdsAt(position(X2),T2),
11      X1 #< 5, X2 #>= 5,
12      sampling_window(W),
13      T2 #< T1 + W, T2 #> T1,
14      infimum(T2, T).
15  happens(gate_close, T) :-
16      gate_angle_lower(A1,T1),
17      gate_angle_lower(A2,T2),
18      A1 #< 90, A2 #>= 90,
19      sampling_window(W),
20      T2 #< T1 + W, T2 #> T1,
21      infimum(T2, T).

22  happens(gate_open, T) :-
23      gate_angle_rise(A1,T1),
24      gate_angle_rise(A2,T2),
25      A1 #> 0, A2 #=< 0,
26      sampling_window(W),
27      T2 #< T1 + W, T2 #> T1,
28      infimum(T2, T).
29  happens(signal_raise, T) :-
30      holdsAt(passing,T1),
31      holdsAt(leaving,T2),
32      sampling_window(W),
33      T2 #< T1 + W, T2 #> T1,
34      infimum(T2, T).
35  happens(train_exit, T) :-
36      holdsAt(position(X1),T1),
37      holdsAt(position(X2),T2),
38      X1 #< 20, X2 #>= 20,
39      sampling_window(W),
40      T2 #< T1 + W, T2 #> T1,
41      infimum(T2, T).
```

With the above modeling, we query s(CASP) to check various properties relative to the train speed and gate angle rotations. We can also ask whether system is safe, i.e., if when the train is passing through the gate area the gate is open (or rising): ?- holdsAt(passing, T), holdsAt(open, T). Similarly, we can check liveness, i.e., if the gate eventually becomes open after becoming closed: ?- holdsAt(closed, T1) holdsAt(open, T2), T2 #> T1

Note that, we consider only a single train crossing the gate area. The system is modeled in a way that there is a single track and the train follows the set trajectory when approaching the gate area. As we describe in Sect. 4, if the gate lowers too slowly, it will still be lowering when the train has crossed the gate area. Such scenarios are easily detected in our modeling.

4 Checking Safety and Liveness of Train-Gate-Controller

We present several scenarios using the TGC to reason about the train and the controller behavior and check whether the system satisfies desired properties.

Note that, requirements *R7* and *R8* from EARS spec are safety and liveness checks, respectively.

– Scenario A: (i) train speed is 1 unit per second, (ii) gate angle lower rate is 30 degrees per second and, (iii) gate angle rise rate is 40 degrees per second:
  • The query, `?- happens(train_in,T)` produces binding `T = 11`, i.e., the train enters the gate area at time 11.
  • The query, `?- happens(train_exit,T)` produces the binding `T = 21`, i.e., the train exits the gate area at time 21.
  • The query `?- holdsAt(passing,T)` yields the binding `T #> 11` and `T #=< 21`, i.e., it represents the interval $(11, 21]$.
– Scenario B: (i) train speed is 1 unit per second, (ii) gate angle **lower rate is 10** degrees per second and, (iii) gate angle rise rate is 40 degrees per second.
– Scenario C: (i) train speed is 1 unit per second, (ii) gate angle lower rate is 30 degrees per second and, (iii) gate angle **rise rate is 10** degrees per second.

4.1   Safety and Liveness Queries

Let us check what happens when the train passes through the gate area, we can check the *safety* of the system. Thus, we define what it means for the system to be unsafe: the system is in an unsafe state if the gate is either open, lowering, or rising when the train is passing through the gate area:

```
1  unsafe :- holdsAt(passing, T), holdsAt(rising, T).
2  unsafe :- holdsAt(passing, T), holdsAt(opened, T).
3  unsafe :- holdsAt(passing, T), holdsAt(lowering, T).
```

For the scenario A, the query `?- unsafe` yields *no models*, therefore, the system is safe w.r.t. the assumed parameters. However, for the scenario B, the query `?- unsafe` produces a model, meaning that the system is unsafe. Similar to safety, we can check *liveness* of the system, i.e., if the gate after being closed at the time of train passing it becomes opened before a threshold Th.

```
live :- holdsAt(passing,T), holdsAt(closed,T), threshold(Th),
        holdsAt(opened,T1), T1 #> T, T1 #< T + Th.
```

In scenario C, the gate will not be open within 30 s, so if we set the liveness threshold to 30 s, the query `?- live` yields *no models*.

Table 1 lists the running times, in seconds, for the above queries to the different scenarios under s(CASP). Running times to check requirements 1 through 6 of TGC are also listed. They are straightforwardly translated into s(CASP) queries. The evaluation is run on a Quad code Intel(R) Core(TM) i7-10510U CPU @ 1.80 GHz with 8-GB RAM. In general, running the discretized versions on the CLINGO ASP system [8] takes a long time at the grounding stage itself due to the huge size of the grounded program. We ran the EC encodings of TGC based on F2LP/Clingo [12]. They produce no results at our timeout value of 40 min. The EC modelling for TGC can be found using this link: https://github.com/sarat-chandra-varanasi/event-calculus-scasp/blob/main/train_example/trajectory/trajectory.lp

Table 1. Run-time (s) comparison of TGC with 3 scenarios under s(CASP).

	Scenario A		Scenario B		Scenario C	
	Answer	Time	Answer	Time	Answer	Time
?- holdsAt(passing, T).	(11, 21]	0.241	(11, 21]	0.304	(11, 21]	0.241
?- unsafe.	×	2.082	✓	1.834	×	2.156
?- live.	✓	0.641	✓	0.607	×	1.972
?- req1.	✓	0.245	✓	0.231	✓	0.275
?- req2.	✓	0.230	✓	0.240	✓	0.245
?- req3.	✓	0.259	✓	0.265	✓	0.245
?- req4.	✓	0.461	✓	0.385	✓	0.441
?- req5.	✓	0.265	✓	0.300	✓	0.289
?- req6.	✓	0.240	✓	0.258	✓	0.249

5 Conclusion and Future Work

We have shown the ease of modeling cyber-physical systems in EC/s(CASP) and verification of their safety and liveness properties. We intend to apply our techniques to the Generalized Railroad crossing problem and industrial examples handled by UPPAAL system [7]. Also, given the EC/s(CASP) description of a cyber-physical system, one should be able to automatically derive the timed-automata implementing the system. For instance, given the railroad crossing system requirements specification, we should be able to synthesize the timed-automata for the various sub-systems, thereby opening doors to generating an implementation directly from requirement specifications that satisfies safety and liveness constraints. This would be a step towards "correct by design" approach to constructing software. In fact, one could go a step further and generate the EC/s(CASP) code directly from requirements specifications written in EARS for cyber-physical systems, and then generate an implementation from that EC/s(CASP) encoding. We leave these explorations for future work.

Acknowledgement. We are grateful to Brendan Hall, Jan Fiedor, and Kevin Driscoll of Honeywell Aerospace for discussions. Authors gratefully acknowledge support from NSF grants IIS 1718945, IIS 1910131, IIP 1916206, from Amazon Corp and US DoD, and MICINN projects RTI2018-095390-B-C33 InEDGEMobility (MCIU/AEI/FEDER, UE). Views expressed are authors' own and not of the funding agencies. We also dedicate this work to the memory of first author's father, Late Prof. Sitaramaiah Varanasi, who was passionate about Number Theory and ever so curious about Theoretical Computer Science.

References

1. Alur, R.: Principles of Cyber-Physical Systems. MIT Press, Cambridge (2015)
2. Alur, R., Dill, D.L.: A theory of timed automata. Theor. Comput. Sci. **126**(2), 183–235 (1994)

3. Arias, J., Carro, M., Salazar, E., Marple, K., Gupta, G.: Constraint answer set programming without grounding. In: Theory and Practice of Logic Programming, vol. 18, no. 3–4, pp. 337–354 (2018). https://doi.org/10.1017/S1471068418000285
4. Arias, J., Chen, Z., Carro, M., Gupta, G.: Modeling and reasoning in event calculus using goal-directed constraint answer set programming. In: Gabbrielli, M. (ed.) LOPSTR 2019. LNCS, vol. 12042, pp. 139–155. Springer, Cham (2020). https://doi.org/10.1007/978-3-030-45260-5_9
5. Arias, J., Carro, M., Chen, Z., Gupta, G.: Modeling and reasoning in event calculus using goal-directed constraint answer set programming. In: Theory and Practice of Logic Programming, pp. 1–30 (2021). https://doi.org/10.1017/S1471068421000156
6. Bansal, A.: Towards next generation logic programming systems. Ph.D. thesis, Department of Computer Science, University of Texas at Dallas (2007)
7. Behrmann, G., David, A., Larsen, K.G.: A tutorial on UPPAAL. In: Bernardo, M., Corradini, F. (eds.) SFM-RT 2004. LNCS, vol. 3185, pp. 200–236. Springer, Heidelberg (2004). https://doi.org/10.1007/978-3-540-30080-9_7
8. Gebser, M., et al.: Potassco: the Potsdam answer set solving collection. AI Commun. **24**(2), 107–124 (2011). https://doi.org/10.3233/AIC-2011-0491
9. Gelfond, M., Lifschitz, V.: The stable model semantics for logic programming. In: 5th International Conference on Logic Programming, pp. 1070–1080 (1988). http://www.cse.unsw.edu.au/~cs4415/2010/resources/stable.pdf
10. Gupta, G., Pontelli, E.: A constraint-based approach for specification and verification of real-time systems. In: Proceedings Real-Time Systems Symposium, pp. 230–239. IEEE (1997)
11. Hall, B., et al.: Knowledge-assisted reasoning of model-augmented system requirements with event calculus and goal-directed answer set programming. In: Hojjat, H., Kafle, B. (eds.) Proceedings of the 8th Workshop on Horn Clauses for Verification and Synthesis, Virtual, Volume 344 of EPTCS, 28 March 2021, pp. 79–90 (2021). https://doi.org/10.4204/EPTCS.344.6
12. Lee, J., Palla, R.: System F2LP – computing answer sets of first-order formulas. In: Erdem, E., Lin, F., Schaub, T. (eds.) LPNMR 2009. LNCS (LNAI), vol. 5753, pp. 515–521. Springer, Heidelberg (2009). https://doi.org/10.1007/978-3-642-04238-6_51
13. Mavin, A., Wilkinson, P.: Big EARS (the return of "easy approach to requirements engineering"). In: 2010 18th IEEE International Requirements Engineering Conference, pp. 277–282. IEEE (2010). https://doi.org/10.1109/RE.2010.39
14. Mavin, A., et al.: Easy approach to requirements syntax (EARS). In: 2009 17th IEEE International Requirements Engineering Conference, pp. 317–322. IEEE (2009). https://doi.org/10.1109/RE.2009.9
15. Mueller, E.T.: Commonsense Reasoning: An Event Calculus Based Approach. Morgan Kaufmann, Waltham (2014)
16. Saeedloei, N., Gupta, G.: A logic-based modeling and verification of CPS. SIGBED Rev. **8**(2), 31–34 (2011). https://doi.org/10.1145/2000367.2000374
17. Saeedloei, N., Gupta, G.: Timed definite clause ω-grammars. In: Hermenegildo, M.V., Schaub, T. (eds.) Technical Communications of the 26th International Conference on Logic Programming, ICLP 2010, Volume 7 of LIPIcs, Edinburgh, Scotland, UK, 16–19 July 2010, pp. 212–221 (2010)
18. Shanahan, M.: The event calculus explained. In: Wooldridge, M.J., Veloso, M. (eds.) Artificial Intelligence Today. LNCS (LNAI), vol. 1600, pp. 409–430. Springer, Heidelberg (1999). https://doi.org/10.1007/3-540-48317-9_17

Parallel Declarative Solutions of Sequencing Problems Using Multi-valued Decision Diagrams and GPUs

Fabio Tardivo$^{(\boxtimes)}$ and Enrico Pontelli

Department of Computer Science, New Mexico State University,
Las Cruces, NM 88003, USA
{ftardivo,epontell}@nmsu.com

Abstract. The resolution of combinatorial optimization problems, especially in the area concerned with the sequencing of tasks (i.e., referred to as *sequencing problems*), is an important challenge. This domain covers a wide breadth of applications, e.g., expressed as scheduling or routing problems. Such problems can often be optimally solved using Constraint Programming techniques; nevertheless, if a "good" solution is needed in a short amount of time, Constraint Programming techniques may not be feasible.

This paper explores the opportunities that the transitional semantics of Multi-valued Decision Diagrams (MDDs) offers in terms of modeling and efficiency. The paper explores the combination of MDDs with Large Neighborhood Search (LNS), as an effective local search strategy. The paper also demonstrates the use of GPU-based parallelism to enhance efficiency in the exploration of the search space. The paper describes the integration of these techniques within a solver, focused on a time-bounded search for high-quality solutions. The solver is evaluated on several classes of benchmarks, with positive outcomes in terms of time and solution quality compared to state-of-the-art constraint-based solvers.

Keywords: Multi-valued Decision Diagram · GPGPU · Local search

1 Introduction

In this work, we focus on solving a class of hard combinatorial problems named *sequencing problems*. They require determining the best order for performing a set of tasks and are common in routing and scheduling applications. These problems are often solved using Constraint Programming (CP) techniques, but in applications where a solution is needed in (almost) real-time, or the problem changes frequently, faster approaches are needed.

This work proposes and implements a fast method to find good quality solutions for sequencing problems. It makes use of the powerful *transitional semantic* of Multi-valued Decision Diagrams (MDDs), the exploration capabilities of Large

© Springer Nature Switzerland AG 2022
J. Cheney and S. Perri (Eds.): PADL 2022, LNCS 13165, pp. 191–207, 2022.
https://doi.org/10.1007/978-3-030-94479-7_13

Neighborhood Search (LNS), and the parallelism offered by the Graphics Process Units (GPU). The contributions of this paper are the following:

- An original approach that makes use of MDDs to repair the partially destroyed solutions in an LNS. Unlike traditional approaches that make use of problem-specific heuristics or generic Constraint Programming, our method is a generic heuristic algorithm.
- The design and implementation of a solver that performs parallel LNS on both CPU and GPU. On the contrary to traditional parallel implementations of LNS, which exploit only the CPU or only the GPU, our solver makes them cooperate for complementary aspects of the search process.

The rest of the paper is organized as follows. Section 2 gives an introduction to the techniques integrated into this work, namely Multi-valued Decision Diagrams, Large Neighborhood Search, and General-Purpose computing on Graphics Processing Units (GPGPU). Section 3 describes how sequencing problems can be easily modeled, how the search is performed, and how the implementation works. Section 4 details the benchmarks we made and analyzes the results. Section 5 concludes the paper.

2   Background

A *sequencing problem* of n tasks can be modeled as a Constraint Optimization Problem (COP) with n variables $x_1, \ldots, x_n$. Each variable x_i has domain $\{0, \ldots, n-1\}$ and represents the position of the i-th task in a possible executions sequence. Such variables are commonly subject to a number of constraints, including an *allDifferent* constraint, to ensure a distinct assignment of items in the sequencing, and a number of precedence constraints of the form $x_i < x_j$. The problem includes a cost function $c : \{0, \ldots, n-1\}^n \to \mathbb{R}$. A solution to the COP consists of an assignment of values to the variables $x_1 = v_1, \ldots, x_n = v_n$ that satisfies all the constraints and minimizes the value of $c(v_1, \ldots, v_n)$. Meta-heuristics, such as the *Large Neighborhood Search*, are proven methods to deal with sequencing problems [12] and *Multi-valued Decision Diagrams* have recently emerged as a promising technique to solve such problems [8].

2.1   Multi-valued Decision Diagrams

Binary Decision Diagrams (BDD) are compact representations of boolean functions [1,21]. They gained popularity as a formalism for canonical representations in the context of verification of logic designs [6]. Not long ago, a generalization of BDD, called *Multi-valued Decision Diagrams (MDDs)* found applications in constraint programming as an effective filtering [2] and propagation [17] technique. MDDs have been applied to obtain bounds in optimization problems [5] and in general branch-and-bound algorithms for discrete optimization [4].

MDDs are extensions of BDDs to multiple values. They can be used to compactly represent the solutions of Constraint Satisfaction Problems (CSP). Let $P = (X, D, C)$ be a CSP such that:

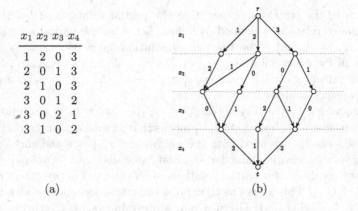

Fig. 1. Solutions of P represented as table and MDD

$$X = \{x_1, x_2, x_3, x_4\}$$
$$D = \{\{0, 1, 2, 3\}, \ldots, \{0, 1, 2, 3\}\}$$
$$C = \{allDifferent(x_1, x_2, x_3, x_4), x_1 > x_3, x_2 < x_4\}$$

Its solutions (see Fig. 1a) can be encoded in an MDD with respect to a given variable ordering. For the order x_1, x_2, x_3, x_4 the MDD is illustrated in Fig. 1b. In the Direct Acyclic Graph (DAG) behind an MDD, we have a root node r and a terminal node t; an edge represents a feasible value for the corresponding variable and a path from the root r to a node v represents a partial solution. A *partial solution* is an assignments $x_1 = v_1, \ldots, x_i = v_i$ such that there are values $v_{i+1}, \ldots, v_n$ that make $x_1 = v_1, \ldots, x_i = v_i, x_{i+1} = v_{i+1}, \ldots, x_n = v_n$ a solution. It follows that every path from r to the terminal node t represents a solution and each solution is represented by a path from r to t.

An MDD can be described as a Labeled Transition System (LTS) defined by the triple $(S, \Lambda, \rightarrow)$ where S is a set of states, Λ is a set of labels, and $\rightarrow$ is a subset of $S \times \Lambda \times S$. A transition from state s to state s' with label ℓ is written $s \xrightarrow{\ell} s'$. Let $P = (X, D, C)$ a CSP and M the MDD encoding its solutions for a fixed variable order $x_1, \ldots, x_n$, then the LTS corresponding to M is such that:

1. The set of states S is partitioned in $n + 1$ *layers*. The first layer L_0 contains a single root state s_r without predecessors, and the last layer L_{n+1} contains a single terminal state s_t without successors.
2. The labels set Λ is defined as the union of the values in the domains $\bigcup_{D_i \in D} D_i$.
3. The transition relation $\rightarrow$ connects only states of adjacent layers L_i, L_{i+1} with labels in the domain of x_{i+1}.
4. For $i > 0$, a state $s \in L_i$ is a non-empty set of partial solutions. Such partial solutions have form $x_1 = \ell_1, \ldots, x_i = \ell_i$ and are defined by the sequences of i transitions $s_r \xrightarrow{\ell_1} \cdots \xrightarrow{\ell_i} s$.

5. For $i > 0$, the states in L_i partition the partial solutions of length i by a equivalence relation $\sim$ defined as follow. Let p be the partial solution $x_1 = v_1, \ldots, x_i = v_i$ and p' be the partial solution $x_1 = v'_1, \ldots, x_i = v'_i$, then $p \sim p'$ iff for every solution $x_1 = v_1, \ldots, x_i = v_i, x_{i+1} = v_{i+1}, \ldots, x_n = v_n$, the assignment $x_1 = v'_1, \ldots, x_i = v'_i, x_{i+1} = v_{i+1}, \ldots, x_n = v_n$ is a solution and for every solution $x_1 = v'_1, \ldots, x_i = v_i,' x_{i+1} = v_{i+1}, \ldots, x_n = v_n$, the assignment $x_1 = v_1, \ldots, x_i = v_i, x_{i+1} = v_{i+1}, \ldots, x_n = v_n$ is a solution.

6. A transition $s \xrightarrow{v} s'$ from L_i to L_{i+1} means that at least one of the partial solutions of s can be extended with the assignment $x_{i+1} = v$ and such extended partial solutions are contained in s'. Point 5. entails that s' is unique, since the contrary means that a partial solutions of length $i + 1$ is present in multiple states of L_{i+1}. This allows us to express the transition relation as a function $t : S \times \Lambda \rightarrow S \cup \{s_\emptyset\}$. Given a pair state-value (s, v), t returns the state s' of extended partial solutions, if present, and the dummy state $s_\emptyset$ without outgoing edges otherwise.

The abstraction given by an LTS enables the top-down construction of an MDD illustrated in Algorithm 1. The algorithm is provided with the variables' domains D, the root state s_r and the transition function t. The output is an MDD M in the form of a DAG. The construction begins initializing L_0 with the root state and proceeds iteratively building the next layer L_i using the function t. In line 7 is calculated a candidate state s' from a state $s \in L_{i-1}$ and a value $v \in D_i$. Line 8 checks if s' is a dummy state and in such a case the iteration is terminated. If s' is a proper state, line 9 verify its presence in L_i

---

Input: Variables domains $D = \{D_1, D_2, \ldots\}$, root state s_r, transition function t
Output: An MDD $M = (V, E)$

```
1  M = ({s_r}, ∅)
2  L_0 = {s_r}
3  for i = 1 to |D| do
4  |   L_i = ∅
5  |   foreach s ∈ L_{i-1} do
6  |   |   foreach v ∈ D_i do
7  |   |   |   s' = t(s, v)
8  |   |   |   if s' ≠ s_∅ then
9  |   |   |   |   if s' ∉ L_i then
10 |   |   |   |   |   L_i = L_i ∪ {s'}
11 |   |   |   |   |   M.V = M.V ∪ {s'}
12 |   |   |   |   end
13 |   |   |   |   M.E = M.E ∪ (s, v, s')
14 |   |   |   end
15 |   |   end
16 |   end
17 end
18 return M
```

Algorithm 1: Top-down algorithm to construct an MDD

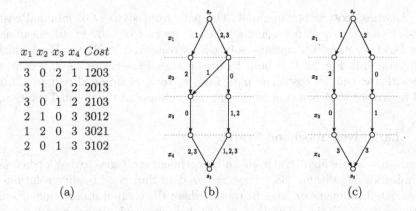

x_1	x_2	x_3	x_4	Cost
3	0	2	1	1203
3	1	0	2	2013
3	0	1	2	2103
2	1	0	3	3012
1	2	0	3	3021
2	0	1	3	3102

(a)   (b)   (c)

Fig. 2. Solutions cost, relaxed MDD, and restricted MDD for P'

(line 9) and in the negative case s' is added to L_i. The iteration terminate with the creation of the transaction (s, v, s') at line 13.

The creation of states that contain only partial solutions is crucial for the algorithm. Hooker et al. [18] analyze the relationship between Decision Diagrams and Dynamic Programming (DP), demonstrating that if a problem is solvable by a DP model, it is possible to define a transition function that does not lead to infeasible states.

The DAG underlying an MDD can grow exponentially in the number of the variables and quickly become too expensive to process. This problem can be contained by limiting the *width* of the graph [4]. When a layer L_i grows too large, it can be reduced by:

Relaxation This approach heuristically chooses some states $S_i \subset L_i$ and merges them in a single state s_m. For every state $s' \in S_i$, each incoming transition (s, v, s') is replaced with a transition ending to new state (s, v, s_m). Similarly, each outgoing transition (s', v, s) is replaced with a transition starting from the new state (s_m, v, s). It follows that there will be some new paths from s_r to s_t and such paths are not solutions.

Restriction This approach heuristically chooses some states $S_i \subset L_i$ and deletes them. For every state $s' \in S_i$, each incoming transition (s, v, s') is deleted, and each outgoing (s', v, s) is deleted too. It follows that there will be fewer paths from s_r to s_t and so fewer solutions.

The usefulness of relaxed and restricted MDDs is more clear in the context of optimization problems. Let P' the constraint optimization problem derived from P and the cost function $c(\cdot)$ that maps a partial solution p to an integer as follows:

$$c(p) = p[1] + p[2] \cdot 10 + p[3] \cdot 100 + p[4] \cdot 1000$$

where $p[i] = x_i$ when x_i is assigned and 0 otherwise (see Fig. 2a). A relaxed MDD for P' of width 2 is illustrated in Fig. 2b. It is built by merging the states

$s \in L_i$ whose cost is not minimal. The path from s_r to s_t of minimal cost is $2, 0, 1, 1$ and despite it not being a solution, its cost of 1102 is still meaningful as a *lower bound* of the optimal solution. A restricted MDD for P' of width 2 is illustrated in Fig. 2c. It is built by discarding all the states $s \in L_i$ except the two with the smaller cost. The path from s_r to s_t of minimal cost is $1, 2, 0, 3$, and its cost of 3021 is meaningful as an *upper bound* of the optimal solution.

2.2 Large Neighborhood Search

Metaheuristics are high-level problem-independent strategies to develop heuristic optimization algorithms [33]. They are used to find good-quality solutions to complicated problems or large instances where the computational time of exact methods is prohibitive. The field of metaheuristics includes a broad range of proposals, such as early methods like simulated annealing [19], tabu search [13], genetic algorithm [14], and more recently ant colony optimization [10], variable neighborhood search [24], and large neighborhood search [32].

In this work, we are particularly concerned with *Large Neighborhood Search* (LNS), which has become one of the most successful paradigms for solving various routing and scheduling problems [12]. LNS gradually transforms a given initial solution, by repeatedly destroying and repairing some of its parts (see Algorithm 2). The destroy method $d(\cdot)$ usually contains some randomness, so that different parts are destroyed each time. The repair method $r(\cdot)$ must balance the quality of the repaired solutions and the repairing time, so it is usually based on some heuristics. The solutions that are obtained by destroying and repairing a solution s are referred to as the *neighborhood* of s. The advantage of LNS is that the neighborhoods can be large, possibly exponential on the size of the destroyed parts, thus enabling broad navigation of the solution space.

Input: Initial solution s_i
Output: Better solution s_b
1 $s_b = s_i$
2 $s_c = s_i$
3 **while** *stopping criterion is not met* **do**
4     $s_t = r(d(s_c))$
5   **if** *accept*(s_t, s_c) **then**
6        $s_c = s_t$
7   **end**
8   **if** $cost(s_t) < cost(s_b)$ **then**
9        $s_b = s_t$
10   **end**
11 **end**
12 **return** s_b

Algorithm 2: Large neighborhood search algorithm

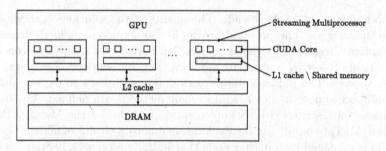

Fig. 3. GPU architecture

2.3 GPGPU with CUDA

General-Purpose computing on Graphics Processing Units (GPGPU) is the use of a Graphics Processing Unit (GPU) to speed up computations traditionally handled by the Central Processing Unit (CPU). In 2007, NVIDIA introduced the *Compute Unified Device Architecture* (CUDA), a general-purpose programming library and APIs that allow programmers to ignore the underlying graphical concepts in favor of more high-performance computing concepts [25]. CUDA has been successfully used to accelerate computations in a variety of fields, such as physics, bioinformatics, and machine learning [26].

The advantages of GPU come from its architecture. While the CPU is optimized to execute a small number of threads with relatively low latency, the GPU is optimized to run thousands of them in parallel and achieve better performance despite the lower speed of the GPU computing units (i.e., high throughput). The architecture of a GPU (Fig. 3) includes a main memory (DRAM), an L2 cache, and an array of Streaming Multiprocessors (SM). Each SM contains a small amount of fast memory, used as L1 cache or scratchpad memory (the *Shared memory*), and several CUDA Cores. The CUDA cores in one SM are in charge of executing groups (referred to as *blocks*) of threads using a Single Instruction-Multiple Data model. In case of control flow divergence among the threads within a block, their execution is serialized.

Designing a CUDA program in blocks of threads guides the programmer in the parallelization process. The problem has to be divided into coarse subproblems that can be solved independently by blocks of threads, and each subproblem into finer pieces solvable by the threads within a block.

2.4 Related Works

The literature has explored a number of approaches to parallelize LNS and its variants. The common idea among all these proposals is the use of parallelism to concurrently explore different neighborhoods. The work in [28] explores the combination of LNS with a portfolio method. The portfolio contains different cost functions, each one with an associated weight. A cost function is selected at each iteration, with a probability proportional to its weight, and used in different neighborhoods by multiple threads. The quality of the solutions is then used to update the weights. The proposal by Ropke [30] explores a generic framework for Adaptive Large Neighborhood Search [31]. Such variation of LNS consists of using a pool of destroy and repair methods that are heuristically chosen based on past success. The implementation uses different threads to explore different neighborhoods, once the destroy and repair methods are defined. The work in [16] presents a distributed LNS implementation that uses the Message Passing Interface (MPI) to parallelize the exploration among a cluster of nodes. The computation is managed by a master node that initially receives a heuristic solution from each worker node. The master node iteratively selects the best solution received, broadcasts it to the workers, and updates the best solution when necessary. The workers repeatedly receive a solution, perform an LNS, and return the solution to the master. The proposal by Campeotto et al. [7] makes use of a GPU to parallelize LNS. The initial solution is found by performing parallel constraint propagation on GPU. After that, the GPU is used to parallelize the LNS. Another approach to parallelize LNS using GPUs is presented in [3]. The initial solution is obtained using the GPU to run several instances of a greedy algorithm, each with different parameters. After that, the GPU is used to parallelize the ALNS.

3   Design and Implementation

3.1   Overview

The overall idea of this work is to use the transitional semantic of MDDs to improve the efficacy of classical LNS. A partially destroyed solution is repaired using a *restricted* MDD of width w. During its construction, we keep the w states of each layer that contains the partial solutions with better costs. Finally, we consider the solution with the best cost as the repaired solution.

This approach has two benefits compared to traditional backtracking for repairing. First, it enables a heuristic cost-driven navigation of the search space, where the more promising regions are explored early. Second, it can be effectively parallelized and efficiently implemented on GPUs since each transition is independent of the others.

To obtain an efficient and general system, we relax some definitions presented in Sect. 2. First, we allow the presence of multiple copies of the same state in the layers (Algorithm 1 line 9). This is because the time required for the presence check may overcome the benefits of having more solutions encoded in a restricted MDD. The resulting structure is a tree, instead of a DAG, with the property that a state contains only one partial solution. By including it in the state representation, we do not need to traverse the MDD to find the best solution since it is stored in one of the states of the last layer. This allows us to perform the entire construction in a very small amount of memory that fits in the fast Shared memory of the GPU. The second change that we made is about the transition function; we allow t to return states made of an assignment that is not a partial solution. This translates into greater flexibility, where t can range

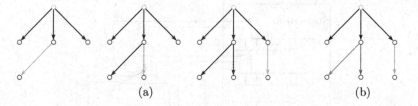

Fig. 4. Calculation of the third layer on CPU and on GPU

from a simple function that just describes if and how to create a state given a state and a value, to a complex function that creates a state only if it contains a partial solution.

We implement our ideas in a generic solver that can be easily made problem-specific providing:

- Problem representation,
- State representation,
- Transition function.

Once these elements are integrated, the solver accepts as input instances of the problem in standard JSON format. After the instance is read, the search for an initial solution begins. Such search greedily explores the complete MDD of the problem using the CPU for a fixed amount of time, and the best solution found becomes the initial solution for the LNS. The LNS explores multiple neighborhoods in parallel using both the CPU and the GPU to find better solutions. When the allotted time has been exhausted, the best solution found to that point is returned.

3.2   LNS Parallelization

Effective metaheuristics are designed to balance two opposite components: intensification and diversification. *Intensification* focuses the search on the region of the search space surrounding the current best solution. Its purpose is to find better solutions that are similar to the current one. *Diversification* spreads the search on unexplored regions of the search space. Its purpose is to find better solutions that are genuinely different from the current one.

The proposed solver distributes components of intensification and diversification as best suited to the specific features of the CPU and GPU architectures. The CPU provides higher speed and access to large cache memory; these features can be used to support the creation of wide MDDs, that consider many values for each variable (i.e., diversification). On the other hand, a GPU supports massive parallelism coupled with access to fast (but relatively small) on-chip memory; these features can be used to build narrow MDDs, with few values for each variable (i.e., intensification).

Both CPU and GPU use a top-down algorithm to build the MDDs. It differs from Algorithm 1 only in the fact that we keep a bounded number of states per

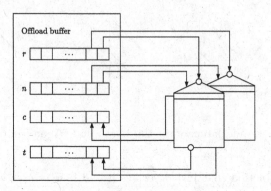

Fig. 5. Usage of offload buffer

layer since we are building restricted MDDs. In order to select states, we use a heuristic based on the cost of the partial solution in such states, discarding the states with higher costs. States with the same cost are randomly shuffled to improve diversification. The CPU applies a simple form of parallelism, where multiple MDDs are built at the same time, each of them in a sequential way. In detail, each MDD is created by a thread that calculates the states of the next layer one by one (Fig. 4a). The GPU applies a more complex form of parallelism, where multiple MDDs are built at the same time, each of them in a parallel way. Each MDD is created by a block of threads, where the states of the next layer are concurrently calculated by the block's threads (Fig. 4b).

The construction of the restricted MDDs is managed by two *offload buffers*, one for the CPU and one for the GPU. An offload buffer is defined as a quadruple $o = (r, n, c, t)$, where r is an array containing the root states, n is an array of neighborhoods descriptions, c is an array used to store the children of the root states, and t is an array dedicated to storing the terminal states. During the computation, each thread/block of the CPU/GPU uses a state from r to build a restricted MDD according to the corresponding neighborhood, saving in c the children of the root and in t the terminal state (see Fig. 5). Because we relaxed some conditions of Sect. 2, there is no guarantee that a terminal state exists or it is unique. In the first case, we save in t a dummy state $s_\emptyset$, in the second case we save the state with the best solution.

The initial solution is found by the CPU using a greedy algorithm. It uses a priority queue Q that sorts states by the cost of their partial solutions, and it is initialized with the root state of the complete MDD of the problem. The algorithm uses Q to fill the CPU offload buffer r array, and without considering any neighborhood, calculates c and t. Then, the states in c are pushed into Q while the states in t are compared with the current best solution. We observed that spending too much time on this loop rarely gives better solutions and subtracts time to the LNS. On the other side, investing too little time leads to initial solutions of sensibly lower quality that the LNS has difficulty improving. We empirically determined that stopping the initial search after 10 s is a valid compromise.

Once the initial search is complete, the LNS starts on both CPU and GPU. It randomly generates the neighborhood descriptions in n using the current best solution. After that, it fills the offload buffers' r arrays with the root state of the problem and builds the MDDs. Finally, the states in t are compared with the current best solution. The algorithm stops when a set timeout is reached.

3.3 Implementation Details

The solver (called LNS-MDD) is written in CUDA C++ and designed to be a generic framework that is made problem-specific using templates [34]. Once compiled with the problem representation, state representation, and transition function, LNS-MDD can solve instances of that problem without further adjustments to the data structures or algorithms.

The state representation adopted is based on triples $s = (p, c, a)$. In such a triple, p encodes the partial solution of the state, c is the cost of the partial solution, and a is the set of admissible values for extending the partial solution. The transition function takes advantage of this representation and works as follows. Given a state s and a value v, the function first checks whether $v \in a$; if that is the case, the function creates a new state s' from s, by extending p with v, removing v from a, and updating c, a according to the problem definition. Otherwise, t returns a default dummy state $s_\emptyset$.

A neighborhood is described by a pair of lists $n = (c, v)$ such that v stores the values of the current solution, and c indicates whatever a variable has to be fixed to the corresponding value in v. The list c is randomly generated depending on a probability threshold $0 \leq lns_= \leq 1$: a random number $0 \leq r \leq 1$ is generated for each variable, if $r \leq lns_=$ then the variable has to be fixed to the corresponding value in v, otherwise it is free to take any value.

From the GPU perspective, there are two important observations. First, because the layer L_{i+1} depends only on L_i, it is possible to build a restricted MDD in a bounded amount of memory. This allows us to calculate the entire restricted MDD on the fast Shared memory instead of using the high latency DRAM [35]. The second observation is that each state of L_{i+1} is calculated using the same transition function t. This is important because different threads can calculate different states with minimal serialization.

The amount of parallelism and other aspects of the algorithm can be tuned to better exploit the available hardware. The following list contains all the parameters that can be changed:

w_c The width of the MDDs built on the CPU.
m_c The number of MDDs built in parallel on the CPU.
w_g The width of the MDDs built on the GPU.
m_g The number of MDDs built in parallel on the GPU.
$lns_=$ The probability threshold used to generate the LNS neighborhoods.

We observed that a good tuning strategy is to start with $w_c = 500$, $m_g = 8$, $w_g = 3$, $m_g = 2500$ and adjust such values so that each LNS iteration takes about 1 s on both CPU and GPU.

4   Results and Analysis

We evaluate our solver in a five-way comparison on three benchmarks drawn from the literature. We compare:

CPU-Only MDD-LNS configured to use only the CPU for the LNS.
CPU-GPU MDD-LNS configured to use both CPU and GPU for the LNS.
Gecode A state-of-the-art constraint solver [11].
Gecode-LNS A Gecode-based implementation of LNS [9].
Yuck A state-of-the-art local-search constraint solver based on simulated annealing [22].

This selection of systems allows us to contrast the proposed design with and without the use of a GPU, and against an efficient constraint solver, another solver using LNS, and a solver using a different local-search technique.

The benchmarks that we use are:

Sequential Ordering Problem (SOP) Let G a weighted directed graph, v_s, v_e two of its nodes, and C a set of precedence constraints among nodes. The sequential ordering problem consists of finding the shorter Hamiltonian path from v_s to v_e that satisfies all the precedence constraints in C. The dataset is from the TSPLib [29] and is a selection of the 9 open instances, all synthetic, with up to 380 nodes. For Gecode, Gecode-LNS, and Yuck, we create a MiniZinc model based on the all_different global constraint.

Open-Shop Scheduling Problem (OSSP) Let $M_1, \ldots, M_m$ machines and $J_1, \ldots, J_n$ jobs where each job consists of m independent operations. An operation O_{ij} of the job J_j is processed on machine M_i for an amount of time p_{ij}. Each job is processed by one machine at a time, and each machine process only one job at a time. The open-shop scheduling problem consists of finding a start time s_{ij} for each operation such that the makespan $max_{1 \leq i \leq m, 1 \leq j \leq n}(s_{ij} + p_{ij})$ is minimum. The dataset is from the literature [15] and is a selection of the 10 bigger instances, all synthetic, with 10 jobs and 10 machines. For Gecode, Gecode-LNS and Yuck, we used the model present in the MiniZinc Benchmark Suite [23].

Cable Tree Wiring Problem (CTWP) Consider m electric boards with a total of b couples of plugs that have to be connected with cables by a robot. Because the presence of a cable can prevent the connection of other plugs, there are precedences among plugs connections. Such precedences can lead to situations where the first plug of the pair is connected but the second can not be immediately connected because other plugs have to be connected first. The resuming from such interruption is not perfect and there is a chance to fail. The cable tree wiring problem consists of finding a plugs connection order that minimizes the failure chance [20]. The dataset is from the authors of the problem and is a selection of 10 hard instances, 5 real and 5 synthetic, with up to 100 cables. For Gecode, Gecode-LNS and Yuck, we used the MiniZinc model provided by the authors of the problem.

These benchmarks give us an insight of how our approach performs on three classes of problems: routing problems with precedence constraints, scheduling problems with big search space, and scheduling problems with disjunctive constraints.

The comparison focuses on hard instances and small timeouts to simulate the cases in which a solution is required in real-time [27]. The benchmarks are performed by running the solvers with 60 s timeout. We solved each instance 10 times and considered the average results.

The CPU-Only configuration is $w_c = 1000$, $m_c = 16$, while the CPU-GPU version includes $w_g = 5$, $m_g = 10000$. Gecode, Gecode-LNS, and Yuck are configured to use 16 threads. The solvers CPU-Only, CPU-GPU, and Gecode-LNS randomly generate their neighborhoods in such a way that each variable has 70% chance to be fixed to the corresponding value in the current solution. Empirical tests directed us to configure Gecode-LNS and Yuck to stop the exploration of a neighborhood after visiting 10000 nodes of the search tree. A smaller value leads to failure in finding an initial solution or prevents exploring the neighborhoods enough to find better solutions. A bigger value leads to exploring fewer neighborhoods within the timeout and often makes the exploration uselessly looks for betters solutions. We disabled the Yuck's pre-solver since it often prevents the solver to find a solution within the timeout.

The system used in the benchmarks has an Intel Core i7-10700K CPU with 8 cores/16 threads at 3.8 GHz, 32 GB of DDR4 RAM at 3200 MHz, and an NVIDIA GeForce RTX 3080 GPU with 8704 CUDA cores at 1.7 GHz and 10 GB of GDDR6X RAM. The system runs Ubuntu 20.10 with Linux kernel 5.8, NVIDIA drivers 465.19, and CUDA 11.3. The versions of the solvers are Gecode 6.3.0 and Yuck 20200923.

4.1 Results

We present the results of the benchmarks in Tables 1, 2, and 3 using three metrics. The first is the best solutions average cost, the second is the best solutions average search time and the third is the optimality gap. This last metric is the ratio between the best solutions average cost and the best know solution cost. The smallest gap of each instance is highlighted using a bold font. If a solver is not able to find a solution within the time limit, then the relative metrics will be omitted.

4.2 Analysis

In the SOP benchmark, the configuration CPU-Only shows promising performance with good solutions for all the instances. Such results are improved in terms of cost and\or search time when also the GPU is used. Both Gecode and Gecode-LNS found solutions of cost sensibly higher than MDD-LNS, and both were not able to provide a solution within the timeout for rbg378a, the bigger instance in the benchmark. The Gecode-LNS implementation was able to provide a solution for kro124p.4 on the contrary of Gecode. This is because

Table 1. Benchmark results for the Sequential Ordering Problem

Instance	CPU-Only			CPU-GPU			Gecode			Gecode-LNS			Yuck		
	Value	Time	Gap	Value	Time	Gap	Value	Time	Gap	Value	Time	Gap	Value	Time	Gap
ft70.2	43527	33	1.08	42979	27	**1.06**	57289	59	1.42	59658	58	1.48	48659	32	1.2
kro124p.1	43176	48	1.1	42767	29	**1.08**	193677	45	4.91	200941	54	5.1	55170	31	1.4
kro124p.2	47263	52	1.14	46132	36	**1.12**	183261	55	4.43	199014	44	4.81	62974	28	1.52
kro124p.3	59946	56	1.21	58621	31	**1.18**	178937	50	3.61	197042	41	3.98	74738	29	1.51
kro124p.4	91427	30	1.2	89898	30	**1.18**				185794	43	2.44	110738	19	1.46
prob.100	2080	9	1.79	2011	21	**1.73**	24085	39	20.71	26224	52	22.55	4145	29	3.56
rbg378a	3744	53	1.33	3722	57	**1.32**							7150	18	2.54
ry48p.2	18652	31	1.12	18301	21	**1.1**	44638	32	2.68	44377	28	2.66	18326	33	1.1
ry48p.3	21909	32	1.1	21525	20	**1.08**	46613	55	2.34	47122	26	2.37	22043	39	1.11

Table 2. Benchmark results for the open-shop scheduling problem

Instance	CPU-Only			CPU-GPU			Gecode			Gecode-LNS			Yuck		
	Value	Time	Gap	Value	Time	Gap	Value	Time	Gap	Value	Time	Gap	Value	Time	Gap
gp10-01	1227	43	1.12	1169	32	1.07	1160	60	1.06	1126	46	**1.03**	5833	56	5.34
gp10-02	1231	40	1.12	1198	22	1.09	1142	58	1.04	1130	20	**1.03**	5827	56	5.31
gp10-03	1290	42	1.19	1221	34	1.13	1141	53	1.06	1106	32	**1.02**	5775	56	5.34
gp10-04	1229	31	1.14	1199	28	1.11	1139	2	1.06	1092	11	**1.01**	5552	58	5.16
gp10-05	1252	49	1.17	1203	31	1.12	1108	2	1.03	1101	33	**1.03**	5666	55	5.29
gp10-06	1319	21	1.23	1211	31	1.13	1187	10	1.11	1107	41	**1.03**	5214	52	4.87
gp10-07	1308	33	1.21	1273	35	1.18	1123	58	1.04	1101	20	**1.02**	5159	52	4.78
gp10-08	1320	3	1.21	1254	19	1.15	1137	1	1.04	1098	10	**1**	5767	59	5.28
gp10-09	1294	32	1.16	1208	26	1.09	1131	6	1.02	1129	28	**1.02**	5715	59	5.14
gp10-10	1348	44	1.23	1302	34	1.19	1153	48	1.06	1106	41	**1.01**	5301	52	4.85

Table 3. Benchmark results for the cable tree wiring problem

Instance	CPU-Only			CPU-GPU			Gecode			Gecode-LNS			Yuck		
	Value	Time	Gap	Value	Time	Gap	Value	Time	Gap	Value	Time	Gap	Value	Time	Gap
A033	5365579	15	1.04	5211220	19	**1.01**	19173142	2	3.72	15648337	49	3.04			
A060	43507543	20	1.08	43110402	19	**1.07**	48428926	10	1.2	48918033	39	1.21			
A066	367173030	32	1.08	357849770	41	**1.05**									
A069	522718858	28	1.08	513712849	36	**1.06**									
A073	324979620	14	1.44	322602988	49	**1.43**									
R192	15338688	8	1.23	15113612	13	**1.22**	49900473	41	4.02	50799513	28	4.09	50705677	55	4.08
R193	10507396	10	1.55	10168835	19	**1.5**	47672071	50	7.03	44620390	58	6.58	40910908	40	6.03
R194	19739047	3	0.82	19736504	11	**0.82**	69350428	49	2.9	68650777	40	2.87	70887876	55	2.96
R195	23121710	20	0.82	22854223	18	**0.81**	63064236	6	2.25	63847011	36	2.27	67483347	50	2.4
R196	18685476	3	1.27	18685476	6	**1.27**	64366748	43	4.38	63704119	35	4.33	68475688	53	4.66

Gecode-LNS restarts the search process also for the search of an initial solution, and doing so, it does not get stuck in an unpromising part of the search tree. Finally, Yuck provided solutions such costs are from slightly to sensibly higher than MDD-LNS.

In the OSSP benchmark, Gecode provides excellent solutions, improved to almost optimal in the Gecode-LNS implementation. Such results can be explained by the optimized model that the solvers use. Such a model contains a strong formulation based on several global constraints coupled with a specific search heuristic. The resulting search process is very effective and can rapidly find high-quality solutions. The generic approach adopted by MDD-LNS provided good solutions of quality comparable to the solutions provided in the other benchmarks. Finally, Yuck provided solutions with costs about 5 times bigger than the solutions provided by the other solvers. Despite it is using the same model of Gecode and Gecode-LNS, the search effectiveness is largely affected by the local search heuristic used in place of the specialized one.

In the CTWP benchmark, the configuration CPU-Only shows excellent performance with good solutions for all the instances. Such results are improved in terms of cost when also the GPU is used. Moreover, MDD-LNS was able to find better solutions than the know best solutions for the real instances R194, R195. Both Gecode and Gecode-LNS found solutions of cost sensibly higher than MDD-LNS, and both were not able to provide a solution within the timeout for A66, A69, A73, the bigger instances in the benchmark. Finally, Yuck provides solutions comparable with Gecode\Gecode-LNS for the real instances, but it did not give solutions for the artificial instances.

5   Conclusions and Future Work

Inspired by the parallelization opportunities opened by the transitional semantic of Multi-valued Decision Diagrams, we presented the design of a solver that uses CPU and GPU to solve sequencing problems by Large Neighborhood Search. We designed it to be a general framework that can be easily made problem-specific.

We tested our implementation on three different benchmarks using random neighborhoods and focusing on small timeouts to simulate the cases in which a solution is required in real-time. The experiments confirmed that the synergetic work of CPU and GPU improves the already good results of the CPU only. On the contrary to the other solvers, our approach was able to provide a solution for all the instances within the timeout. Such solutions are consistently good among the benchmarks and, on average, just 15% more costly than the best known solutions. For a couple of instances, our approach returned solutions even better than the best know solutions.

There are many ways to extend and improve this work, such as to further parallelize the search using a cluster of CPU\GPU, make use of problem-specific neighborhoods, etc. The one that has our attention is to integrate a learning mechanism. Two possibilities in such direction are the integration with Monte Carlo Tree Search and the integration with Reinforcement Learning.

References

1. Akers, S.: Binary decision diagrams. IEEE Trans. Comput. C-27 (1978). https://doi.org/10.1109/tc.1978.1675141
2. Andersen, H.R., Hadzic, T., Hooker, J.N., Tiedemann, P.: A constraint store based on multivalued decision diagrams. In: Principles and Practice of Constraint Programming – CP 2007. Springer, Berlin (2007). https://doi.org/10.1007/978-3-540-74970-7_11
3. Bach, L., Hasle, G., Schulz, C.: Adaptive large neighborhood search on the graphics processing unit. Eur. J. Oper. Res. **275** (2019). https://doi.org/10.1016/j.ejor.2018.11.035
4. Bergman, D., Cire, A.A., van Hoeve, W.J., Hooker, J.N.: Discrete optimization with decision diagrams. INFORMS J. Comput. **28**(2016). https://doi.org/10.1287/ijoc.2015.0648
5. Bergman, D., Ciré, A.A., van Hoeve, W.-J., Hooker, J.N.: Optimization bounds from binary decision diagrams. In: O'Sullivan, B. (ed.) CP 2014. LNCS, vol. 8656, pp. 903–907. Springer, Cham (2014). https://doi.org/10.1007/978-3-319-10428-7_64
6. Bryant, R.: Graph-based algorithms for Boolean function manipulation. IEEE Trans. Comput. C-35 (1986). https://doi.org/10.1109/tc.1986.1676819
7. Campeotto, F., Dovier, A., Fioretto, F., Pontelli, E.: A GPU implementation of large neighborhood search for solving constraint optimization problems. In: ECAI (2014). https://doi.org/10.3233/978-1-61499-419-0-189
8. Cire, A.A., van Hoeve, W.J.: Multivalued decision diagrams for sequencing problems. Oper. Res. **61** (2013). https://doi.org/10.1287/opre.2013.1221
9. Dekker, J.J., de la Banda, M.G., Schutt, A., Stuckey, P.J., Tack, G.: Solver-independent large neighbourhood search. In: Hooker, J. (ed.) CP 2018. LNCS, vol. 11008, pp. 81–98. Springer, Cham (2018). https://doi.org/10.1007/978-3-319-98334-9_6
10. Dorigo, M., Maniezzo, V., Colorni, A.: Ant system: optimization by a colony of cooperating agents. IEEE Trans. Syst. Man Cyber. Part B (Cybernetics) **26** (1996). https://doi.org/10.1109/3477.484436
11. Gecode team: Gecode, https://www.gecode.org
12. Gendreau, M., Potvin, J.-Y. (eds.): Handbook of Metaheuristics. ISORMS, vol. 272. Springer, Cham (2019). https://doi.org/10.1007/978-3-319-91086-4
13. Glover, F.: Future paths for integer programming and links to artificial intelligence. Comput. Oper. Res. **13** (1986). https://doi.org/10.1016/0305-0548(86)90048-1
14. Goldberg, D.E.: Genetic algorithms in search, optimization, and machine learning. Choice Reviews Online 27 (1989). https://doi.org/10.5860/choice.27-0936
15. Guéret, C., Prins, C.: A new lower bound for the open-shop problem. Ann. Oper. Res. **92** (1999). https://doi.org/10.1023/A:1018930613891
16. Hifi, M., Negre, S., Saadi, T., Saleh, S., Wu, L.: A parallel large neighborhood search-based heuristic for the disjunctively constrained knapsack problem. In: 2014 IEEE International Parallel & Distributed Processing Symposium Workshops (2014). https://doi.org/10.1109/ipdpsw.2014.173
17. Hoda, S., van Hoeve, W.-J., Hooker, J.N.: A systematic approach to MDD-based constraint programming. In: Cohen, D. (ed.) CP 2010. LNCS, vol. 6308, pp. 266–280. Springer, Heidelberg (2010). https://doi.org/10.1007/978-3-642-15396-9_23
18. Hooker, J.N.: Decision diagrams and dynamic programming. In: Gomes, C., Sellmann, M. (eds.) CPAIOR 2013. LNCS, vol. 7874, pp. 94–110. Springer, Heidelberg (2013). https://doi.org/10.1007/978-3-642-38171-3_7

19. Kirkpatrick, S., Gelatt, C.D., Vecchi, M.P.: Optimization by simulated annealing. Science 220 (1983). https://doi.org/10.1126/science.220.4598.671
20. Koehler, J., et al.: Cable tree wiring - benchmarking solvers on a real-world scheduling problem with a variety of precedence constraints. Constraints **26**, 56–106 (2021). https://doi.org/10.1007/s10601-021-09321-w
21. Lee, C.Y.: Representation of switching circuits by binary-decision programs. Bell Syst. Tech.l J. **38** (1959). https://doi.org/10.1002/j.1538-7305.1959.tb01585.x
22. Marte, M.: Yuck. https://github.com/informarte/yuck
23. MiniZinc Team: The minizinc benchmark suite. https://github.com/MiniZinc/minizinc-benchmarks
24. Mladenović, N., Hansen, P.: Variable neighborhood search. Comput. Oper. Res. **24** (1997). https://doi.org/10.1016/s0305-0548(97)00031-2
25. Nvidia Team: CUDA toolkit documentation. https://docs.nvidia.com/cuda/cuda-c-programming-guide, (Accessed on 04/22/2021)
26. Nvidia Team: GPU accelerated applications. https://www.nvidia.com/en-us/gpu-accelerated-applications. Accessed 22 Apr 2021
27. O'Neil, R.J., Hoffman, K.: Decision diagrams for solving traveling salesman problems with pickup and delivery in real time. Oper. Res. Lett. **47** (2019). https://doi.org/10.1016/j.orl.2019.03.008
28. Perron, L., Shaw, P., Sa, I.: Parallel Large Neighborhood Search. Tech. rep, ILOG SA (2003)
29. Reinelt, G.: Traveling salesman problem library. http://comopt.ifi.uni-heidelberg.de/software/TSPLIB95/index.html
30. Røpke, S.: PALNS - a software framework for parallel large neighborhood search. In: Metaheuristic International Conference (2009)
31. Ropke, S., Pisinger, D.: An adaptive large neighborhood search heuristic for the pickup and delivery problem with time windows. Transp. Sci. **40** (2006). https://doi.org/10.1287/trsc.1050.0135
32. Shaw, P.: Using constraint programming and local search methods to solve vehicle routing problems. In: Maher, M., Puget, J.-F. (eds.) CP 1998. LNCS, vol. 1520, pp. 417–431. Springer, Heidelberg (1998). https://doi.org/10.1007/3-540-49481-2_30
33. Sörensen, K., Glover, F.W.: Metaheuristics. In: Encyclopedia of Operations Research and Management Science. Springer, Boston (2013). https://doi.org/10.1007/978-1-4419-1153-7_1167
34. Tardivo, F.: MDD-lns, https://github.com/95A31/MDD-LNS
35. Wong, H., Papadopoulou, M.M., Sadooghi-Alvandi, M., Moshovos, A.: Demystifying GPU microarchitecture through microbenchmarking. In: 2010 IEEE International Symposium on Performance Analysis of Systems & Software (ISPASS) (2010). https://doi.org/10.1109/ispass.2010.5452013

Green Application Placement
in the Cloud-IoT Continuum

Stefano Forti[✉][ID] and Antonio Brogi[ID]

Department of Computer Science, University of Pisa, Pisa, Italy
{stefano.forti,antonio.brogi}@di.unipi.it

Abstract. Green software engineering aims at reducing the environmental impact due to developing, deploying, and managing software systems. Meanwhile, Cloud-IoT paradigms can contribute to improving energy and carbon efficiency of application deployments by (*i*) reducing the amount of data and the distance they must travel across the network, (*ii*) by exploiting idle edge devices to support application deployment. In this article, we propose a declarative methodology and its Prolog prototype for determining placements of application services onto Cloud-IoT infrastructures so as to optimise energy and carbon efficiency, also considering different infrastructure power sources and operational costs. The proposal is assessed over a motivating example.

1   Introduction

The energy demand from Information and Communications Technology (ICT) could possibly reach 14% of the total worldwide footprint by 2040 [3]. As climate scientists agree on the urgency of reducing the human impact on the environment, *green software engineering* is getting increasing attention as a possible way to contain ICT energy usage and carbon emissions, through achieving a more sustainable software life-cycle [8]. While much work has focussed on embedding sustainability principles in software design phases, less work has proposed methodologies and tools to improve and assess software lifecycle sustainability [21], i.e. from application testing to deployment and runtime management. Meanwhile, Cloud-IoT computing paradigms – e.g. Fog, Edge computing [7] – have been proposed to improve on the Quality of Service (QoS) of emerging latency-sensitive and bandwidth-hungry applications. As highlighted by some authors [18,23], those paradigms can also represent greener alternatives to the Cloud paradigm as they can exploit pervasive and possibly idle computational devices closer to the IoT, thus improving on energy efficiency of those idle resources and reducing unnecessary data transfer from/to the Cloud.

To achieve the above sustainability goals, it is crucial to place application services so to meet all their requirements *and* by determining the best trade-off between the operation costs of their deployment and the expected energy consumption and carbon emissions, which very much depend on the characteristics of the target deployment nodes (i.e. energy profile, power sources, power usage effectiveness). While the problem of placing application services onto Cloud-IoT

© Springer Nature Switzerland AG 2022
J. Cheney and S. Perri (Eds.): PADL 2022, LNCS 13165, pp. 208–217, 2022.
https://doi.org/10.1007/978-3-030-94479-7_14

infrastructure to meet their software, hardware, IoT and network requirements has been extensively studied [5,19], the problem of determining energy- and carbon-aware placements was only marginally addressed until very recently [1].

In this article, based on our previous work [10,11], we illustrate a declarative programming solution to the problem of determining energy- and carbon-aware application placements in Cloud-IoT settings, also capable of estimating operational deployment costs. The methodology of [10,11] permits determining eligible application placements that meet software, hardware, IoT, latency and bandwidth requirements. We extend it so as to estimate deployment costs, energy consumption and carbon emissions of eligible application placements, by relying on data disclosed on the available Cloud-IoT nodes. Being declarative, our approach is easy to understand and extend, e.g. by employing alternative formulas to estimate all of the above. A Prolog open-source prototype, GFogBrain, is assessed over a motivating example based on lifelike data.

The rest of this article is organised as follows. Section 2 describes the model and methodology of GFogBrain, while showcasing its functioning over a lifelike motivating example. Section 3 briefly discusses some closely related work, and Sect. 4 concludes by pointing to some directions for future work.

2   GFogBrain in Action

In this section, we illustrate GFogBrain's prototype and methodology by means of a lifelike motivating example from *smart environments* [4]. GFogBrain extends our previous work in the field of context- and QoS-aware placements of Cloud-IoT applications, to also determine energy- and carbon-aware placements. Particularly, we extend the model prototype of [10] to consider all necessary ingredients to estimate energy consumption and carbon emissions of running applications, and operational costs (i.e. due to leasing computational resources to keep application services up and running).

Our goal is to support application operators, enabling them to informedly identify placements that can reduce energy consumption and carbon emissions, while assessing the impact that *being greener* could have on the operational costs of their deployments. In the next paragraphs, we detail our declarative application and infrastructure model and the declarative programming methodology implemented by GFogBrain to achieve such a goal.

Applications Requirements – As in [10], application A made of services S1 ... Sk is declared as

```
application(A, [S1, ..., Sk]).
```

The software, hardware[1] and IoT requirements of service S are declared as

```
service(S, SoftwareReqs, HardwareReqs, IoTReqs).
```

---

[1] For the sake of simplicity, we represent hardware units as integers as in [10].

Finally, interactions between services S1 and S2 with associated maximum end-to-end latency and minimum bandwidth requirements are declared as

```
s2s(S1, S2, MaxLatency, MinBandwidth).
```

Example 1. The application of Fig. 1 consists of two interacting services – Lights Driver and ML Optimiser – for optimising ambient lighting in a museum based on processing real-time video footage. The Lights Driver requires 2 GB and Ubuntu to run, and to reach out a video-camera and a lights hub. Similarly, ML Optimiser requires 16 GB of RAM and the availability of Ubuntu, MySQL and Python on the deployment node, which must also be equipped with a GPU for processing streamed data. Finally, the interaction from the Lights Driver to the ML Optimiser requires at least 16 Mbps of available bandwidth and tolerates at most 20 ms latency. On the other hand, the interaction from the ML Optimiser to the Lights Driver needs only 0.5 Mbps, with a latency lower than 50 ms. Such an application can be simply declared as in Fig. 2.   □

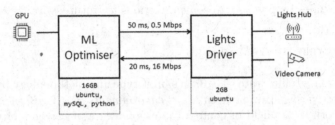

Fig. 1. Example application.

```
application(lightsApp, [mlOptimiser, lightsDriver]).
    service(mlOptimiser, [mySQL, python, ubuntu], 16, [gpu]).
    service(lightsDriver, [ubuntu], 2, [videocamera, lightshub]).
    s2s(mlOptimiser, lightsDriver, 50, 0.5).
    s2s(lightsDriver, mlOptimiser, 20, 16).
```

Fig. 2. Example application declaration.

Infrastructure Capabilities – Complementarily to application service requirements, Cloud-IoT nodes can be declared along with their software, free hardware and IoT capabilities, and with the unit hourly cost for leasing hardware resources:

```
node(NodeId, SoftwareCapabilities, FreeHW, IoTCapabilities).
cost(NodeId, UnitHWCostPerHour).
```

Similarly, end-to-end links between nodes N1 and N2 are declared, along with their FeaturedLatency and FeaturedBandwidth, as in

```
link(N1, N2, FeaturedLatency, FeaturedBandwidth).
```

The *power usage effectiveness* (PUE) associated to a node is the ratio between the overall energy needed for keeping the node working and the energy that the node uses for actual computation. For instance, a PUE of 1.5 indicates that for every 1 kWh spent in computation, another 0.5 kWh is needed for non-IT tasks (e.g. cooling, lighting, network) that keep the server working. Typical values of the PUE range between 1.2 and 1.9. Extending the model of [10], we assume that node operators can disclose information about the total hardware (free and in use) at each node and the associated PUE as in

```
totHW(N, TotalHardware).                pue(N, PUE).
```

Node operators can then specify the energy consumption profile of each node via predicates like

```
energyProfile(N, Load, EnergyConsumption) :- ...
```

where EnergyConsumption is obtained in kWh as a, possibly non-linear, function of the current percentage Load at node N. Existing processors show a baseline energy consumption even when they are idle, which increases as the node workload increases [20].

Last, the percentages of the energy mix of each node can be specified as in

```
energySourceMix(N, [(P1,Source1), ..., (PK,SourceK)]).
```

where PJ is the percentage of electricity that node N receives from SourceJ.

We finally assume that average CO_2 emissions for each source are declared in a public knowledge base of facts like emissions(Source, Mu), where Mu are the emissions in $kgCO_2/kWh$ for Source, e.g. as those reported in Table 1.

Note that, when energy-related information is not disclosed, GFogBrain easily allows to employ default data or data taken from public audits such as [14].

Table 1. CO_2 emissions per power source [17].

Power source	Emissions [$kgCO_2/kWh$]
Gas	0.610
Coal	1.100
On shore wind	0.0097
Off shore wind	0.0165
Solar	0.05

Example 2. Consider the Cloud-IoT infrastructure of Fig. 3 to deploy the application of Example 1. Figure 4 epitomises the declaration of the capabilities and energy information of all three nodes. Due to space limitations, we only show the declaration of the link between Private Cloud and Access Point.

Note that, for instance, node Private Cloud currently features 128 free hardware units (out of the 150 totally available), each offered for 0.0016 cents per hour, and that its energy consumption in kWh is given by a function $\phi(L)$ of the current workload L such that $\phi(w) = 0.1\,\mathrm{kWh} + 0.01 \cdot \log(L)$ with $L \in [0, 100]$. Besides, Private Cloud is powered by an energy mix coming for 30% from a solar plant and for 70% from a coal plant, as declared by energySourceMix/2. Last, the PUE of Private Cloud is 1.9.　　□

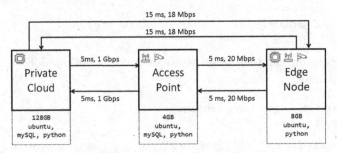

Fig. 3. Example Cloud-IoT infrastructure.

```
node(privateCloud,[ubuntu, mySQL, python], 128, [gpu]).
    cost(privateCloud,0.0016).        totHW(privateCloud,150).
    energyProfile(privateCloud,L,E) :- E is 0.1 + 0.01*log(L).
    pue(privateCloud,1.9).
    energySourceMix(privateCloud,[(0.3,solar), (0.7,coal)]).
node(accesspoint,[ubuntu, mySQL, python], 4, [lightshub, videocamera]).
    cost(accesspoint,0.003).        totHW(accesspoint,6).
    energyProfile(accesspoint,L,E) :- E is 0.05 + 0.03*log(L).
    pue(accesspoint,1.5).
    energySourceMix(accesspoint,[(0.1,gas),(0.8,coal),(0.1,onshorewind)]).
node(edgenode,[ubuntu, python], 8, [gpu, lightshub, videocamera]).
    cost(edgenode,0.005).        totHW(edgenode,12).
    energyProfile(edgenode,L,E) :- L =< 50 -> E is 0.08; E is 0.1.
    pue(edgenode,1.2).
    energySourceMix(edgenode,[(0.5,coal), (0.5,solar)]).

link(privateCloud, accesspoint, 5, 1000).
```

Fig. 4. Example infrastructure declaration.

Energy-, Carbon- and Cost-Aware Placements – Figure 5 shows[2] how the GFogBrain prototype determines energy- and carbon-aware application place-

---

[2] Due to space limitations, we only show the main predicates of GFogBrain. Full code is open-sourced at https://github.com/di-unipi-socc/fogbrainx/tree/main/green.

ments in Cloud-IoT settings. Predicate placements/2 (lines 1–3) determines all Placements that satisfy software, hardware, IoT and network QoS requirements of the application by means of gFogBrain/4, along with the associated hourly deployment Cost, energy consumption E and carbon emissions C (line 2). The obtained placements are sorted by increasing estimated carbon footprint, cost, and energy consumption, considered in this order of priority[3] (line 3).

Predicate gFogBrain/4 (lines 4–6) exploits the placement/2 (line 5) and the allocatedResources/2 (line 6) predicates of [10] (see Appendix A) to determine a placement that satisfies software, hardware, IoT and network QoS requirements of a given application, and the associated hardware and bandwidth in use, respectively. Then, Energy consumption and Carbon emissions associated to the placement are computed via the footprint/4 predicate (lines 6, 7–11).

Based on the deployment nodes used by P (line 8), the predicate footprint/4 computes hardware- (line 9) and network-related (line 10) energy consumption and carbon emissions and sums them, respectively (line 11). GFogBrain employs an extended version of the model from Kelly et al. [17] to associate an estimate of energy consumption to a piece of computation running on a given node. The overall energy E_s consumed by service s at node n is computed as

$$E_s = E_n \cdot PUE_n \quad [\text{kWh}] \tag{1}$$

where E_n is the energy consumption (in kWh) of running s on n excluding non-IT tasks, and PUE_n is the PUE of n. As aforementioned, E_n is a (non-linear) function of the current node load. For each node N involved in placement P, hardwareFootprint/4 (line 9, 12–17) exploits hardwareEnergy/4 (line 14, 18–23) to first retrieve the node load OldL before placing the services in placement P, and the associated energy consumption OldE (line 20). Then, it retrieves the node load NewL after placing the services as per P (line 21), and computes the associated energy consumption NewE (line 22). The difference between NewE and OldE, multiplied by the PUE of N, estimates the Energy consumption of P on node N as per Eq. (1) (line 23).

Based on this, GFogBrain also estimates the associated carbon emissions. To this end, extending [17], we consider the case in which multiple energy sources are combined at node n – each with an associated mix percentage $p_1, \ldots, p_k$ such that $\sum_i p_i = 1$ – producing $\mu_1, \ldots, \mu_k$ emissions, respectively. Predicate hardwareEmissions/3 (line 15, 24–27) recursively scans the energy mix declared for node N and computes carbon emissions as

$$I_s = E_s \cdot \sum_i p_i \mu_i \quad [\text{kgCO}_2] \tag{2}$$

Finally, following the approach of [20], networkFootprint/3 (lines 10, 28–31) estimates the carbon emissions to transmit traffic flows allocated by P. Transmitting 1 MB of data over the Internet requires around 0.00008 kWh (kWhPerMB/1)

---

[3] By suitably rearranging output tuples, it is possible to prioritise differently among the estimated metrics. For instance, the order (Cost,E,C,P) at line 2 would give priority to cost over energy consumption and carbon emissions.

[15] and the average *global carbon intensity* (averageGCI/1) of electricity is of 475 gCO2/kWh [16]. Then, the network energy consumption E_N and carbon emissions I_N for transmitting M MB for one hour can be estimated as

$$E_N = 450 \cdot 0.00008 \cdot M \text{ [kWh]} \quad \text{and} \quad I_N = 0.475 \cdot E_N \text{ [kgCO}_2\text{]} \qquad (3)$$

also considering that 1 Mbit/s = 450 MB/h. Equations (3) are computed at lines 30 and 31 of the code of Fig. 5, respectively.

```
1   placements(A,Placements) :-
2       findall((C,Cost,E,P), (gFogBrain(A,P,E,C), hourlyCost(P,Cost)), Ps),
3       sort(Ps,Placements).

4   gFogBrain(A,P,Energy,Carbon) :-
5       application(A,Services), placement(Services,P),
6       allocatedResources(P,Alloc), footprint(P,Alloc,Energy,Carbon).

7   footprint(P,(AllocHW,AllocBW),Energy,Carbon) :-
8       deploymentNodes(P,Nodes),
9       hardwareFootprint(Nodes,AllocHW,HWEnergy,HWCarbon),
10      networkFootprint(AllocBW,BWEnergy,BWCarbon),
11      Energy is HWEnergy + BWEnergy, Carbon is HWCarbon + BWCarbon.

12  hardwareFootprint([(N,HW)|Ns],AllocHW,Energy,Carbon) :-
13      hardwareFootprint(Ns,AllocHW,EnergyNs,CarbonNs),
14      hardwareEnergy(N,HW,AllocHW,EnergyN),
15      energySourceMix(N,Sources), hardwareEmissions(Sources,EnergyN,CarbonN),
16      Energy is EnergyN + EnergyNs, Carbon is CarbonN + CarbonNs.
17  hardwareFootprint([],_,0,0).

18  hardwareEnergy(N,HW,AllocHW,Energy):-
19      totHW(N,TotHW), pue(N,PUE),
20      OldL is 100 * (TotHW - HW) / TotHW, energyProfile(N,OldL,OldE),
21      findall(H,member((N,H),AllocHW),HWs), sum_list(HWs,PHW),
22      NewL is 100 * (TotHW - HW + PHW) / TotHW, energyProfile(N,NewL,NewE),
23      Energy is (NewE - OldE) * PUE.

24  hardwareEmissions([(P,S)|Srcs],Energy,Carbon) :-
25      hardwareEmissions(Srcs,Energy,CarbSrcs),
26      emissions(S,MU), CarbS is P * MU * Energy, Carbon is CarbS + CarbSrcs.
27  hardwareEmissions([],_,0).

28  networkFootprint(AllocBW,BWEnergy,BWCarbon) :-
29      findall(BW, member((_,_,BW),AllocBW), Flows), sum_list(Flows,TotBW),
30      kWhPerMB(K), BWEnergy is 450 * K * TotBW,
31      averageGCI(A), BWCarbon is A * BWEnergy.
```

Fig. 5. Main predicates of GFogBrain.

Example 3. By querying `placements(lightsApp,Placements)` over the inputs of Examples 1 and 2, we obtain the two eligible placements for application LightsApp listed in Table 2, along with their estimated hourly carbon emissions, energy consumption, and cost. Based on those and on business considerations, application operators can then informedly decide whether to enact P_1 or P_2. While P_1 saves more than 9% CO_2 emissions compared to P_2, and consumes 5% less energy, it incurs in an 11% cost increase (i.e. +0.004 €/h $\simeq$ +3 €/month). It is also possible to exploit GFogBrain to perform *what-if* analyses and to possibly evaluate *greener* infrastructure operators, thus improving on target metrics.   □

Table 2. Example placement results.

Id	Placement	Emissions	Cost	Energy Cons.
P_1	on(lightsDriver, edgenode), on(mlOptimiser, privateCloud)	0.29 kgCO$_2$	0.0356 €/h	0.60 kWh
P_2	on(lightsDriver, accesspoint), on(mlOptimiser, privateCloud)	0.32 kgCO$_2$	0.0316 €/h	0.63 kWh

3   Related Work

Much work targeted the problem of placing multi-service applications in Cloud-IoT computing scenarios, e.g. as surveyed in [5,19]. Only some works featured some aspects of energy-awareness but did not consider carbon footprint or relied on simple linear models for energy consumption (e.g. [2,18,24,26]). To the best of our knowledge, [1] is the first work including carbon emissions in the trade-off analyses to determine optimal Cloud-IoT application placements, via mixed integer linear programming. A limitation of [1] resides in the fact that it only considers linear energy consumption for infrastructure nodes. On the contrary, energy consumption is usually a non-linear function of a computational node load [20,25]. Last, [1] does not consider the possibility to estimate energy consumption based on combined sources, does not account for operational costs estimates, and requires full knowledge of the physical network topology and employed routing algorithms, which is not always available in real scenarios.

Focussing on declarative approaches, Casadei et al. [9,22] devised a declarative approach to service coordination based on *aggregate computing*, managing opportunistic resources via a hybrid centralised/decentralised solution by relying on a self-organising peer-to-peer architecture to handle churn and mobility. We have exploited logic programming to assess the security and trust levels of application placements [13], and to determine them [10,11] also in Osmotic computing settings [12]. Finally, we very recently proposed a fully decentralised solution to write and enforce QoS-aware application management policies written in Prolog [6]. None of those declarative solutions, however, considers energy consumption nor carbon emissions, as GFogBrain does.

4　Concluding Remarks

In this article, we have presented a declarative methodology and its prototype, GFogBrain, to determine eligible multiservice application placements and to estimate their carbon emissions, energy consumption and operational costs. The prototype determining application placements that satisfy all software, hardware, IoT, and network QoS constraints, and to informedly decide on the best trade-off placement considering its estimated impact on the environment and its deployment operational costs, which oftentimes represent contrasting objectives.

Future work includes extending GFogBrain with *continuous reasoning* (as in [10]) and assessing it via simulation or over testbeds, also employing different formulas to estimate energy consumption and carbon emissions (e.g. considering deployment duration and workload). Last, we intend to enable placing services in different *flavours*, as in Osmotic computing [12], to better meet set targets.

References

1. Aldossary, M., Alharbi, H.A.: Towards a green approach for minimizing carbon emissions in fog-cloud architecture. IEEE Access **9**, 131720–131732 (2021)
2. Barcelo, M., Correa, A., Llorca, J., Tulino, A.M., Vicario, J.L., Morell, A.: IoT-cloud service optimization in next generation smart environments. IEEE J. Select. Areas Commun. **34**(12), 4077–4090 (2016)
3. Belkhir, L., Elmeligi, A.: Assessing ICT global emissions footprint: trends to 2040 & recommendations. J. Clean. Prod. **177**, 448–463 (2018)
4. Bisicchia, G., Forti, S., Brogi, A.: Declarative goal mediation in smart environments. In: 2021 IEEE International Conference on Smart Computing (SMART-COMP), pp. 389–391 (2021). https://doi.org/10.1109/SMARTCOMP52413.2021.00079
5. Brogi, A., Forti, S., Guerrero, C., Lera, I.: How to place your apps in the fog - state of the art and open challenges. Softw. Pract. Exp. **50**(5), 719–740 (2020). https://doi.org/10.1002/spe.2766
6. Brogi, A., Forti, S., Guerrero, C., Lera, I.: Towards declarative decentralised application management in the fog. In: ISSRE Workshops, pp. 223–230 (2020). https://doi.org/10.1109/ISSREW51248.2020.00077
7. Brogi, A., Forti, S., Ibrahim, A., Rinaldi, L.: Bonsai in the fog: an active learning lab with fog computing. In: 2018 Third International Conference on Fog and Mobile Edge Computing (FMEC), pp. 79–86. IEEE (2018)
8. Calero, C., Piattini, M.: Green in software engineering, vol. 3. Springer, Cham (2015). https://doi.org/10.1007/978-3-319-08581-4
9. Casadei, R., Viroli, M.: Coordinating computation at the edge: a decentralized, self-organizing, spatial approach. In: FMEC 2019, pp. 60–67 (2019). https://doi.org/10.1109/FMEC.2019.8795355
10. Forti, S., Bisicchia, G., Brogi, A.: Declarative Continuous Reasoning in the Cloud-IoT Continuum. J. Logic Comput. **19** (2021, in press)

11. Forti, S., Brogi, A.: Continuous reasoning for managing next-gen distributed applications. In: Ricca, F., et al. (eds.) Proceedings 36th International Conference on Logic Programming (Technical Communications), ICLP Technical Communications 2020, (Technical Communications) UNICAL, Rende (CS), Italy, 18–24th September 2020. EPTCS, vol. 325, pp. 164–177 (2020). https://doi.org/10.4204/EPTCS.325.22, https://doi.org/10.4204/EPTCS.325.22

12. Forti, S., Brogi, A.: Declarative osmotic application placement. In: Polyvyanyy, A., Rinderle-Ma, S. (eds.) Proceedings of the Advanced Information Systems Engineering Workshops - CAiSE 2021 International Workshops, Melbourne, VIC, Australia, June 28 –July 2, 2021, Lecture Notes in Business Information Processing, vol. 423, pp. 177–190. Springer (2021). https://doi.org/10.1007/978-3-030-79022-6_15

13. Forti, S., Ferrari, G.L., Brogi, A.: Secure cloud-edge deployments, with trust. Fut. Gener. Comput. Syst. **102**, 775–788 (2020). https://doi.org/10.1016/j.future.2019.08.020

14. Greenpeace: Clicking green. who is winning the race to build a green internet? (2017)

15. IEA: The carbon footprint of streaming video: fact-checking the headlines. https://www.iea.org/commentaries/the-carbon-footprint-of-streaming-video-fact-checking-the-headlines

16. IEA: Global energy & co2 status report 2019. https://www.iea.org/reports/global-energy-co2-status-report-2019/

17. Kelly, C., Mangina, E., Ruzelli, A.: Putting a Co2 figure on a piece of computation. In: 11th International Conference on Electrical Power Quality and Utilisation, pp. 1–7 (2011). https://doi.org/10.1109/EPQU.2011.6128960

18. Kopras, B., Idzikowski, F., Chen, W.C., Wang, T.J., Chou, C.T., Bogucka, H.: Latency-aware virtual network embedding using clusters for green fog computing. In: 2020 IEEE Globecom Workshops (GC Wkshps, pp. 1–7. IEEE (2020)

19. Mahmud, R., Ramamohanarao, K., Buyya, R.: Application management in fog computing environments: a taxonomy, review and future directions. ACM Comput. Surv. **53**(4), 1–43(2020)

20. Microsoft: The principles of sustainable software engineering. https://docs.microsoft.com/en-us/learn/modules/sustainable-software-engineering-overview/

21. Mourão, B.C., Karita, L., do Carmo Machado, I.: Green and sustainable software engineering - a systematic mapping study. In: SBQS: Proceedings of the 17th Brazilian Symposium on Software Quality, ACM (2018)

22. Pianini, D., Casadei, R., Viroli, M., Natali, A.: Partitioned integration and coordination via the self-organising coordination regions pattern. Fut. Gener. Comput. Syst. **114**, 44–68 (2021). https://doi.org/10.1016/j.future.2020.07.032

23. Sarkar, S., Misra, S.: Theoretical modelling of fog computing: a green computing paradigm to support IPT applications. IET Netw. **5**(2), 23–29 (2016)

24. Souza, V.B., Masip-Bruin, X., Marín-Tordera, E., Ramírez, W., Sánchez, S.: Towards distributed service allocation in fog-to-cloud (f2c) scenarios. In: 2016 IEEE Global Communications Conference (GLOBECOM), pp. 1–6. IEEE (2016)

25. Xiao, Y., Zhang, Y., Kaku, I., Kang, R., Pan, X.: Electric vehicle routing problem: A systematic review and a new comprehensive model with nonlinear energy recharging and consumption. Renew. Sustain. Energy Rev. **151**, 111567 (2021)

26. Yu, Y., Bu, X., Yang, K., Wu, Z., Han, Z.: Green large-scale fog computing resource allocation using joint benders decomposition, Dinkelbach algorithm, ADMM, and branch-and-bound. IEEE Internet of Things J. **6**(3), 4106–4117 (2018)

Author Index

Printed in the United States
by Baker & Taylor Publisher Services